BEHIND THE COSMIC VEIL

A New Vision of Reality,
Merging
Science, the Spiritual and the Supernatural

THOMAS P. FUSCO

NⓋP
NEW VISION PRESS

www.cosmicveil.com

Acknowledgments

It has been observed that an author's first book is often a reflection of that person's inner self. I suppose this could be said here as well. The experiences, education, and moments of personal discovery during the many years of its preparation have all played a role. The picture of reality described in this book is what I see when I look out on the vast landscape of God's creation, or into the deepest parts of my inner self.

Along the way I've met many people who contributed to this work in some way. They either challenged me, inspired me, supported me, and/or served as a sounding board for the many ideas presented here. Although space does not allow me to name them all, I want to thank each and every one for helping to shape both this book and its author.

Several teachers from my school years have made important contributions, although they're not aware of it. My fourth grade teacher Miss Carmen (forgive me my dear lady, but your first name has been lost to me in the ashes of my childhood) took this troubled child under her wing and made him believe he could achieve whatever he imagined. I never forgot Lawrence Carter's raw enthusiasm, which taught me that a genuine love for your subject is infectious. Richard Caruso demonstrated that persistence and determination coupled with a high moral and professional standard could overcome most any obstacle.

A thank-you also goes to Jeff "Woodsy" Wooten, who taught me how to set goals and obtain them through adherence to discipline and organized planning, which is the foundation for all human achievement.

The tireless work of Dr. Thelma Moss in the field of paranormal research was truly inspiring. Her words of support those many years ago as well as her offer to provide the Kirlian photographs for this book are both deeply appreciated.

My younger brother Anthony Fusco created the wonderful illustrations found in this book. Words cannot fully express my deepest gratitude for all the editorial, technical, intellectual and emotional support he has given me throughout this process.

I also wish to thank my beloved wife Sharon, who among other things tolerated the sleepless nights, the endless re-reads, and my many eccentricities. She celebrated with me during my moments of excitement, gave me moral support when I was discouraged, offered sound advice and served as my greatest fan. Though she has joined me in my life and my endeavors late in my walk, her contribution is no less significant.

No acknowledgment for a work such as this would be complete without making mention of the late, great Albert Einstein, whose revolutionary vision of reality blazed the trail for all modern theorists. He had the courage to challenge the firmly entrenched belief system of Newtonian physics, and dared to mention the name of God in his writings at a time when the atheistic worldview championed by Charles Darwin was all the rage in the scientific community.

Finally, I owe my very life to Jesus of Nazareth, whose power of spirit and divine wisdom saved me from my former self, and revealed to me the true nature of His Father and His Creation.

Contents

Introduction

During my sophomore year in high school, a classmate with whom I had just recently made acquaintance invited me to her house for lunch. As I was waiting in the living room for sandwiches from the kitchen, my attention was drawn to one of the paintings on the wall. While studying the painting, I suddenly felt an excruciating pain in my left forearm. I immediately called my friend into the room. Without revealing my physical discomfort, I began to ask what seemed at the moment to be such a natural question. Yet I hesitated, being torn between my need to know and my schooled logic, which screamed that such an inquiry made absolutely no sense. As usual, my innate curiosity won this internal debate. "Did the person who painted this ever injure their arm?" She glared at me in astonishment. After recovering from her initial shock, she told me that her older brother had painted it, and recounted how several years prior he had indeed injured his left forearm severely with a chainsaw. I was so sure the painter had suffered such an injury that I received her answer casually as a matter of fact with no sense of alarm or surprise.

It was this event that first forced me to personally confront the reality known as the paranormal.

Behind The Cosmic Veil

My limited exposure to the subject of paranormal phenomena had come mostly from the books of Frank Edwards, who collected numerous accounts of such strange happenings. Being a very scientifically minded student, I read these books mostly for entertainment and curiosity's sake. I had never heard the subject discussed within the halls of higher education, which only confirmed my belief that these stories were either fictional or could be explained through conventional means. After my experience however, I no longer had the option of simply dismissing them. My mind churned as I replayed every detail of that fateful day, searching for how I might have subconsciously picked up subliminal clues that told me her brother had both painted the picture and had suffered this injury. But I didn't even know she had a brother until this incident! And how many people have hanging art painted by someone they know? I was therefore forced to concede that I had encountered a truly paranormal event that defied any conventional explanation.

I began to recall a few other times in my life when some hidden piece of knowledge seemed to have popped in my mind from nowhere. I'd never given these spontaneous revelations much thought, believing that I had somehow reasoned them out in my intellect, perhaps even on a subconscious level. But certainly not from some "psychic" mumbo jumbo! The earliest one I could recall occurred when I was six. My father arrived home from work later than usual one day with a strange withdrawn look in his eyes. I instantly ran to my older brother of eight and declared to him, "Grandma's dead." I can still see my brother and I milling around in the hallway as if it were yesterday. I always thought it was my reason alone that me led to conclude this as the only possible explanation for my father's expression. But now as I looked back upon the event, I realized there was no way this six-year-old had enough information to form that conclusion. For one, my grandmother's death was sudden. To my knowledge, she was suffering no extended illness that would cause one to expect her imminent demise. The

2

subject of death had never been discussed before in my house, so why would a six-year-old even think of it? Though it made me uneasy, I was forced to conclude that this too might have been another instance of a paranormal experience.

It should have been no surprise that the paranormal was never mentioned in the classroom. Such disquieting controversies are typically avoided in these institutions, which have long since abandoned earnest inquiry in favor of benign security. The several teachers whom I now approached with the subject either quickly pleaded ignorance or dismissed it as nonsense. This of course didn't discourage me, for I had already come to learn that authority figures were more often motivated by personal agenda than pursuit of truth. I also knew that just because an authority declared a thing to be or not to be did not in itself make it so. I was determined to find the truth, and so I committed myself to absorb all I could about this scholastic taboo known as the supernatural.

I soon discovered that most people were too uncomfortable to speak about the paranormal beyond a passing comment. In the innocence of my young age, it had never occurred to me that intelligent people might be afraid to probe so deeply into the mysteries of the world around them, preferring instead the blissful intoxication of ignorance.

Fear was not the only adversary I faced in my quest for this damnable realm of the paranormal. The available books on the subject seemed pathetically inadequate. These were mostly just collections of alleged paranormal accounts with the added nonsense of hype and sensationalism thrown in to help sell them. Those that did try to explain the possible causes behind these bizarre phenomena offered vague and speculative opinions that differed widely between one author and the next. None of these suppositions had any tangible correspondence to solid physical theory. Though interesting, these proved to be of little use in my scholarly pursuit.

Scientific inquiry into paranormal phenomena was still in

3

its infancy, and so there were few books containing any credible investigative work. Of these, most were written by reputable scientists whose clear intent was to discredit the entire field of paranormal research by any means necessary. This came to me as no surprise, since I was growing ever more familiar with the establishment's snubbing of anything not fitting neatly into its prevailing belief system. The books that were devoted to serious investigation were each so narrowly focused on one particular phenomenon (such as ghosts or telepathy) that it was virtually impossible to draw from their findings any broad conclusions about the natural mechanism behind paranormal events. The dominant theme in much of this literature was the perennial debate between established science and paranormal investigators as to whether or not these events were even legitimate phenomena. Unfortunately, the impact of my own personal experiences had denied me the luxury of indulging in any such academic debate.

I then turned my attention toward religion and spirituality. Surely, here was a discipline that embraced the supernatural and suffered no hesitation in forming conclusions about the nature of the universe at large based on those phenomena. Perhaps if there were no truth to be had from the physical sciences (in which I had also immersed myself), I could at least arrive at a philosophical or spiritual one. So I began an extensive study of many diverse religions. But here too my efforts were met with frustration. I found that for a single phenomenon, ten different religions had ten different ways to define it, and ten different explanations as to how or even why this might occur. To make matters worse, most religions asserted that these phenomena were only possible under their discipline, and only in the way they prescribed. All other paranormal phenomena outside their own narrow view were presented as outright fiction, delusion or works of the devil.

Still, I *knew* the paranormal effect was real. By setting aside the prejudices of each religion, I could easily see that they all acknowledged the existence of the same kinds of supernatural phenomena. Modern science's inability to validate them only meant that we were not yet advanced enough in our reasoning to do so. I became increasingly convinced that there must indeed exist a single set of laws or principles as yet undiscovered that would explain the realm of the paranormal while being scientifically consistent with known physical reality. With this conviction, however, also came the possibility of conceding that such a set of laws might be beyond the reach of our human understanding.

Finally, in my late 20s, I found the breakthrough I had been looking for. Call it inspiration, gestalt or spiritual revelation—it certainly made a believer out of me. In any event, I came to realize that the reason no one had been able to convincingly tie together both religion and the paranormal with science is that we have all been looking at the evidence in the wrong way. It really wasn't possible to tightly relate these three in their current forms. One had to look instead for the common source, the primordial principles from which they had all originated This was the missing ingredient, the elusive invisible key.

For centuries we had little knowledge as to the origins of the continents. We could deduce a few things from certain isolated bits of common information, but we couldn't grasp the greater scheme. Then came the guiding principles of tectonic plates and continental drift. Suddenly, the veil lifted, and our eyes were opened to a totally new frontier of understanding. When we finally realized that the continents were once a single large land mass that separated into different plates and drifted apart, all the pieces of this once impossible puzzle fell together. Not only that, but it also revealed to us the natural processes behind phenomena like earthquakes, volcanoes, the formation of mountains and even species migration between continents. All this incredible wealth of knowledge came from the discovery of a single, elementary principle.

In this very same manner, this hidden key I had stumbled

upon unlocked for me a revolutionary way to approach the existing evidence. The strong common threads joining these three disciplines that were only hinted at by philosophers of the past now emerged as well defined principles and processes.

The ensuing years were spent developing and organizing this newly acquired body of data into an orderly system with the necessary scientific and logical supportive arguments. This ongoing work led to the development of cutting-edge concepts and terminology, the first truly functional physical model of the invisible mechanics behind the paranormal, and an innovative perspective on existing scientific laws and theories, all culminating in the entirely new vision of reality presented in this book.

It is my sincerest prayer that you too might receive through this work satisfying answers to questions upon which your heart and mind may have long pondered.

1

Quest for the Theory of Everything

*The end of all exploration will be to ar-
rive where we started; and to know the
place for the first time.*
                                    —T.S. Elliot

Since the time humans first appeared on this earth, we have
sought the ultimate truth about the world in which we live. This
deep-rooted need to explain the mysteries of existence compelled our ancestors to deify the elements—sky, water, sun and
moon were all raised to godhood. The myths they spun around
these natural gods gave them a sense of security in a world that
was often dangerous and unpredictable. By crediting floods,
earthquakes, and other natural disasters to the "anger of the
gods," the ancients found meaning to those events beyond their
reason or control and satisfied their thirst for truth.

Homo Sapiens has come a long way since the time of our
low-browed forebears. We no longer see the natural elements
as a race of super-beings who command us like playthings for
their own perverse amusement. We have plumbed the depths of

the oceans, harnessed the building blocks of matter, and have set foot upon the face of another world. Yet this impressive volume of knowledge does not seem to satisfy our need, for we are still driven by an insatiable lust to find what new truth awaits us over the next horizon.

Our thirst for knowledge appears to stem from the way in which we humans approach survival. Animals in nature survive by adapting to their environment. The better they can fit into their ecosystem, the greater chance they have at survival. Their specialized adaptations enable them to run faster, jump further, climb higher, bite harder, and conceal themselves better so that they can compete more effectively. We humans are designed differently. We don't survive by adapting to our environment, but by overcoming and conquering it. The more knowledge we acquire about the environment, the better we can subdue it and harness its resources for our own purposes. Since the survival instinct is one of the strongest drives within us, the desire to learn more about how to manipulate our surroundings occupies the greater part of our thought processes.

Our ultimate goal as a species seems to be the acquiring of a final truth, that singular, ultimate set of principles that could explain the workings of all things. Truth with a capital "T" if you will. Absolute Truth. Only such an all-encompassing concept would have the power to quench our intellectual thirst.

The pursuit of this Truth has given rise to our physical sciences by which we probe the depths of the subatomic realm and peer out to the very edge of the universe. Its underlying theme is the search for what physicists call the Theory of Everything or TOE, a single philosophy or set of laws by which the true nature and behavior of all things can be accurately described. With such a universal formula in hand, we might shape the elements of this world into anything we imagine, thereby permanently securing the survival of our species in this vast and often unforgiving universe.

There is another world, however, that we also must master

to insure our survival. It is the world within us, that dark and secret place of thoughts, emotions, impressions and impulses. For such spiritual matters, religion has traditionally been our discipline of choice. By adhering to the principles of faith, the practitioner seeks mastery over the chaotic inner self thereby gaining a greater control over one's own life, and with it a much better chance at survival and prosperity. Without the discipline of adherence to higher ideals and a higher authority, building the kind of large, peaceful human societies that lead to civilization would be virtually impossible.

In this author's case, that faith is Christianity, with its God who established the nature and order of the universe at the time of its creation, its principles to help guide us through this order, its message of faith that gives us the strength to discipline ourselves to those principles, and its promise of eternal survival through spiritual salvation. The teachings of Christ provide a kind of spiritual TOE that can explain the causes behind life's challenges and furnish solutions that lead to final victory over them. Obedience to God also brings with it the prospect of receiving divine favor, which has the power to mystically alter the fabric of reality itself to our benefit. The miracles performed by Jesus are the evidence that our material realm was created in such a way so that it can be re-configured by means other than technology. While physics seeks to tame the environment by manipulating its elemental building blocks, Christianity overcomes the world by tapping into its essence at its source—the supreme force that shapes those elements and binds them all together.

Today we tend to alternately apply the principles from each of these two disciplines to different aspects of our reality—faith for understanding the spiritual inner realm and science for describing the outer realm of the physical. Yet there is a serious, fundamental flaw in this dual approach to reality. If there is only one universal creation, then there can be only one reality to which these spiritual and physical worlds must both belong.

We should then need only one set of principles to describe them both. The failure of either discipline to *fully* explain and accommodate the elements of the other implies that neither alone is able to satisfy the requirement for Absolute Truth.

This failure does not necessarily mean that either system is fundamentally flawed, or that one should be embraced while the other is discarded. Clearly, each approach has its necessary place, since our drive to conquer applies to our inner selves and the outer world around us. The problem is that both appear to be missing certain necessary ingredients to form a *complete* picture of both the inner and outer together, or in other words, the *complete* Truth. If the knowledge we possess about the Creator cannot reveal to us the nature of created things like gravity or subatomic particles, and if our understanding of gravity and subatomic particles cannot fully reveal to us the nature of their Creator, then that collective body of knowledge must be incomplete in some way.

Unfortunately, when faced with this great paradox, we tend to retreat behind the same outworn dogmatic answers that have served to perpetuate the rift between science and faith. Most physicists simply maintain that matters of faith have no place within cold, pragmatic science. Some who are deeply religious hold a similar view concerning the relevance of science. Then there are atheists who dismiss the whole subject of religion as foolish self-delusion.

These traditional positions are not only short-sighted, but are also at times insincere. Physicists often conveniently forget that several of those who actually laid the groundwork for our contemporary sciences—persons like Isaac Newton and Albert Einstein—were believers in the existence of a creator and applied this faith to their work. Einstein by his own testimony would have never devised the Theory of Relativity without his firm belief in a God who created a world of order. Christians who dismiss science as a viable means to describe the physical universe must admit that the Word of God also fails to do so, even though according to the faith the universe was fashioned through that same Word. It cannot be denied that the physics behind the cars we drive, the telephones over which we speak, and the system of lighting that illuminates our houses at night are not described in the Scriptures. The atheist in turn, by dismissing as nonsense the entire realm of religious experience, only manages to reduce the weight of human ignorance by a few "foolish" questions. None of these rigid positions bring their adherents any closer to finding Absolute Truth. They simply provide a convenient excuse for avoiding the discomfort of examining one's own established beliefs in the exposing light of other possibilities.

It would seem then that the only practical way to come upon a single, accurate description of reality is by combining both spiritual and physical into a unified approach. The idea is by no means a new one. There was actually a time when science and Christianity in the form of the Catholic Church were intimately joined in this manner. Western science was once so closely linked to Christianity that it was considered an important subcategory of Christian thought. There were of course other ancient cultures that developed their own sciences such as those in Egypt, China, Arabia, and India. But these either perished with the falls of their respective civilizations or were too distant or isolated to exert any widespread influence. Modern science— the science that was built upon the remnants of the ancient Greek philosophers and mathematicians, re-emerged after the Dark Ages, and matured into a discipline based on controlled methods, meticulous experimentation, careful observation and peer review—is primarily of Western origin. Early explorers of this science like the mathematician Johannes Kepler, the cleric Copernicus and the astronomer Galileo were not faithless men attempting to oppose or discredit Christian doctrine, but were instead searching for an even deeper understanding of the mysteries of God by observing and analyzing the creation that He wrought.

When Church and Science Were One

The marriage between Church and Science began with the first Western TOE conceived by the Greek philosopher Aristotle in the third century BC. According to him, the universe was created by the Prime Mover or God who placed the earth, unmoving and fixed, at the center of everything. The planets and the entire firmament of stars were each imbedded in their own huge crystal spheres that surrounded the earth like the layers of an onion. The celestial spheres were then set into eternal circular motion by the mighty hand of God. Because the motion of these crystalline spheres was both eternal and unvarying, Aristotle considered them to be in *natural* motion. To him, it was this very smooth harmonious motion that allowed the heavenly bodies to exist forever in a perfect unaltered state.

In contrast, the earth was designed by God to be a fixed, motionless object. This meant that all earthbound objects were likewise motionless in their natural state. Earth-bound forces like weather, fire, flooding and earthquakes acted on these stationary objects and forced them into motion. Aristotle assumed that this *forced* motion was artificial, and therefore *unnatural*. Any object thus moved by force would suffer some damage each time it was dislodged from its natural state of rest, even if the damage was so small as to be imperceptible. The damage over time from the cumulative effect of many forced movements would eventually wear down all objects and ultimately destroy them. It was this unnatural movement that caused tools to become dull and break, buildings to collapse, trees to fall and rot, soil to erode and even our own living flesh to grow sick, die and decay.

Aristotle's view of the universe appeared to be so similar to the cosmology of the Bible that the Church embraced it as the only accurate model of creation. Within it, the Church fathers found a scientific basis for the Biblical portrayal of an earth perishing in constant turmoil where everything was subject to corruption and decay—creatures died, seasons changed, and the "unnatural" worldly forces rearranged landscapes. This view of reality appeared to be confirmed in a number of Scriptural passages such as Paul's description of Satan as *the prince of the power of the air*. The heavens, on the other hand, were eternal and incorruptible, being set into perpetual motion at the time of creation by the Almighty—again, exactly as the Bible seemed to depict. The Church therefore elevated the Aristotelian system from theory to dogma, and decreed it a matter of faith. To question Aristotle was to challenge the Holy Church and God Himself.

Divisions Arise

Aristotle's cosmology dominated western thought for over 1500 years. But there were serious flaws in this ancient system that led to some striking anomalies. One of these arose from Aristotle's assertion that the circular motion of the heavens was a fundamental aspect of its eternal nature. To him, circular motion and eternity were synonymous. His observations of the natural world seemed to confirm his position, in that nothing on the earth appeared to be eternal like the heavenly bodies. Every earthbound thing underwent changes, even if in some cases these changes were miniscule or took place only over long periods of time. Based on these observations, Aristotle jumped to the erroneous conclusion that since nothing on earth was eternal, nothing on earth could ever move in a circular path. If any earth-bound object ever happened to be set into circular motion, it would immediately be 'transmuted' to an eternal state, which to him would have been an impossible violation of physical law. The only type of movement available to earthbound objects therefore was straight-line motion.

According to this concept, it was impossible for an object thrown into the air to curve back to earth as it fell. The object instead traveled straight out in the direction it was thrown until the force that launched it was expended, after which it then fell straight back to earth, tracing a path like an inverted letter V. Belief in this system was so profound that people denied the evidence of their own eyes. When a projectile like a cannonball or a hurled stone was seen curving back to earth, the "illusion" was thought to be due to some limitation in the human eye's ability to detect what was actually taking place.

However, the severest of these anomalies—the ones finally responsible for Aristotle's undoing—were discovered through astronomical observations. For one, the planets periodically reversed their orbits through the sky, an impossible feat if the Aristotelian model was correct. The Divine crystalline spheres would certainly not have allowed their embedded captives to whimsically change course amid God's eternal heavens. Serious inquiries into such anomalies by early pioneers of the Modern Age forced the Church into the awkward paradox of encouraging the fledgling sciences while at the same time defending the increasingly troublesome Aristotelian system.

Ironically, the Church itself was also having its own problems with the ancient philosopher's earth-centered cosmos. As long as the true relationship between the sun, moon, and earth remained a mystery, it was impossible to design a calendar that would synchronize solar and lunar cycles without the need for constant periodic adjustments. The celebration of feasts, festivals, and holy days was crucial to Catholicism, and the lack of a dependable calendar made it extremely difficult for Rome to coordinate its activities throughout its wide geographical range of influence. A more functional model of the solar system had to be devised.

The Sun-Centered System of Copernicus

One of the persons involved with revising the calendar was a Polish mathematician named Niklas Koppernigk, whom we more commonly know as Copernicus. In 1514 he set forth the idea of a sun-centered system in an unpublished manuscript called *The Little Commentary*. By attributing this heretical idea to ancient scholars, Copernicus escaped the wrath of religious fundamentalists who fervently defended the earth-centered system. His full thesis, *On the Revolutions of the Celestial Spheres*, was published around the time of his death in 1543. The Church in 1582 officially adopted a reformed calendar based in part on the Copernican calculations.

Despite the superiority of his own work, Copernicus did not directly challenge Aristotle's cosmology. As a Catholic cleric, he was certainly aware of the sensitive nature of his subject, and may not have wanted his work to be rejected on theological grounds. He instead maintained that his system was merely an imaginary model fabricated solely for the purpose of solving certain mathematical problems in reforming the calendar. He presented it more as a demonstration that an earth-centered system was not the only way celestial movement could be represented. He stopped short of claiming that the solar system was *actually* configured this way. He also retained in his system certain Aristotelian features such as the celestial spheres. By doing so, he managed to attract a wider audience for his ideas while avoiding immediate persecution.

It was a free-thinking Italian mathematician who finally shattered the crystalline spheres of Aristotle, and with it the alliance between Church and science.

The Heresy of Galileo

Galileo constructed the first complete telescope in 1609, which was essentially an improved version of the more primitive Dutch nautical spyglass in use on ships at the time. After increasing its power to thirty diameters, he began a systematic study of the heavens. Through careful observation of celestial phenomena, Galileo was now able to conclusively prove the Copernican model of a sun-centered solar system. His discovery of moons freely orbiting around Jupiter dismissed forever the notion that the planets were fixed to the surfaces of crystalline spheres. With the observation of sunspots that progressively moved across the solar disk, Galileo demonstrated that the sun was not only flawed, but that it was also rotating on an axis, thus refuting the Jesuits' contention that the heavenly bodies were perfect and unchanging.

In one fell swoop, Galileo demolished the universe of Aristotle, and with it the apparent harmony between the physical world and the sacred Scriptures. The impact of this was far more devastating than the work of Copernicus, which had been merely a thesis on paper subject to intellectual interpretation and debate. Scholars everywhere were confirming Galileo's observations by simply gazing through one of the telescopes he was now manufacturing and offering for sale.

To their credit, some officials in the Church were not initially opposed to these revolutionary ideas. The clergy were among society's most educated persons, and many actually welcomed these kinds of scientific advancements. The challenge was not in squelching this new information, but how to best manage its dissemination. There was a real danger that publishing these findings in their entirety might weaken people's faith in the Scriptures, thereby threatening to loosen the religious ties that helped hold society together. Galileo was therefore charged by the Church fathers to carefully present only bits and pieces of his observations over a span of time to allow people to become gradually acclimated to such a radical concept.

With the ascension of a new Pope who seemed to be more progressive in his thinking than his predecessor, Galileo unwisely assumed papal tolerance and boldly published his entire thesis in a work called *The Dialogue on the Two Chief Systems of the World*. He cast the character Simplicio—the defender of the Aristotelian system—as somewhat of a fool, which offended many of the clergy. He also ignored Pope Urban's instructions to present the Copernican system as hypothesis only. The Pope responded by outlawing as heresy any work promoting a sun-centered creation. He ordered Galileo tried before the Inquisition, and forced him to publicly denounce his own work. The Inquisition placed Galileo's description of planetary motion on The Index, decreeing, "To assert that the sun, immobile and without local movement, occupies the center of the world is an absurd proposition, false in philosophy, and more over, heretical, since it is contrary to the testimony of the Scriptures."

This unfortunate incident marked the first significant rift between science and Christianity. Before this, the predominant view among scholars and ecclesiastics alike was that the world could be understood only through adherence to the word of God and the inspiration it provided. The Church's position on the subject was "through faith comes knowledge." After the persecution of Galileo, scholars began to distance themselves from Rome, adopting instead the viewpoint that "through knowledge comes faith." No longer would the Church be allowed to dictate what the established belief system should be. Scholars would now formulate their own system founded on observations and reason alone. They thus became the pioneers of our modern age, and the new standard-bearers in the quest for the Theory of Everything. The Church in turn increasingly withdrew from matters scientific until it was confined almost exclusively to spiritual, social, and political issues.

Unfortunately, as the discipline of science advanced and matured, it too became an institution much like the Church before it. As its history shows, it too has sometimes exercised the same stubborn dogmatism when confronted with facts that threatened its established belief systems.

The Clockwork Universe of Isaac Newton

Perhaps no other work did more to firmly establish science as an institution than the TOE devised by Sir Isaac Newton. Building on the efforts of such men as Descartes and Kepler,

Newton introduced for the first time the concept of physical law. In his *Principia* published in 1687, Newton described the universe as a giant clock-like machine that performed according to fixed laws and principles established at the beginning of creation. These laws were immutable, and all things from comets to cannonballs were subject to them. The well-known adage, "for every action there is an equal and opposite reaction," is one of Newton's famous Laws of Motion. He also confirmed the existence of gravity (whether or not this had anything to do with an apple falling on his head is uncertain), and developed equations for calculating the orbits and relative masses of the planets. He demonstrated that the laws governing both the heavens and earth were the same. The only pure absolutes were space and time, which were separate elements both infinite and unchanging. Space was an empty infinite void without any substance or features. Time ticked by with a constant, unwavering meter, and would continue to do so until the end of creation Physical matter in contrast was not infinite, and so was not an absolute like space and time. Finite matter occupied infinite space, and underwent changes as it moved through the continual cadence of time.

Newton's new physical principles destroyed all that was left of the old belief systems. No longer were the planets kept in motion by the hand of God, but were held in their orbits by the force of gravity. Objects behaved as they did, not because of their individual God-given nature, but according to the universal laws that governed all other objects as well. There was now a consistent set of principles and mathematical formulas by which seemingly every aspect of the physical world could be measured and analyzed.

Armed with this new model of the universe, science made extraordinary and unprecedented progress in deciphering the mysteries of the natural world. There was, however, a serious flaw in this seemingly perfect system that was to eventually lead to its downfall. Newton had derived his laws primarily from the study of gravitational and mechanical forces, but had neglected to include within his framework a detailed examination of light and electricity. There was also little understanding in his time of what we know today as electromagnetic fields. He simply surmised that such energy was composed of tiny bits of matter (later named photons and electrons) that were subject to the same laws that governed all other matter. Subsequent research into the nature of energy was to reveal a new set of anomalies that—like Aristotle before him—would prove his assumption to be in error.

Newton's Clock Unwinds

Early in the nineteenth century, researcher Thomas Young conducted his famous "two-slit" experiment with light. In order to study how photons traveled through space, he split a light source into separate beams by projecting it through a pair of slits in a board and onto a screen. He was attempting to trace the paths of the photons in the separated beam by repeatedly altering the distance between the slits and observing the results from each change. Instead of the random variations predicted by Newtonian physics, the two beams mysteriously produced alternating bands of light and dark on the screen. It appeared as if the separate light beams were somehow colliding with each other after passing through the board and producing a pattern of ripples or waves. But if a beam of light was made up of tiny particles of matter as Newton had claimed, how could it also behave like a wave? If the pellets from two shotgun blasts collided in midair (which is what particle beams should be like), they could not produce any sort of organized wave pattern, but only a scattered random pattern resulting from the sum total of all the individual collisions. On top of that, if space was truly the empty void that Newton proclaimed it was, how could anything produce waves in it? After all, empty space was not supposed to be a material substance like a body of water where one

19

could make waves by tossing in a pebble. Space was an absolute emptiness, and so light particles should travel straight through without incident. This was indeed a very perplexing anomaly.

Research into the nature of electricity was also producing some disturbing anomalies. It was discovered, for example, that an electrical current flowing through a metal wire produced a field of energy around it. It was easy to understand how electric particles could be conducted through a solid physical wire by passing from atom to atom, but how could empty space act as a conductor for an energy field? According to Newton, space was not physical, and so could not act as an electrical conductor like a solid metal wire.

Unfortunately, physicists who were trying to unravel these mysteries suffered from a huge mental block brought on by a false assumption. Newton's principles had been so effective at explaining the workings of the physical world that no one could imagine they might be flawed or deficient in some way. The scientific community's complete adoration of Newton had led them to raise his work from theory to dogma in the same way the Church before them had deified the Aristotelian system. The *Principia* was now more important than the Truth it was intended to describe. Instead of simply allowing these new observations to carry them to a deeper understanding of reality, scientists searched frantically for a way to explain them away while preserving the Newtonian universe.

The "solution" these scientists eventually conjured up took the form of an imaginary, invisible substance that would serve the need for a physical conductor to carry both light waves and electrical fields. This hypothetical substance, or *ether* as it was called, allegedly occupied all of space and acted as the medium in which light produced ripples and through which electrical fields were conducted.

In 1865, physicist James Maxwell published *A Dynamical Theory of the Electromagnetic Field* in which he discussed the similarities between light, magnetism and electricity. He concluded that these energies created disturbances or waves in the ether, and it was these ethereal waves that traveled through space, not the energy itself. In Maxwell's universe, the light from a star in the night sky was not a stream of photons from millions of miles away entering into our eyes. Instead, the star's energy output produced a wave pattern in the ether, and it was these ethereal waves that moved across space and into our eyes (this is something like the waves from an object dropped into a lake reaching a distant shore where an observer can see the pattern of waves hitting the beach, but not the original object). The reason why it took time for these waves to travel through empty space was that the ether was thick enough to slow their progress.

It now seemed that all was well again with the universe. Newtonian faith had been successfully defended. But there was still no direct evidence that this ether really existed. All was speculation aimed at explaining away anomalous phenomena. Maxwell and his contemporaries were indeed on a search for Truth, but only if it could be found within the framework of Newtonian physics.

One inquisitive scientist decided to settle the question of this ether once and for all. In a moment of inspiration, Albert Michelson reasoned that the earth must encounter resistance against the ether as it rotated through space, and this resistance should therefore be measurable. A beam of light projected in the same direction as the earth's rotation should run head-on into the ether and be slowed by the resistance. Likewise, a light beam projected in the opposite direction should move much faster because it would then have the ethereal "wind" at its back. Augustin Fresnel had already demonstrated that the velocity of a light beam projected through water was influenced by the speed and direction of the water's flow. It seemed logical that light would be similarly affected by the flow of ether across the surface of the earth.

With the help of his colleague Edward Morley, Michelson

devised an experiment to measure this proposed variance in the speed of light caused by ethereal resistance. He used mirrors to split a light source into two separate beams and caused them to travel at right angles to each other across a large square slab of sandstone. He then suspended the slab on a pool of mercury so that it could be easily rotated in any direction. By positioning the stone so that one of the beams faced in the direction of the earth's rotation and thus into the ether, he could compare its speed with that of the second perpendicular beam and conclusively demonstrate the existence of the ether.

Three days and sixteen rotations later, the results were negative. Not a single variation was detected between the speed of the two beams. It was as if the ether didn't exist at all! Since this just could not be (i.e., Newton could not be wrong), it was then assumed that the failure to detect the either was due to some fault in the equipment itself. A few scientists even proposed that the equipment's movement through the earth's magnetic field compressed its molecular structure in such a way as to cause the device to shrink in exact proportion to the anticipated resistance of the ether (talk about "bending" the facts to fit the story). The slower beam would then appear to be moving at the same speed as the faster one because the distance it had to cross was shorter due to this shrinkage. Today we might be tempted to look back at this dogmatic thinking with a degree of amusement, but it is alive and well, and still makes occasional appearances on the stage of scholastic vocation.

All Things Become Relative

It was Albert Einstein who finally put to rest the debate surrounding the ether. After carefully considering all the available evidence, he decided to accept the experimental results at their face value, and concluded that the ether simply did not exist. By daring to challenge the Newtonian worldview, he took a crucial step toward formulating his legendary theory of Relativity. In

Einstein's universe, there were no absolutes of time or space as Newton had claimed. The only absolute was the speed of light. All things and events were variables that could be measured only in relation to other things and events (thus the saying that *all things are relative*). Time was no longer a fixed, cosmic rhythm, but was now relative to velocity. A clock ticking away at the North Pole kept different time than one located at the Equator because the equatorial timepiece was traveling through space much faster as the earth rotated.

In order to place anything in the universe with any degree of accuracy, one not only needed to define it spatially (i.e., its x, y, and z co-ordinates), but in time as well. Space and time could therefore not be the separate, absolute entities that Newton had claimed. Instead, they were intrinsically interwoven into a new concept called *space-time*. The famous equation $e=mc^2$ demonstrated that matter and energy were not absolutes, but were merely two varying forms of the same substance. Because light took time to travel, it was impossible to say with certainty what was going on elsewhere in the universe at any given moment, since the light of a star in the night sky had left its source perhaps thousands of years earlier.

The brilliance of this new system arose from Einstein's fantastic vision of the cosmos. Instead of the traditional collage of materials and forces, he perceived the universe as being a single immense unified field. What was previously thought of as empty space was actually vast expanses in this field where its density was very thin. The physical objects that occupied this field were in fact areas of much greater density within its fabric, or what he called *matter points*. In Einstein's universe, everything was interconnected, just as religious sages had been saying for centuries. Moreover, everything in the universe was made of this same fabric field, so that matter and energy were merely two forms of the same substance.

Gone forever was Newton's rigid universal machine with its individual mechanical parts. Its many cogs, gears and wheels now merged together into a continuous expanse of lumpy soup (hence the name *continuum*) with all its ingredients in constant flux. The measurements of any portion of this continuum now varied according to what place in the soup the observer was, which part of the soup was under observation, and how fast or slow the observer was traveling relative to the spatial and temporal co-ordinates of the portion being observed. Oh, and the results could vary significantly depending on *when* the measurement was taken.

Relativity became the new status quo, the new Absolute Truth. With it's help, physicists were now able to resolve the anomalies inherent in the old Newtonian system. Yet relativity too would soon have its own set of anomalies to contend with. Research into the nature of subatomic particles was about to challenge this freshly laid cornerstone of twentieth century science.

The Uncertain World of the Quantum

Physicists who were trying to determine both the momentum and location of individual electrons were running into an experimental dilemma. Since an electron is such a tiny particle, normal light could not be used to detect its location because the electron would become lost between the much larger light waves. It was then discovered that gamma radiation (which has a much smaller wavelength than visible light) could be used to pin down the exact location of an electron. But this created another problem in that the more tightly packed gamma rays now deflected the electron from its previous course and speed, making it impossible to determine the particle's momentum at the time of measurement. Other types of energy beams with larger wavelengths were only effective at measuring momentum, while those with tighter wavelengths could only reveal location. The best that the frustrated scientists could achieve was the ability to mathematically predict the *probability* of a given particle to be in a certain location and at a certain velocity at any given time. It was ultimately concluded that determining the precise natural state of any given particle was impossible because the very act of measuring or even observing it would invariably alter that state. This *uncertainty principle* laid the foundation of quantum mechanics, an entirely new theory of physics aimed at describing the newly discovered subatomic world.

Herein lay the dilemma. Einstein, like Newton before him, believed that the universe had a fixed order or set of laws that could never be broken, even though the relationships between its elements were in constant flux. This belief was fundamental to his thinking when he formulated the theory of relativity. Einstein saw beneath the workings of the cosmos Aristotle's Prime Mover (he called God "the Old One") that established the order of all things at the beginning of creation. He maintained that, given enough information, everything about that order was ultimately knowable and predictable. Everything was the result of cause and effect, being ultimately traceable back to the Prime Cause. Unable to accept a creation-by-chance picture of the universe, Einstein denounced the new philosophy of uncertainty, asserting that "quantum mechanics is impressive, but I am convinced that God does not play dice."

Those physicists siding with Einstein argued that this apparent uncertainty was due to certain limitations of the measuring instruments available at that time, and that given enough information, the exact future state of any given subatomic particle was indeed predictable. The opposing school of thought held that unpredictability was an inherent part of reality. According to them, the current state of the universe was not a result of predictable cause and effect, but the product of random-chance occurrences.

There was yet an even deeper, more fundamental quandary arising from this debate, and one that science had never before encountered. Unlike the past progression of TOEs, this new theory of quantum physics was not able to overthrow its prede-cessor. Although it was true that relativity could not explain the random nature of the micro-universe of subatomic particles, neither could quantum physics explain the predictability of the world at large. What was it that made the orbit of a planet cer-tain and predictable, but not the orbit of an electron? Why did the laws of physics appear to change during the transition from the subatomic to the macroscopic?

This obvious inconsistency between these two theoretical systems has remained largely unresolved to this day. Whereas relativistic theory is the best at explaining the macro-universe, quantum theory provides a more accurate description of the subatomic world. Although this dual expression of physical law serves us for the present, it also holds us back from making even greater scientific progress. Neither gives us the complete picture of reality, and consequently neither can be the Truth that we seek. Both must inevitably succumb to the same chal-lenges that dethroned Aristotle and Newton before, and in turn be replaced by a single TOE that will accept more pieces of the universal puzzle.

Where Do We Go From Here?

Physicists today recognize that in order to reconcile the conflicts between relativity and quantum mechanics, they must first determine the process by which the universe came into being and how it evolved into its present state. The pursuit of this cosmology has led science to perhaps the greatest challenge it has ever faced. It may ultimately prove to be a challenge that science alone cannot overcome.

A perfect example of this can be seen in the research being done on the Grand Unified Field Theory. It is believed that at the moment of creation, all that was to become the universe was concentrated into a single, infinitely tiny compact nucleus that for some unknown reason suddenly exploded. Physicists and astronomers call this event the *Big Bang*. At the exact instant of this grand explosion, a single unified field of energy was released. Within the next fraction of a second, the expanding energy field began to cool and coagulate into various elemental particles and forces. The four forces known to us today—electromagnetism, gravity, and the strong and weak nuclear forces—are all offspring of this first primordial field. The Grand Unified Field Theory attempts to demonstrate by experimentation and mathematical proofs how these four fundamental forces were originally fused together. If this theory is correct, then by reproducing the proper temperatures and particle velocities, the four forces can be joined back together into a single field of primordial energy.

Two-fold unification between the weak nuclear force and electromagnetism has already been demonstrated, and so many scientists believe that we are on the right track. But no known furnace or vessel could ever re-create or contain the incredibly high temperatures necessary to verify even three-fold unification. To prove a complete four-fold unification would require a particle accelerator of such proportions as to be on a galactic scale, which of course is an engineering impossibility. The estimates are that such an accelerator would be required to trace a circular path one trillion kilometers in circumference—a light beam would take a month to travel its length. To demonstrate total unification (i.e., the re-assembling of *all* cosmic particles and forces into the pre-Big-Bang nucleus) would require an accelerator with the incredible circumference of one-thousand light-years. By comparison, the circumference of our entire solar system is only one light-*day*.

Attempts at demonstrating other possible TOEs suffer from the same physical limitations. We are fast approaching a stage in our search for Truth where scientific proof of a new TOE may be physically impossible. An entirely new way of assessing the universe might be required if we are to make any progress in solving this cosmic puzzle. Physicists may be forced to lay aside

27

their measuring instruments and instead place their hopes on a TOE that will answer the greatest number of questions about the universe, but will probably remain scientifically unproven.

A few prominent physicists have already come to embrace this inevitability. Professor G. Chew of the Physics Department at Berkeley once stated in a lecture that, "our current struggle [with certain aspects of advanced physics] may thus be only a fore-taste of a completely new form of human intellectual endeavor, one that will not only lie outside physics, but will not even be describable as 'scientific.'" We thus have every justification—yes, even a compelling need—to seek Truth in areas previously considered out-of-bounds by mainstream science.

The Dogma of Exclusionism

If our instruments will truly fail us, how will we gather the additional information from which to construct this ultimate TOE? Actually, there is already a wealth of data usually ignored by science that can assist in our reckoning. But to make use of it, another scientific hurdle must first be overcome, an obstacle of science's own making.

When scholars first distanced themselves from the Church, they decided to establish a dogma of their own—a dogma of science, by science, and for science. *They* would be the final judges as to what constituted Truth. *They* would hand down the edicts of what must be accepted and what must be excluded from consideration. This elitist demeanor, although perfectly understandable given the circumstances, has trickled down into our modern time as a subtle but intrinsic part of the scientific mindset. Just as had been the case with the Newtonian system, scholars now often adopt the very same prejudicial attitude for which they condemned the Church, refusing to entertain ideas and evidence that might threaten their beliefs.

The writer Charles Fort described this scientific snobbery as *exclusionism*, or the practice of disregarding or demeaning any observable phenomena or anomaly that does not fit into the established belief system. It was this same exclusionistic mindset that dreamed up the imaginary ether of the nineteenth century. The scientific community has all too often championed such exclusionism, embracing the prevailing TOE not merely as a working theory, but as a fortress complete with gunners and moat behind which the establishment can find security while repelling all challengers.

It is not easy to overcome centuries of this scholastic bigotry. Science has rarely been an institution that readily submits to change. Even when anomalies that challenge the establishment are confirmed by numerous qualified observers, the data is still often ignored or rejected simply because it threatens to bring down the current system. Take for example the scientists in the 19th century who scoffed at the widespread reports of meteor falls. Brushing aside such stories as the spawn of ignorance or lies, these men of science assured the poor misguided citizenry that no rocks can fall from the sky simply because there are no rocks in the sky! After all, wasn't it a hoard of uneducated peasants who were claiming aerial bombardment? It was inconceivable that these simple folk were knowledgeable about something of which the distinguished and learned professors knew nothing.

From a strictly self-serving perspective, this prejudicial attitude is at least understandable. How many of us would eagerly embrace a concept that might render an entire career's worth of education, research and dedication meaningless or irrelevant? And if such data came on the lips of ignorant laypeople, wouldn't it be much easier to use one's scholastic credentials as an authoritative club with which to crush these silly rumors and those who spread them?

History is littered with examples of this exclusionistic posture being adopted in the face of new facts that contradicted the prevailing belief system. The Church, for instance, was not Galileo's only antagonist. Francesco Sizzi, a fellow astronomer and contemporary, actually refused an invitation from Galileo to observe the moons of Jupiter through his new telescope, replying that these satellites ".... are invisible to the naked eye and therefore can exercise no influence on the earth, and therefore would be useless, and therefore do not exist."

The scholar Ticinelli, having excluded from his reasoning the future possibility of manned flight, ridiculed the ideas of his contemporary Leonardo Da Vinci, writing, "I have decided to proceed to the disproving of another widespread fallacy: to wit, the notion that in future centuries it will be possible for men to fly by mechanical means."

Now one might say that science has come a long way since the days of Ticinelli. Exclusionism, however, has never been confined to any particular age. In 1957, the noted astronomer Richard vander Riet Wooley proclaimed that the idea of space flight was "utter bilge." Within the year, the Russians launched Sputnik 1.

Thomas Edison fared no better against the exclusionists. When his new talking machine was first demonstrated before the prestigious Paris Academy of Sciences, many of the learned men in attendance declared it to be a hoax performed by ventriloquism.

A periodical no less reputable than *Scientific American* once published an editorial in which physical and mathematical evidence was given to demonstrate that heavier-than-air flight was impossible. The only problem was that the Wright Brothers had already made their first flight prior to its publication.

It is easy for those shut safely behind the fortress walls of institutions and universities to scoff at reports of falling rocks. It is far more difficult to accept evidence that can shatter one's own personal notion as to how things really are. However, there must come a time for even the most stubborn when the cumulative weight of such anomalous evidence becomes irresistible and irrefutable. It is at such times that the old Order must fall and a new one erected in its place.

"Unscientific" Data

The frontiers of human knowledge have never been solely defined by the limits of our science and technology. There are many undeniable truths for which no scientific proof is possible. Take for example the concept of beauty. Many think that Da Vinci's *Mona Lisa* is beautiful. But how would you prove her beauty scientifically? An opinion poll showing what percentage of the population favors Mona is not the type of evidence normally accepted by science. Yet there is little doubt that in many people's eyes, Mona's beauty is an irrefutable fact.

The same argument can be made concerning the emotion of love. The significance of this powerful force is beyond question in spite of the absence of a proof derived through the scientific method. Just because science is unable to construct a device capable of measuring love, does it mean that love is less a part of physical reality than the specific gravity of water or the number of electrons in a hydrogen atom? Do scientists go home to their spouses and refuse to show them love solely because the equipment back at the laboratory fails to detect its presence?

How about the functions of our own minds? The scientific model of the human brain maintains that thoughts and emotions are only intangible abstracts. The products of the human psyche are not believed to have any objective reality apart from the physical brain that generates them. In other words, it is the brain itself that is seen as the physical reality, while its psychological constituents—thoughts and emotions—are merely a description of how that reality behaves. Yet if we set aside for a moment this common prejudice (or misconception if you will), it can easily be shown that, despite our lacking instrumentation that can weigh and measure them, thoughts and emotions are indeed real tangible artifacts in and of themselves.

One of the basic scientific tests for objective reality is the concept of cause and effect. Every event in the universe has a definite cause, and every cause in the universe has physical consequences or effects. Apply this law to human emotions, and you will quickly realize that these "abstracts" certainly do cause physical consequences. Hitler harnessed the emotion of hate, and with it changed the physical face of Europe. Edison took an active imagination coupled with determination and persistence, and created a whole new world around him. Even something as simple as driving a car with an aggressive attitude will produce the physical consequence of an accident far more often than driving while in a more passive state. Therefore, by science's own criteria, emotions are not just imaginary intangibles, but are indeed aspects of objective reality in their own right. They are real physical things that produce real physical actions that in turn cause real physical consequences.

The argument for thought being its own physical reality is even more compelling than for emotions. Whereas emotions behave like a force, thought acts more like a structure or form. Think for a moment (no pun intended) about the invention of the light bulb. We could embark on a lengthy discussion about the theory behind it, as well as the methods and materials used in its construction. But after all is said and done, one fact would remain—the creation of the light bulb began with a thought. The light bulb is the direct physical consequence or effect of the original idea first formed in the mind of the inventor. Moreover, the structure of the physical light bulb has a one-to-one correlation with the structure of the thought that caused its existence. Although the physical brain conducted the thought through itself and into the physical hands that then shaped the physical light bulb with its physical fingers, the object would never have come into being without the thought image or model as its original causality.

Throughout history, there have been billions upon billions of physical brain/hand combinations that have taken place within us. But only one of them produced the first light bulb. The single, solitary difference between the billions and the one was the quality of the thought. Therefore, the very physical existence of the light bulb itself is the indisputable evidence that the thought originally containing its image had an object-ive reality independent of the physical structure (i.e., the brain) through which it was conducted—otherwise, we would expect every human brain that ever existed to also produce light bulbs automatically.

Consider this too: throughout the entire span of the cosmos to the very end of time itself, no amount of chemical reactions, forces of energy, evolutionary processes or random occurrences will ever combine to naturally self-assemble a light bulb all on its own. It had to first assemble an intelligent, visualizing brain with articulating hands as its creative instruments. The human mind is a very unique cosmic construction indeed, the full capa-bilities of which extend beyond any attempt to define it mater-ially, electrically or genetically.

Science must come to terms with such "unscientific" truths if it ever hopes to arrive at a TOE that will transcend the limits of its technology. If we accept as reality such intangibles as hu-man thoughts and emotions, then we must find a place for them within the framework of the ultimate theory, even though they cannot be reduced to mathematical equations or measured with scientific instruments.

More Unscientific Data

Physicists painstakingly dissect matter into increasingly smaller fragments in the hope that by learning how the pieces fit together they might somehow unlock the secrets of creation. Yet throughout their labors, they have consistently overlooked the one piece of matter that continuously displays the process of creation they seek to understand. The human brain has the ability to transform invisible thought into visible reality, or in other words, to create something tangible from something that is intangible. Both science and religion have long been in agree-ment that the creation of the universe resulted from a similar process of tangible reality arising from intangible obscurity. If so, then discovering how the human creative faculty works may lead to a deeper understanding of how the universe itself came into being.

If everything in the entire universe is built according to a single set of fixed physical laws, and if the human brain is a component of that universe, then the brain must also be designed according to those same laws that govern every other universal element and component. These universal laws form a type of invisible cosmic pattern or blueprint by which all substances, energies and processes are accordingly shaped. It's unreasonable to believe that the brain could function outside the physical laws that shaped it. Isn't it then logical to conclude that the creation mechanism within the brain operates along the same lines as the mechanism that created the universe itself? Could it be that the cosmos, through the process we call evolution, shaped our brains in its own creational image? This notion may at first seem too fantastic, but it appears even more unlikely that our own creative processes operate in some fundamentally different manner than those that brought about the creation of the greater universe.

Alternative Realities

It might be tempting at this point to offer the creation of the light bulb from invisible thought as a proof for the relationship between human creativity and universal creation. But there would be a subtle flaw in making that kind of deductive leap. Although the human creative faculty might certainly mimic that of the universal creation, it falls short in that it is not spontaneous. In other words, the mind indeed creates the original thought spontaneously, but it does not immediately create the actual physical light bulb directly from that thought. The mind is exerting no direct effect over physical reality to produce the light bulb, but is merely commanding the hands to re-arrange the already created compounds in the earth into the desired shape. It can therefore be said that this process is not one of creation, but a form of manipulation. To actually demonstrate the relationship between mind and matter, a more convincing example must be found in which the human mind directly and immediately exerts its influence over physical reality without the use of a set of hands as intermediaries.

Fortunately, there is a category of evidence that can furnish us with such examples. It goes by a variety of names—ESP, psi, parapsychology, psychic phenomena, and the like. These are grouped under the general heading of *paranormal phenomena*. Paranormal occurrences like telepathy and telekinesis display the type of creative spontaneity that illustrates the mind's ability to directly effect physical reality.

Consider a common example of ESP. You are thinking of someone you have not heard from in a long time. Immediately the phone rings and the caller is that person. Most people have had an experience like this at least once in their lives. We could of course have a debate as to whether the recipient's thoughts caused the caller to dial, or the caller's dialing cause the recipient to think of that person. In either case, a process in the one person's mind causes an immediate effect on the mind of the other without the two being in physical contact. This is certainly more than mere physical manipulation, since there is no physical implement being used by one mind to manipulate the workings of the other. This is an example of true spontaneous creation.

The most remarkable aspect of these paranormal mental phenomena is that they appear to accomplish their spontaneity by operating outside the confines of space and time. In normal space, two interacting events must be physically connected in some way. You cannot turn on a light, for instance, without first physically touching the light switch. The bulb itself will not light without power being fed to it by a hard-wired connection. Even a television receives its signals over a physical carrier wave that connects the broadcasting tower to the set's receiving antenna. But in the above example of ESP, one mind produces a direct effect on the reality of other mind from a remote distance without any physical contact between them. This should not be possible according to the laws of conventional physics. Yet we know it happens.

Admittedly, the paranormal is perhaps the most damned and excluded subject in modern history. Its very existence is diputed among distinguished scientists and psychologists alike. Most attempts at reproducing paranormal phenomena under controlled laboratory conditions have yielded inconsistent and inconclusive results, leading mainstream science to reject the paranormal as scientifically unprovable. Yet the thousands of well-documented accounts of strange phenomena reported by credible witnesses from all walks of life, as well as the evidence recorded on film, tape and digital media, force us to seriously contend with this body of data. The paranormal experiences of others cannot be ignored merely because these phenomena do not readily submit to scientific scrutiny. How can we surrender an entire body of human experience to a mere handful of laboratory formulas and procedures? Should we now enslave ourselves to our own creation, becoming the servants of science instead of our science serving us?

It is precisely because these strange events escape the grasp of today's sciences that they deserve a place in our search. They are just the type of anomalous evidence that can lead to a new and more complete Theory of Everything.

The Spiritual Cosmos

In addition to including an honest study of the paranormal in its quest for Truth, science needs to once again take a fresh look at Judeo-Christianity. There is much evidence worthy of consideration within the domain of God. For example, there are well-documented cases of individuals having undergone an increase in supernatural experiences through spiritual devotion. If adherence to Biblical principles can somehow amplify the creational forces of the human psyche, then the Scriptures must also contain information that will shed more light on the universal creation.

Imagine the brain as a complex computer. If a computer is programmed with "garbage"—programming that is incorrect or inaccurate—it will produce worthless results. But if the brain is programmed with accurate information and instructions, the results can be quite impressive. If there were no Truth in the Scriptures, then no power would ever be realized by adhering to its precepts. Since our brains are built along the same physical principles as all other matter in the universe, the fact that Biblical teachings produce an increase in the brain's spontaneous creative faculty indicates that Biblical "programming" (designed for our own human computers) contains accurate information regarding the order of creation.

There are still other reasons to include the Scriptures in the search for Truth. Few other literary works delve more thoroughly into the relationship between the Creator and the human mind. The Scriptures were mostly penned by individuals who were both observers of and participants in supernatural events. And let's not forget that the very founders of modern science—Copernicus, Galileo, Kepler, Newton, and Einstein—strongly believed in the existence of God or a Prime Creator, and in their religious faith sought to unravel the mysteries of His creation. We shall at the very least be in good company.

Still More Exclusionism

The introduction of spiritual elements in this work compels us to also address the dogma of ecclesiastical exclusionism. The religious snubbing of modern science is rooted primarily in fundamentalist extremism, which maintains that the Scriptures contain the sum total of all Truth regardless to what additional information or evidence might be available. Take for example the belief that the earth is only about 6000 years old in spite of the abundance of geological and archaeological evidence to the contrary. Among the proofs presented by its proponents is a passage from the book of Psalms (90:4): *For a thousand years in your sight are like a day that has just gone by, or like a watch in the night.* The reasoning here is that if the earth was created in six days as is stated in the book of Genesis, and if a day of God is equal to 1000 years, then the earth must be 6000 years old. Any evidence that cannot be made to conform to this scriptural sum must be discarded or re-evaluated.

But the last part of this passage referring to "a watch in the night" proves this interpretation faulty. The ancient Hebrews divided the night into sentry periods or *watches* of four hours each. By using the same formula as before, the following alternative can be calculated: one watch of four hours = 1000 years; six watches per 24-hour period × 1000 years = 6000 years per day; 6000 years per day × the six days of creation = 36,000 years of earth age. So, according to these passages, the six days of God devoted to the creation could be for us either 6000 years or 36,000 years. Take your pick. The significant difference in the two sums clearly shows that the ancient writer composed this passage as a metaphor, not as a literal, precise unit of time.

There is a second possible interpretation of these passages that indicates the numbers are not to be taken literally. The number 1000 was sometimes used in ancient times as a loose equivalent for the concept of infinity. To say, for example, that a person owned 1000 goats might simply mean that the number of goats in his herd were too numerous to count. Today we sometimes jokingly use fictitious numbers to express the same idea like "He has a 'ga-zillion' of them." Therefore the phrase "for a thousand years in your sight are like a day" was no doubt intended to mean "an immeasurable period of time" instead of a specific number.

As a Christian, this writer agrees in principle that the Bible is Truth. But one must admit that it's not always a simple task to establish exactly what those words are saying.

There are still those of religious faith who view physics as a "profane" science. Yet the very Scriptures themselves oppose this view, proclaiming, *Ever since the creation of the world, His invisible nature, namely, His eternal power and deity, has been clearly perceived in the things that have been made* (Romans 1:20). Are we not then meant to scientifically study His creation —the things that have been made—so that we might better understand the nature of its Creator? The apocryphal book of Wisdom (13:9) seems to almost taunt us into pursuing just such an analytical course, *for if they had the power to know so much that they could investigate the world, how did they fail to find sooner the Lord of these things?* Those who claim a sincere love of Truth cannot simply dismiss hard scientific data. After all, it is the earth that indeed revolves around the sun.

Scientists, like other mortals, can be profane. Their findings, if accurate, cannot.

Being both a Christian *and* a rationalist, I have always found the clash between faith and science to be both disturbing and unnecessary. If there is but one set of physical or empirical laws governing all things, then both science and religion must eventually reach the same conclusions, even if arrived at by opposite approaches. Christian faith indeed dictates that the Scriptures need to be accepted by the believer as Truth. But those same Scriptures in no way forbid scientific study. After all, scientific data is nothing more than a highly detailed description of various aspects of God's Creation.

Perhaps if the Church had received the ideas of Galileo with less hostility, both disciplines would have continued to work together in greater harmony over the last four centuries to unlock the secrets of the universe. Instead, each party now seems bent on inhibiting the growth and advancement of the other in the belief that one will eventually triumph while the other is discredited. This long-trodden position is not only untenable, but also entirely unnecessary, and what will ultimately prove to be an exercise in futility.

The Inclusionistic World View

Why not practice inclusionism in our reckoning of the cosmos? Must Biblical concepts be taboo to the physicist or the parapsychologist? Must religious fundamentalists reject the findings of science without further consideration merely because they seem at first sight to conflict with their spiritual beliefs? Must the paranormal be renounced out-of-hand by physicists because they cannot measure it, or by ecclesiastics because they fear it? Can we not, if our searching is both diligent and earnest, devise a system that will satisfactorily accommodate the critical elements of all these fields?

It can be said that the entire scientific process is an attempt to solve the equation, "Given the universe, derive God." Science has made great strides toward this goal, yet certain fundamental problems remain. Christianity on the other hand has been following the course indicated by the inverse equation, "Given God, derive the universe." Both approaches have their merits, yet both lack some essential ingredient necessary to describe the whole of what we humans observe and experience. The challenge is to establish a median where these two opposing disciplines can be joined in harmony. Only then can a theory be formulated that will describe both the entire body of physical phenomena *and* human experience, encompassing all that is scientific, spiritual, and supernatural.

The task is by no means simple. Great pains must be taken not to fall into the same intellectual traps as those ecclesiastics, philosophers, and theorists before us who, in their reckoning of the cosmos, excluded facts and evidence that according to their preconceived logic cannot possibly exist. The facts do indeed exist. It is our duty to allow those facts to tell their story and take their rightful place within the greater cosmological picture.

Nor will it be a casual journey. Some aspects of this subject are very deep, and at times will require an uncommon measure of contemplative commitment. Any soul who dares a peek behind the cosmic veil of creation must be prepared for focused meditation upon the very roots of reality itself. This is no intellectual stroll through the park, nor a path for the weak-willed and idly curious.

Judeo-Christianity, modern science, and the paranormal have never before been successfully brought together into one homogenous system. This fact alone, however, should not dissuade us. Those who have tried before have been shackled with the conventionalistic thinking of their specific fields of study. We, on the other hand, need not be constrained by the dogma of any individual discipline save that of the search for Absolute Truth. We should therefore make the most of this speculative liberty.

Whatever theoretical system or super-science awaits us at the end of our journey, the path that leads to it should incorporate the findings of modern science, embrace the body of religious principle, and accommodate the world of the paranormal. We shall then have practiced true Inclusionism.

Galileo would have wanted it that way.

Behind The Cosmic Veil

2

Scientific Anomalies and Misnomers

Disquieting Data that Science Cannot Yet Explain

*Science is a turtle who says that its
own shell encloses all things.*
—Charles Fort

Imagine you are a human of 40,000 years ago. You are ignorant of everything we today deem scientific. Your world is a mystery explained entirely through myth and fable. What primitive knowledge you may possess has been acquired from your personal interactions with the natural world.

Now imagine you are standing in an open field on a windy day. You feel the breeze against your face as you have so many times before. But on this occasion, a question enters your mind. How is the wind driven? Is it pushed, or pulled along? From your perspective in the field it's impossible to tell. Either way, the wind would appear to act in the same manner and would feel the same against your skin. Everything would behave exactly the same in your immediate surroundings whether the wind "blows" or "sucks" along.

But the conclusions you could derive about the world at

large would be far different from one than from the other.

Conventional thinking—conclusions that we draw based on similar circumstances with which we are already familiar—tells us that the wind is pushed along. We can make our own miniature winds by pushing the air with the wave of a hand, or blow it out our lungs through puckered lips. Even our common name for air movement—the wind is *blowing*—exhibits the conventional notion that the wind pushes along. This convention can also be seen in historic artwork and maps where clouds with human-like faces blow their blustery breath across the face of the earth.

Global air currents are influenced by a combination of many factors. But the predominant mechanism behind the wind is the movement of air from an area of high pressure to an area of low pressure. Although it appears at first to be a pushing effect, this assumption is not quite right. Scientifically speaking, it is more correct to say that a vacuum pulls air into itself. The vacuum of a low-pressure zone sucks air into it from adjacent areas of higher pressure, thereby producing the effect known as wind.

Conventional thinking is wrong. The wind is *pulled* along.

We can easily forgive ourselves for such errors in judgment, blaming it on a simple lack of information. We would certainly not expect those in the scientific community to make such elementary missteps in reasoning. But sometimes scientists also lack the necessary information from which to draw accurate judgments. They, like all other humans, do their best in such cases to fill the gaps with educated guesses or assumptions. These assumptions are often based on conventional thinking.

Take for example the established view of gravity. Science has long maintained that gravity is one of the four elementary forces in nature. This idea was championed in the early part of the 19th century by Michael Faraday, who successfully demonstrated that both electricity and magnetism were actually two different forms of the same energy (hence the name *electromagnetism*). He then assumed that since gravity appeared to work much like magnetism, it too must be a manifestation of that same force.

Science has embraced Faraday's basic concept down to the present day, and not without justification. Gravity does indeed seem to behave like a magnetic force. Its influence over physical masses can be measured, calculated, and accurately predicted. But what some may not realize is that there is no direct, hard physical evidence to confirm that gravity actually *is* an element-al force. According to the standard model of the universe, a force must convey its effect in the form of particles or waves. But after decades of intensive research, we have yet to detect the existence of either a gravity wave or a graviton (a particle of gravity). In the absence of hard proof, scientists *assume* that gravity must be an elemental force, especially since convention-al thinking tells us it behaves like one.

But what if gravity is not a force at all generated by physical matter? What if gravity is merely a consequence of the dimen-sional geometry of space?

Albert Einstein suggested a fascinating model of gravity. He asserted that all masses from protons to planets bend the geo-metry of the surrounding space, thereby creating curvatures or depressions in the otherwise featureless fabric of empty space. To illustrate this, imagine a thin rubber sheet stretched over the mouth of a large bowl. This rubber represents the flat plane of empty space. Next, take a large heavy marble to serve as a mod-el for a planet and place it on the center of the rubber sheet so that the weight of the marble produces a cone-like depression in the rubber. This depression represents the curvature in the fabric of space caused by the mass of our marble-planet.

Now imagine we take a much smaller marble and start it rolling around the bowl near the outer edge of the rubber sheet as if it were orbiting the larger marble. As the smaller marble rolls, it begins to spiral down the incline of the depression in the sheet toward the larger marble. Eventually, the smaller mar-ble will impact the larger one and come to rest against it at the bottom of the depression.

In Einstein's model, the smaller marble might represent a meteor traveling along a path in space. When it encounters the spatial depression surrounding a larger object like a planet, the meteor gets trapped in the gravity well and 'falls' inward, spiraling down the curvature of the depression toward the planet's surface. This model perfectly illustrates the effect we know as gravity.

If this is so, then gravity is not so much a force, but more a function of the curvature in space associated with the mass of a planetary body. Larger masses like the sun have much stronger gravitational fields simply because their greater mass displaces a proportionately larger depression in the geometry of space.

When astrophysicists employ the complex gravitational calculations necessary to formulate the flight paths of satellites, their resulting equations may not represent the measurement of a force at all, but instead may actually describe the geometric landscape of a solar system littered with potholes of planetary depressions—road hazards in the highway of space.

This doesn't mean these gravitational calculations are inaccurate. If gravity were indeed a consequence of the geometry of planetary space instead of an elemental force, its effect would be unchanged. Gravity would still behave in the same way, exerting its influence in the precise, predictable manner to which we are accustomed. Just as in the case of our prehistoric human and the wind, everything we can observe about the behavior of gravity would be exactly the same in either scenario. But the understanding we might derive as to the true nature of the universe would be quite different from one perspective than from the other. Our view of the cosmos might change considerably when we fully grasp the true nature of gravity.

Sometimes scientific ideas like those pertaining to gravity are presented to the general public as verified facts when they are instead merely assumptions or hypotheses. Although those presenting these concepts are well aware of a theory's unproven status, the air of professional authority with which these self-edifying assertions are made leaves the layperson with the impression of indisputable certitude. My high school text books were littered with such scientific misnomers. For instance, no mention was ever made in my classes about the uncertainties surrounding gravity, a fact of which those learned scholars who authored those books were certainly aware. Yet all the books pronounced unequivocally that gravity was an elemental force virtually identical to electromagnetism. Perhaps this subtle disinformation was due to a belief that oversimplification was necessary when addressing high school students. But regardless to the reason, the impression conveyed to the students was one of indisputable truth. It was only years later—through self-education—that I learned about the ambiguities regarding this and certain other scientific "facts."

The instruction I received on the subject of astronomy was no less tainted. Speculation and educated guesses were presented at every turn as absolute truth—the moon was formed in such-and-such a manner, the atmosphere of Jupiter comprised such-and-such, the surface of Venus was this-and-that, and so on. Many students were taught as late as the 1950s that moon craters might actually be the remnants of giant bubbles that formed in its early molten surface and then subsequently popped and hardened in the cold of space. Today we know that such ideas were nothing more than fantasy. But they weren't presented in the classroom that way.

Some scholars would like to think that they can predict the nature and behavior of most anything with science, and are willing to twist the facts to prove it. A case in point is that of the French astronomer Urbain LeVerrier. According to the official party line, LeVerrier predicted in 1846 the discovery of a planet beyond Uranus through calculations based on certain irregularities in its orbit. I remember being quite impressed when first learning about this in school. It was only years later that I came upon the inconvenient truth that had been excluded from my education. It seems that when the planet Neptune was finally discovered by astronomers Johann Galle and Heinrich d'Arrest, its actual position differed so much from its predicted location that LeVerrier himself questioned whether it was the planet of his calculations! Excluded too from my "education" was that Le-Verrier, using the very same methods of calculation, also predicted the location of a previously undiscovered planet between the Sun and Mercury. He was so confident of his findings that he took the liberty of pre-naming this intra-mercurial planet *Vulcan*. On March 22, 1877, Vulcan failed to show at the location LeVerrier predicted. We're still waiting.

Astronomers soon began to find similar irregularities in the orbits of the other planets but could offer no explanation, since additional planets that might cause such LeVerrien deviations simply weren't there. It fell to Albert Einstein and his relativity theory to finally explain these orbital anomalies. Relativity also exposed why Neptune's orbit was much further from Uranus than LeVerrier calculated, and why there was no planet Vulcan. The embarrassing truth was now exposed—LeVerrier predicted nothing, and the fact that there happened to be a planet beyond Uranus was pure coincidence. LeVerrier was merely the beneficiary of a stroke of dumb luck. In spite of their knowledge of this truth, the scientific community perpetuates this fantasy, and chants the praises of LeVerrier at every opportunity.

Perhaps such disquieting facts are concealed from students to prevent any tarnishing of the glory of Modern Science in the minds of such tender age. But this kind of scholastic trickery and deceit-by-omission must be exposed if real progress is to be made toward uncovering the Truth. How can you prepare and motivate students to ponder the mysteries of the universe when you deceive them into believing those mysteries have already been solved?

Please do not think that I am launching an attack on the discipline of science. On the contrary, this writer has devoted much time to its study. Science continues to inspire me with fascination and wonder, making my imagination soar as it first did during my grade school years. I am only trying to emphasize the difference between proven fact and hypothesis, and how easy it is to mistake one for the other, and how destructive it is to humanity's advancement to falsely portray one as the other. Scientific authorities, emboldened by science's many successes, have often presented mere theories to the public with an air of conviction normally associated with hard fact, thereby giving the false impression that science has mastered all it has surveyed. The problem here is not in the scientific method, but with human integrity. In reality, there is so much we still do not understand. Many uncertainties and anomalies remain, numerous theories continue unverified, and faulty representations both innocent and intentional persist. It is the study of these anomalies—not the concealment of them—that will lead us to new horizons in the pursuit of Truth.

What follows is a selection of scientific anomalies that don't quite fit into the conventional model of creation, and so are among the best indicators of what we do not know about the universe. It is vital for the purpose of this book—as well as for any sincere pursuit of the Truth—that we examine and ponder these mysteries in some detail. They are the hard evidence that something very significant is missing from our current picture of the universe, something of great importance beyond the sum total of all the physical things we can see and measure. As the universal model proposed in this book unfolds, we will revisit these scientific puzzles and attempt to provide reasonable explanations for them.

EVOLUTION

Perhaps no scholastic subject has spurred more heated controversy than the theory of evolution. The idea that man came from apes still has religious fundamentalists in an uproar. They also criticize evolution on moral issues, citing several evils to which the theory has given birth. The ruthless dog-eat-dog predation often exhibited by modern capitalism, as well as the Nazi belief of Aryan Supremacy, both find their justification rooted in the concepts originally introduced by Darwin in his *Origin of Species*.

Evolution makes a great case study in our quest for several reasons. First, it is a subject about which its basic concepts are familiar to most, especially through the often-publicized details of the perennial clash between the extremists of both evolution and creationism, the latter of which is more commonly presented today in a less extreme form called *intelligent design*.

Second, it illustrates how some in the scientific community occasionally engage in intellectual dishonesty by concealing irregularities in their data behind professional credentials and an air of assertiveness. While it is difficult for us to detect this subtle deceptiveness in scientific fields without direct access to the relevant experimental data, the conclusions of evolutionists are more easily scrutinized because they are based primarily on subjective argument.

Finally, and perhaps most importantly, there are real mysteries here to solve. For example, how did life "evolve" from inanimate matter and into the almost unimaginable complexity of systems and structures found in living things? As long as the theory of evolution fails to provide a rock-solid solution to the origins of life itself, then by definition it must be incomplete or inaccurate in some way (an embarrassing truth that you'll rarely if ever see openly discussed).

Then there's the problem with predictability. Scientific laws allow us to make accurate predictions about future events, such as how much force it might take to move a particular object, or what the position of the stars will be 100 centuries from now. The ability to derive accurate predictions based on the precepts of a given theory is at the heart of the scientific method. But no evolutionist can declare with absolute precision—or even vague approximation—what a squirrel will look like after ten million years of evolution.

This lacking in predictability brings us to another scientific quandary with evolution. Virtually all the modern sciences have a solid foundation in physics. Since evolution deals with living things, and therefore natural, physical processes, we should at least expect part of its underpinnings to be rooted in physical law. This foundational shortcoming is directly linked with its failure to formulate or even hypothesize the physical laws that define the process by which living tissue can evolve from inanimate matter. Think about it—any such physical process must be governed by physical laws. What are they? Something big is obviously missing here.

So, even if we were to completely disregard the arguments of religious antagonists and examine it from a purely scientific perspective, the fact remains that the theory of evolution is just that—a *theory*. Although it's a good one with much supporting evidence, a number of anomalies, gaps and inconsistencies prevent anyone from credibly stating that the theory of evolution *in its entirety* and *in its precise, current form* is established fact or law, regardless to the certitude with which it is publicly pronounced or delivered in a classroom.

Scholastic Sleight-of-Hand

Sometimes the very statements made by evolutionary experts expose the subtle deception that occasionally infects scholastic reasoning. In one segment of a popular public television documentary series aired some years ago on the subject of dinosaurs, a recognized paleontologist stood next to the mounted skeleton of a large reptile that went extinct just prior to the age of the dinosaurs. After citing a number of supposed flaws in the creature's anatomical design, the paleontologist proudly proclaimed that the animal "was an experiment in evolution that failed."

I'm sure many viewers were duly impressed, accepting in

trust this imperial scholastic edict. But in light of the actual facts, it was shocking and somewhat disturbing to hear such an educated man make so outrageous a statement! To begin with, this creature's bones have been found in many geographical locations and in geological strata spanning millions of years. If this species were so widely distributed, and survived in its final evolutionary form for all those years (and was therefore quite successful), how then could this magnificent beast be so arrogantly dismissed as a mere defective, failed experiment?

Secondly, this huge animal was the result of an evolutionary process of incremental changes over the course of many millions of years from a pint-size ancestor to the spectacular creature whose bones were being displayed—at least according to the theory of evolution. If so, then its immediate ancestor must have differed only slightly. How then did this ancestor survive the millions of years necessary to slowly evolve into its final "defective" form? What subtle change caused this animal to fail while its predecessor thrived? And if this subtle evolutionary adjustment produced an *inferior* creature, how did this "failed experiment" overtake and subsequently replace its superior ancestor? If its final stage of development resulted in a form *less* adapted to its environment than its predecessor, wouldn't that be an example of *de*-evolution?

Finally, paleontologists openly admit they cannot agree on a definite reason why the whole family of giant lizards vanished just prior to the appearance of the first dinosaurs at the beginning of the Triassic Period. How is it then that any one of them, in their self-confessed ignorance, could conclusively pronounce that this particular animal's disappearance was the result of some flaw in its anatomy?

It's these kinds of examples of intellectual pride carried to the level of delusion that need to be challenged and confronted in science wherever they're found. Perhaps members of the scientific community occasionally make such pretentious statements because they believe it is expected of them. Perhaps they must do so to assure us that real progress is being made. Perhaps they feel an inner need to justify the time and expense afforded to them by the rest of us to support a lifetime of digging around in the dirt for old bones. But regardless to the reason, it is intellectually and scholastically dishonest. And it's a stern reminder that just because an intellectual authority proclaims a thing to be does not necessarily make it so.

Trade Secrets

There are two fundamental anomalies within the current theory of evolution that some in the field have privately dubbed the "trade secrets"—facts that if discussed too openly could be bad for business. The first has to do with the origin of genera (the first name in the familiar Latin genus + species titles like *Homo* Sapiens, *Homo* Habilis, *Homo* Erectus, etc.). What is at issue is not the subtle changes within a *species* like variations in coloration or size from one environment or another, but major transformations into a dramatically different *genus* so distinct from its distant ancestor that successful mating between them would be genetically impossible.

The problem with this scenario is that the fossil record does not entirely substantiate the evolutionary hypothesis of *gradual* change from one distinct genus to another. For example, large land animals like the elephant supposedly evolved in gradual increments over many millions of years from tiny shrew-like mammals that first appeared at the end of the age of dinosaurs. While the fossil evidence certainly gives some hint of this, firm confirmation would have to come from establishing a continuous, unbroken line displaying perhaps dozens or even hundreds of transitional creatures, each having progressively larger ears, snout, body size and so on, evolving gradually from tiny ancient shrew to modern elephant. Attempts to arrange remains found in the fossil record in such a sequential order of gradual change have been beset with frustration. Instead we find more dramatic changes marked by large gaps between successive forms. The fossil record skips from one distinct genus to the next. In most cases, a new species sprouts from nowhere, thrives for awhile, then goes extinct, its final form remaining virtually identical to the time it first made its appearance. There is an extraordinary lack of fossil specimens showing the gradual, subtle changes between successive genera predicted by traditional evolutionary theory.

The Paradox of Archaeopteryx

Hailed as one of the most sensational archaeological discoveries of all time, the fossilized remains of Archaeopteryx seems upon first examination to confirm the theory of the evolution of genera once and for all. Here is a creature that looks to be half dinosaur and half bird, sporting the dinosaurian features of a tooth-filled mouth and a long spindly tail, but with the large feathered wings of a modern bird. To all appearances, this odd creature is a perfect intermediary form representing a missing link in the chain of evolution between dinosaur and bird.

In the television series mentioned earlier, a whimsical animation illustrates the supposed evolution of Archaeopteryx. A small animated dinosaur runs on its long powerful hind legs through a dense forest. As it is running, the dinosaur begins to magically mutate—legs slowly shrink, arms gradually elongate, and feathers start to sprout. By the time the metamorphosing creature reaches the edge of the forest, it has transformed into a bird-like animal, which then takes off and goes soaring into the air. The animation then fades into a film clip showing a modern bird in flight.

Impressive, but there's one snag—the above transformation would require many dozens of intermediate forms, each displaying in turn the gradual increments from land animal to sky animal. No such succession of intermediaries leading directly to this particular creature has ever been found. A specimen of a dinosaur having appendages halfway between arms and wings, and/or having a covering of growth halfway between scales and feathers has never surfaced. Similarly, no specimens have been unearthed showing the gradual transition from Archaeopteryx to modern birds. Archaeopteryx just mysteriously appears on the scene, then vanishes suddenly, leaving no evidence of immediate predecessors or descendants.

But, based on *conventional thinking* and the *preconceived notion* that the standard theory of evolution *must be true and complete,* paleontologists *assume* that such intermediate genera *must have existed.*

Among the multitude of creatures living on the earth today, there exists an abundance of evidence for what might be called *microevolution,* or variations of species within a given genus. The case for *macroevolution*—the transformation of a distinct genus into another—is a much different matter. For instance, among fishes, the genus *Esox* (the pike family) has numerous sub-variations that clearly point to a past common ancestor. Muskellunge, northern pike, chain pickerel, redfin pickerel and grass pickerel are all so similar (aside from size and modest coloration differences) that the inexperienced eye might not be able to distinguish between them. But they are all pike—they are not salmon. There are no specimens, either living or extinct, that are an obvious common ancestor or missing link between the two, nor does the fossil record show a gradual lineage of successive forms from an obvious extinct ancestor to either a pike or a salmon. They are all indeed fishes, but they are all distinct genera, both extinct ones and living ones.

Now conventional thinking would dictate that since these are all fishes, they *must* all have a common ancestor. Although I agree with the reasoning of this assumption, it should never be represented as anything more than that—assumption and educated guess. To do so is less than honest. And no one can dare say with certainty precisely from what genus the very *first* ancestral fish emerged.

Of Chickens and Eggs

The second evolutionary trade secret is the apparent co-evolution of different characteristics within a single animal. According to evolution, each characteristic of a given species is the result of a lone, random change. Yet many animals possess two or more distinct characteristics that are inextricably co-dependent. This would necessitate multiple features to simultaneously mutate along an intelligent, synchronized progression, which is not provided for in standard evolutionary theory. The question of "what came first, the chicken or the egg?" is moot, since both are co-evolutionary so that one could not possibly exist without the other. The first chicken laid eggs, and the first chicken egg hatched a chicken.

In most cases, a creature developing only one co-dependent characteristic would gain no significant advantage, and might even suffer a detriment. For example, female whales possess a highly specialized nipple to suckle their young under water. Its design is such that the organ could simply not function correctly except in its present, fully developed state. Other features like fins, tail, and blowhole are also necessary for the creature's success in its aquatic environment. Now evolutionary theory maintains that whales were once land animals that gradually adapted to a watery way of life. This seems reasonable at first until you really think about it. How could the gradual loss of its arms and legs, its nipples for land suckling, and its developing a respiratory "leak" on its back benefit a transitional creature? Any intermediate ancestral form would have had to retain the ability to return to dry land for suckling its young while at the same time losing by mutation into fins and tails the very appendages that it requires for such land excursions. Such intermediate limbs—not quite fins or legs, but something in between—would have crippled the ancestor in its efforts to either swim in water or walk on land. And how do you explain the advantage of developing a vulnerable blowhole at the base of the skull while still breathing through its nostrils? It is difficult to defend the viability of such an anatomically convoluted and disabled creature by arguing that each of these incremental variations provided the next creature with a superior environmental adaptation over its predecessor.

There are just so many examples of these co-evolutionary oddities that it is difficult to know where to begin. The giraffe possesses a complex hydraulic control system that maintains proper blood pressure in its brain during the raising and lowering of its huge neck. It could not have developed its long neck without first having this system. Yet without the neck, development of the necessary specialized heart muscles and vessels would have been pointless and a waste of the animal's precious resources. Traditional evolution cannot account for the two co-evolving so that the genes controlling both heart-muscle specialization and neck elongation simultaneously and continually mutated in a synchronized manner as if one was aware of the other's progress. To assert instead that the giraffe's blood pressure system evolved in *anticipation* of its neck would imply the existence of some greater "cosmic consciousness" or intelligent design overseeing the process—a concept far more Mosaic than Darwinian.

More About Eggs

The human bot fly is so named because its larvae develop to maturity under the skin of humans. Yet unlike other types of parasitic insects that lay their eggs directly on their hosts, the human bot fly has no direct contact with humans. Instead, the fly waits next to water where mosquitoes are emerging from their larval stage. As a freshly hatched mosquito pauses to allow its new skin and wings to harden, the bot fly quickly moves in and seizes it. Being careful not to harm it, the bot fly lays its eggs on the mosquito's underside at strategic points so as not to interfere with the mosquito's movement or its ability to fly. It then releases the mosquito and begins searching for its next victim. When the "loaded" mosquito bites a human, the host's body heat induces the larvae to break out of their eggs (another evolutionary oddity) and begin boring through the skin.

How did evolution force the human bot fly to seek such an indirect means to deliver its eggs? It would certainly be much simpler to lay its eggs directly on its host as do other parasitic insects. The success of these other species proves that the direct approach is quite effective, and so it can't be argued that the bot fly's indirect and painstaking technique is necessary for its survival. Granted, one might argue that because of our intelligence and the dexterity of our hands and arms, humans present a more challenging target than four-legged mammals, and therefore require such extraordinary tactics to exploit them. But if this were the case, then what advantage accrues to the insect by selecting such a formidable host in the first place, when other mammals were far more plentiful and so much more easily compromised?

How did the larvae of the human bot fly first acquire its responsiveness to mammalian body heat? If the sensitivity developed gradually in stages, then the eggs of its ancestors would have been unable to hatch at the proper moment for successful procreation, and the species would have perished long before the modern version of the fly came into being. Moreover, how could these eggs begin to develop this strange ability prior to the fly's use of a human host for reproduction? Did some obscure species of fly in the distant past suddenly begin laying its eggs on warm-blooded mammals in a determined attempt to force its offspring to learn this trait? Could its eggs develop this characteristic in advance of the need for it, as if in prophetic anticipation of the future method of reproduction its progeny were destined to adopt?

And how did this species finally happen upon the mosquito as its means of delivery? Did the bot fly use "reasoning" to make the connection between egg, mosquito, and human? Did its larvae "learn" to hatch in the proximity of mammalian body heat without the ability to see its potential host through its egg-shell? How did the fly "learn" the precise spots on a mosquito to lay its eggs so as not to hinder the creature's movements? And in the unlikely event that some distant ancestor did learn these tricks, how were they passed on to other bot flies, since it is not a social creature and therefore would not likely acquire the techniques by watching others? If it were truly capable of such higher levels of reasoning, and were also able to communicate this knowledge to others of its kind, then we would be forced to conclude that the human bot fly—in spite of its tiny, unsophisticated brain—possesses a mental capacity far beyond all other species in the insect world, as well as most in the animal kingdom.

And finally, how did it "evolve" to prey on a species with which it has no direct contact?

The Birds....

One of the more stunning challenges to traditional evolution can be found in the common woodpecker. This unique creature possesses several highly specialized and co-dependent characteristics that distinguish it from all other birds, past and present. First, there is the incredibly tough beak that is capable of chiseling through wood so hard as to bend nails. Next, strong neck muscles serve as the powerhouse to drive its jackhammer-like blows. It also sports an unusually thick skull that is able to withstand the kind of constant pounding that would be fatal to other birds.

Also unique among the avian family is the woodpecker's feet. All birds possess four toes, three at the front of the foot, and one at the rear. But the toes of the woodpecker are positioned two in front and two in back, an arrangement absolutely necessary to maintain a vice-like grip on a tree during its intensive hammering sessions.

Strangest of all is the woodpecker's tongue, which is rooted in the right nostril! It divides in two as it proceeds back, wrapping around the woodpecker's skull under the skin on either side of the neck, then re-uniting as it comes up through the lower jaw and out the beak. Another unique feature is the sticky fluid it exudes, which allows the woodpecker to catch insects hiding deep within a tree.

Evolution suggests that such a bird evolved into its highly specialized form from earlier, more generalized specimens like blackbirds or robins. If so, how many suicidal robins smashed their heads against trees for untold thousands of years before one was born with a skull thick enough to withstand the blows? And how could they hang onto the tree without the specialized feet? And even if certain robins came into being with the proper beak, skull thickness, and feet, how many of them starved to death before one was born with the weird talent of secreting glue from its tongue?

As to how or why the root of the woodpecker's tongue migrated via evolution from its usual place among birds to the inside of the right nostril, splitting in two and wrapping around the skull in the process....evolution falls silent.

.... And the Bees

Corianthes is a species of orchid native to South America. Only a single type of bee called the orchid bee can pollinate it. The flower's interior is shaped in such a way as to permit only an insect with the body shape of an orchid bee to gain access to the pollen. The flower in turn secretes a waxy perfumed substance that acts as the male bee's only means to attract a mate. Neither the flower nor the bee can reproduce without the help of the other. This extreme interdependency does not appear to be in the best interest of either species, as the decline of one would be disastrous for the other. Can such a deep symbiotic relationship be the product of mere random changes?

More about Birds

While we're on the subject, flight itself is an evolutionary quirk. All creatures were once bound to the earth and sea by gravity, which was also where all their needs were being met quite nicely. What caused them to leave this and take to the air? It's easier to understand leaving the oceans for the land or vice versa, but how did animals aspire to a realm where they could not rest nor hide nor reproduce nor raise young? An evolutionist might speculate that birds took wing to exploit the insects there. What then propelled insects to flight? Consider the highly complex form of insect and bird wings, the incredible structure of bird feathers and their hollow bones to reduce weight. What advantages did the intermediate forms of these features provide until they were sufficiently developed to enable flight? Think of the required thousands of intermediary forms over millions of years, each differing slightly from the last, all progressing toward some unforeseeable future as if guided by an invisible hand. It's as if the air called to the animals, and the genes of their flesh gradually migrated with outstretched arms toward the sound, not adapting to their surrounding environment like they're supposed to, but responding instead to one in which they did not yet live, nor for which they had any pressing need to navigate for survival.

Has anyone stopped to think about this?

The Problem With Humanity

Humanity itself flies in the face of Darwinism. Naturalist Alfred Russell Wallace, who came upon the notion of evolution independently of Darwin, vigorously disagreed with his more famous counterpart when it came to the development of the human species. Unlike Darwin, Wallace had spent much time on remote islands with primitive human populations. These primitive tribal peoples required little more than the skills and intelligence of animals to survive in their lush environment. Yet these peoples developed complex abilities such as music and simple mathematics, qualities impossible to explain according to the evolutionary criteria of survival and adaptation. Wallace viewed this fact as a serious anomaly, observing, "Nature never over-endows a species beyond the demands of everyday existence." He therefore concluded that when it came to humanity, an influence other than those in the natural world must be responsible for the development of a brain far in excess of its owner's needs. Historical circumstances led to the widespread dissemination of Darwin's interpretation, while Wallace's opposition has been largely forgotten (they didn't teach this fact in school either).

Our brain is not the only human bone to get lodged in the Darwinian throat. During his cataloging of hundreds of species, Darwin noticed that animal appendages were highly specialized to meet the needs of their particular environment. A horse's hoof, for example, is ideal for carrying a sizable creature over many types of terrain, while its herbivore molars are the perfect tools to grind the fibers of its vegetarian diet. A lion instead fills a very different ecological niche, and so developed other various specializations like sharp teeth for tearing flesh and padded feet with articulating toes and claws for chasing down and subduing prey.

Following conventional thinking, Darwin came to conclude that since humans were the most advanced of all creatures, our appendages must also be the most specialized. Instead, humans are unique in that we are the ultimate generalists. While carnivores have mostly sharp, cutting teeth while herbivores mostly flat, grinding ones, we have a more or less even distribution of both—perfect for the generalized omnivore we are. Rather than growing at a specialized angle as in other animals, human teeth grow straight up and down.

Our hands are also the most generalized appendages when compared to the rest of the animal kingdom. They do not allow us to run faster, climb trees more easily, or provide bigger claws with which to better kill our prey, features that evolution would classify as superior adaptations to environmental conditions. Instead they are universal or non-specialized, permitting us to perform a wide variety of tasks, many of which are not essential to our survival.

If we follow the evolutionary doctrine stating that features such as appendages always evolve toward greater specialization and adaptation to specific environmental factors, then we must conclude that our teeth and hands represent an evolutionary step backward—yet another example of de-evolution.

Why Pick On Evolution?

It may seem that I've spent a lot of time criticizing evolution in a book that's devoted to a subject more aligned with physics. Believe me, there's no veiled agenda to promote fundamentalist creationism as an alternative. If you eliminate any thought of creationism, the criticisms would still be the same. The point is that these issues are at the very heart of what this book seeks to accomplish. The controversy over evolution illustrates these issues in a very striking way.

We know our current model of reality is flawed. Studying the anomalies in our sciences is the only way we can arrive at a better system that will resolve these flaws. The natural processes that evolution attempts to describe are a part of this system, but it's a part that physicists entirely ignore in their theorizing. This to me is a fatal oversight, since any Theory of Everything will also have to describe the process by which living flesh arose from non-living matter. This disturbing detail must be brought to the table of Absolute Truth, no matter how it further complicates physicists' search for the ultimate TOE. Once included, the anomalies of evolutionary theory—and there are some troublesome ones as we have seen—must also be addressed along with those from the other sciences.

Discussing the defects in evolution also brings to light another dark enemy of Truth, which is the tendency of scientific authorities to conceal and gloss over the awkward anomalies that threaten the status quo of their own chosen discipline. Perhaps no other field of study displays this kind of close-minded dogma and intellectual dishonesty in a manner that's so easily recognized and exposed. Sadly, this dogma is not the exclusive domain of evolution, but is at work in other sciences as well. The study of how it subliminally operates in the field of evolution helps to develop a healthy skepticism that more readily recognizes when mere speculation is being pawned off to you as hard fact.

Evolution is a functional theory that answers many of the questions posed to it in a consistent and sensible way. But its several serious anomalies—not the least of which is its failure to explain the origin of life—are equally strong evidence to indicate that something deeper and more complex is also at work here. In Truth, to herald the whole of evolutionary theory as complete and absolute proven fact requires a genuine leap of faith, perhaps almost equal to that of believing that all species both past and present spontaneously arose during six 24-hour periods 6000 years ago.

PHYSICS AND COSMOLOGY

The anomalies of evolution are by no means the only evidence that exposes what's missing from our knowledge of the universe. Recent findings in both the fields of particle physics and astronomy have given rise to an array of new evidence that seems to contradict long-established scientific principles and laws. We've already covered several such anomalies involving light and gravity. What follows are a few more examples that point us in the direction of where we need to look for solutions to the cosmological puzzle.

Are Matter and Energy Immortal?

One of the dictums you may remember from school is that "matter can neither be created nor destroyed." This statement is a simplified version of the law of conservation of mass-energy, also known as the first law of thermodynamics. The law states that the total amount of mass and energy in the universe has always been and always will remain the same. Though mass can be converted into energy and energy into mass, the combined cosmic total of these two never changes. Matter and energy are considered to be effectively immortal.

Modern theory, however, has shed doubt on this previously immutable law. Scientists working on grand unification theories now believe that protons, one of the basic building blocks of matter, are subject to decay. A proton consists of three smaller particles called quarks. During the process of decay it looses one of these quarks. Yet without all three quarks, the proton cannot sustain its form, and so promptly disintegrates. Without protons there can be no atoms. Without atoms there can be no matter. If this new theory is correct, then given enough time, most of the matter in the universe will eventually dissolve.

Another anomaly in the laws of conservation comes from the field of astronomy. A black hole is allegedly a collapsed star whose gravitational field is so intense that not even light can escape it (hence the name "black" hole). It is believed that when matter and energy get sucked into a black hole, they are hurled out of space-time itself, and thus into nonexistence. Although not as universally fatal as proton decay, the theory of black holes represents another instance where matter and energy can indeed be destroyed.

If these theories prove to be correct, then the traditional laws of conservation are wrong, and science will have to seek yet another TOE to describe physical reality.

Is the Hole Black or Just Empty?

Speaking of black holes, here's another concept that astrophysicists toss around as established fact when in reality it's mostly educated assumption. Black holes are supposed to be objects in which the gravity is so strong that even light cannot escape, hence the name. According to the classical view of black holes, anything sucked into one can never escape. Once the unfortunate victim travels past the point of no return (known as the black hole's *event horizon*), it's crushed into a "singularity" that is infinitely dense and infinitely small.

The trouble is, even though such gravity wells are possible according to general relativity, they are not easily integrated into quantum mechanics or the classical laws of conservation. The biggest problem is the loss of information. Physicists in the computer age have come to realize that all matter and energy is assembled from bits of information. So, just as matter cannot ever be destroyed, neither can the information from which it is constructed. When something is swallowed by what we define as a black hole, the information about that object is also lost forever to the rest of space-time, which the law of conservation doesn't allow. Another deal-breaker is the physical impossibility of anything in the universe having a value of infinity, as would be the case with the quantum singularity allegedly at the core of every black hole. Moreover, the gravitational field of a forming black hole bends space in such ways that according to quantum mechanics prevents local matter and energy from completely collapsing into an infinite black hole singularity.

In an effort to somewhat shore up this tenuous classical representation of a black hole, Stephen Hawking proposed that minute amounts of matter must somehow occasionally escape its gravitational grip in the form of randomly emitted particles. But this *Hawking radiation* as it is called can carry almost no information with it out of the singularity, and therefore does not satisfy the law of "information conservation" (also known as quantum unitarity).

Contrary to public perception, Hawking's theories are by no means universally accepted in the scientific community. Noted theoretical physicists like Leonard Susskind of Stanford University hotly dispute Hawking's notion of black holes (his book, *The Black Hole Wars* presents a detailed discussion of this controversy). To resolve these theoretical conflicts, some physicists have proposed alternative models for the bodies we call black holes bearing names like fuzzballs, gravastars, and black stars that would display similar characteristics to classical black holes but are more consistent with quantum theory. Each of these models, however, have other problems that prevent them from being wholly satisfactory.

Even the prevailing opinion that a black hole exists at the center of every galaxy is fraught with contradiction. While proclaiming this to the public as gospel, physicists privately cannot agree on whether the black hole formed its galaxy or the galaxy formed its black hole. And neither camp can explain why these black holes don't tear apart the galaxies they reside in, even though their alleged properties would demand it.

The bottom line here is that black holes are yet another example of the scientific community feeding hypothesis to the general public for years as absolute fact, when they know full well it's not. There is no way getting around how intellectually dishonest this truly is. Complete conviction extrapolated from wholesale uncertainty....this is science?

Lumps in the Soup

The tendency of mixed gases to reach equilibrium through the chaotic interaction of their molecules is a basic physical principle taught in elementary science classrooms around the world. To illustrate this principle, imagine a sealed box filled with air. The air is made up of many gases including oxygen, hydrogen, helium, and nitrogen. The atoms and molecules of this mixture of gases rush about chaotically, colliding with the sides of the box and with each other producing a very uniform mixture This homogenous mixture is said to be in a state of *equilibrium*. But this mix is also understood scientifically to be in a highly *disorganized* state. Throughout the box, everything is in a state of disorder—no ordered structure can exist anywhere in the box because the random, violent collisions make the formation of any distinct structure virtually impossible.

Now imagine that for some mysterious reason, all the oxygen atoms in the box suddenly begin to separate themselves out from the other gases and collect in one corner to form a pocket of pure oxygen. There is now a highly *organized* structure in the box established by the segregation of the gases into two distinct areas. But this order is also defined as being a most *improbable* state, as there aren't any naturally occurring forces local to the box's interior that could cause such a separation to take place. In the highly unlikely event that such a separation spontaneously occurred through some stroke of random chance, the violent movement of the molecules in the gases would quickly destroy the newly forming structure, forcing the air in the box back into its most *probable* state of disorder and equilibrium.

The Big Bang produced just such a giant gas cloud in the form of a hot, uniform soup of particles and radiation. Yet when astronomers peer out into the cosmos, they find a cosmic landscape remarkably ordered and structured. For some inexplicable reason, this primitive soup got "lumpy" and segregated into areas of greater density from which the galaxies were born. But this state of lumpiness was highly improbable, as the laws of equilibrium would have been continually working to break up any newly developing structures within the primordial cloud. There are numerous theories as to how the universe escaped chaotic disorder, but none provide a workable explanation on which most scientists can agree.

Then there's the question of temperature. The supercharged particles in the primordial cloud emitted incredible amounts of heat energy. Scientists have calculated the extreme temperatures in this cloud and have estimated the degree of cooling that should have taken place over the course of billions of years. Yet the ambient temperature of our universe today is quite a bit cooler than what these calculations indicate. Curiously, if the universe was actually as hot as the equations say it should be, life as we know it could not survive.

How the universe became so highly organized and so cool in defiance of known physical laws remains one of the greatest of cosmological mysteries.

Whence Came Universal Order?

How did this remarkably ordered universe with its uniform structure of physical laws emerge from the chaotic beginning of the Big Bang? The universe is in fact so orderly that a collection of molecules, each comprising two atoms of hydrogen and one of oxygen, and at the correct temperature and pressure, will always produce a clear liquid we call *water* regardless of where in the universe these molecules might form and collect.

Where did this intrinsic order come from? What force or influence established the physical laws that govern it? The behavior of matter and energy *conforms* to these physical laws, and therefore the laws themselves must have been in place *before* matter and energy came together. For instance, protons, neutrons, and electrons all combine to form atoms according to fixed, established guidelines. When the first atom coalesced, it did so in conformity to these very same rules. There is no escaping the conclusion that physical law must therefore pre-date matter. To believe differently would be to propose that matter established its own laws as it assembled itself. But even if we were to allow for such an illogical possibility, then from where came the primordial command that kick-started this process of self-assembly, since matter and energy did not yet exist to issue any commands to itself?

If matter had indeed established its own physical laws, then those laws might have changed each time matter "decided" to vary the way in which it assembled itself. This idea can spawn speculations about multiple universes having each a different set of physical laws. But for our own universe—the only one we know exists for certain—science has proved repeatedly there is but a single set of principles governing the assembly of atomic structures. As the primordial cloud expanded and cooled, untold trillions of particles extending across countless light years began to simultaneously assemble themselves all in accordance with this singular set of principles. There was no evolutionary trial-and-error process where particles randomly came together and fell apart until the first patriarchal atom materialized, which then gave birth to all other atoms. Nor was there any "parent" galaxy that likewise gave birth to all the rest. Instead, particles began to assemble into atoms everywhere throughout the early universe at about the same time and according to the same guidelines. Similarly, galaxies everywhere began to form independently, yet all in conformity to a same set of underlying, predetermined laws.

According to the laws of thermodynamics, it's unimaginably improbable for the exact same order to suddenly form everywhere in the primordial cloud at the very same instant in time (remember our sealed box of air). The laws governing quantum mechanics further stipulate that the behavior of all subatomic particles is always random and unpredictable. There is virtually no possible scenario that would allow many trillions of particles separated by vast distances to suddenly begin performing the exact same self-assembly procedure. Yet in violation of all these laws, the particles of the early universe did just that.

So again, it must be concluded that the cosmic recipe for assembling atoms was somehow programmed into all primordial matter *before* the first atom ever came into being. From the moment of the Big Bang, the subatomic constituents were pre-destined by their very nature to become atoms, molecules, stars and galaxies.

Therefore, if the universe cannot be a product of quantum chaos, what "intelligence" pre-established its underlying order? From whence did the original blueprint come?

The Universe Grows Dark

Every high school student learns that gravity is what holds the universe together. The laws of gravity establish the shape of galaxies and the orbital paths of planets. Yet in recent years, astrophysicists have discovered a disturbing fact. It seems that the combined total of all the matter in the universe is not sufficient to generate the amount of gravity needed to shape and hold all the structures in the cosmos together. Current estimates place the material deficit incredibly at about eighty-five to ninety percent. That's quite a big gap in our current understanding of the universe.

To account for all the missing gravity-generating material, physicists have proposed the existence of a hypothetical substance known as *dark matter*. This dark matter is supposed to be invisible and undetectable, yet can generate gravity just like normal matter, and is distributed throughout empty space in varying density. The idea that matter could be invisible to every means of detection is contradictory to all that is established science. Yet astronomers have discovered no other source for the additional gravity their formulas tell them must be there. To balance their gravitational equations, physicists just pour into the cosmic mixing bowl the required amount of dark matter (about six parts dark to one part normal matter) and presto! All is right again with the universe.

Now comes the assumption. Astrophysicists have conjured this artificial solution from their adherence to the conventional view that gravity *must* be a physical force like electromagnetism and therefore *must* be generated by a physical substance. The problem is that there is not a shred of hard evidence to demonstrate that such invisible matter has any reality to it at all. Dark matter is essentially the 21st century equivalent of the 19th century ether, and also just as imaginary. The Michelson-Morley experiment described in the first chapter proved conclusively that there is no cloistered substance floating around in empty space. Yet from the writings of contemporary scientific circles, you'd think that the evidence for the existence of dark matter is fully established.

I recently watched another of those television documentaries, this one on the universe, where three astrophysicists spoke of dark matter unhesitatingly as if its existence was verified fact and a foregone conclusion, even though they all know it's pure speculation. But it sure made them sound like they really knew their stuff.

For the sake of honesty, the only thing here that science has discovered beyond a doubt is the *need* for something like dark matter. Their calculations prove only that there is much more gravity at work in the cosmos than there is physical matter to generate it. Period. The rest is nothing more than speculation and supposition. To arrogantly present dark matter as factual is merely a ruse to disguise our embarrassing level of ignorance.

Hey, all you kids in school! Don't even bother to engage your young minds in contemplating such cosmic puzzles—we already have it all figured out. Just give us a few more decades and there's a remote chance we might even be able to prove it.

Physicists claim that dark matter must be a type of particle similar to a neutrino (making it more of a dark "energy" than matter). But particles that can escape detection from our current instruments would be too small or too few to cause the amount of gravity attributed to them. The estimated concentration of these particles in our own galaxy is about 10^5 particles per cubic meter, a huge amount of material to remain hidden in empty space. Another hypothesis proposes a particle 100 times heavier than a proton—which is itself quite a large chunk of subatomic matter—but fails to explain how such a mega-particle might elude detection. Some have let their speculation run wild, claiming that we experience dark matter "seasons" as the earth's rotation causes us to move with or against the flow of this invisible substance—the very kind of ethereal ocean that the Michelson-Morley experiment convincingly disproved over a century ago.

One of the "proofs" offered by astronomers for the existence of dark matter is derived from observations of a cosmic structure known as the Bullet Cluster (so-called because of its shape) that was formed by the collision of two smaller galaxy clusters. Recall that the force of gravity produces curves in the fabric of space. Consequently, the light that shines through these curvatures is bent as if by a gigantic cosmic lens. The degree of this *gravitational lensing* as it is called is used as a reliable gauge for how much gravity is at work in a particular region of space. The Bullet Cluster has sufficient concentration of gravitational fields to make this phenomenon very pronounced. Since the total mass of matter and hot plasma in this cluster cannot on its own generate sufficient gravity for the amount of lensing observed, proponents argue that dark matter must be generating the rest. But if this dark matter had the ability to bend light, shouldn't this have been observed in the light beams of Michelson-Morley? And if the density of dark matter is too small to have been detected in that landmark experiment, how can it now account for about 90% of the universe's gravity?

Using 3-D rendering software, scientists have mapped the regions where they believe dark matter is concentrated. The resulting map corresponds very closely to the pattern of distribution of visible matter in the universe. This matrix of galactic material has come to be known as the *cosmic web*. Nearly all of the material in the universe appears to be concentrated into its branch-like structure, while the remainder of space is virtually empty. Astrophysicists claim that this web is composed of dark matter, and the resulting gravity is what holds all the galactic material within its matrix. According to this model, dark matter served as some sort of universal cure-all in the early stages of universal development that allegedly provided the gravitational scaffolding around which the galaxies were formed and shaped. This is supposedly what made the "lumps" in the primitive soup of the early universe.

Yet this solution itself raises other insolvable questions, like which kind of matter (invisible or visible) came first, how did it come into being, and by what process did one give rise to the other?

In reality, the branches of this so-called cosmic web only map the areas where nine times more gravity-generating matter should be, but is not—that is, of course, if our present understanding of how gravity is generated and the role it plays in the shaping of our universe is correct. The whole concept of dark matter is based on the belief that our notion of gravity in relationship to the behavior of astronomical bodies and the fabric of space is accurate and reasonably complete (which we are well aware it is not). This hypothetical model of dark matter distribution is in reality more a map outlining the boundaries of our own ignorance than the actual location of some cosmic secret sauce.

There is another imaginary character playing on this stage of cosmic speculation, which goes by the name of *dark energy*. According to the Big Bang theory of creation, the universe has been continually expanding since the time of its creation. The problem is that our measurements show this expansion to be accelerating for some unknown reason. This is contrary to what the gravitational forces of all the matter in the universe that are collectively pulling on the fabric of space-time should be doing, which is to produce a *slowing* of this expanding cosmic balloon. This cosmic paradox is considered by many to be among the most profound mysteries in physics today.

To explain this anomaly, astrophysicists have offered up this dark energy as the unseen power pushing the expansion of the fabric of space-time against the force of gravity. But once again, the only evidence for the existence of such an invisible energy is the observation of a phenomenon for which we have no good material explanation.

All this talk about dark matter and energy really boils down to one thing. Physics is about materialism, or in other words, about the physical makeup of the universe. Physicists are the ultimate materialists. The problem here is that we have come to a point in our sciences where we have simply run out of cosmic material with which to attribute all of what we are now able to observe. That's the actual anomaly at the core of this controversy—it's as much a perceptual problem as it is a physical one. Since physicists cannot perceive a non-materialistic solution, they must dream up an additional material substance that they can plug into their materialistic model to explain this mystery in a materialistic way. This materialistic void is the stuff from which dark matter and dark energy are made.

What will ultimately prove effective is to devise a new and more precise definition of gravity that is consistent with both relativity and quantum mechanics, which will then provide a better explanation for these inexplicable phenomena. We're working on it, but we're not there yet.

Anomalies Ad Infinitum

We could continue to list many more anomalies that challenge our established physical, cosmological, and evolutionary models. Indeed, there are already volumes loaded with such scientific curiosities and freaks. Gross repetition, however, does not necessarily make a thing more certain. One need only observe the arrival of a single meteorite to conclude that rocks do indeed fall from the sky. The anomalies that we've covered are the ones that will point us in the right direction in our quest for the final TOE.

Einstein proposed a standard by which to judge the soundness of a physical theory [italics are Einstein's]:

> Whatever the meaning assigned to the term *complete,* the following requirement for a complete theory seems to be a necessary one: *every element of the physical reality must have a counterpart in the physical theory.*

To achieve this completeness, every observable phenomenon must have a corresponding place within a theory. The theory must also remain consistent with itself, accommodating all data within the system it proposes without having to make exceptions to the rules for individual observations.

If this is the benchmark, we've got our work cut out for us. Quantum theory, one of the very cornerstones of our modern physics, fails this test. Quantum theory has no correlation with what is actually observed in the world at large. At its very core lies a doctrine asserting that all events are unpredictable, and so proclaims that the future can be anticipated only in terms of statistical probability. But there are many things in our universe that are predictable with certainty. A glass of pure liquid water, for instance, will always be a clear fluid at 70° F and sea-level air pressure no matter where, when, or how the water molecules are assembled. We are obviously not going to solve this paradox by plodding the same worn paths.

Fortunately, new discoveries are being made almost daily that call into question established theory. Whether it is astronomy, geology, medicine, evolution or physics, every discipline has its anomalies that do not quite fit into the standard models. So we have no shortage of material with which to reckon. Only by confronting and resolving these unknowns can we ever hope to arrive at the complete TOE that Einstein envisioned.

There is still another "unknown" that needs to be addressed in our search for a more complete Truth. It is perhaps the most damnable scientific anomaly of all—the world of paranormal phenomena.

3

Enigma of the Paranormal

The Strangest Anomaly of All

*If I had to live all over again, I should
devote myself to psychical research.*
—Sigmund Freud

There was a time when information on the paranormal was available only to those who sought it on dusty library shelves or in the New Age rack at the paperback bookstore. It was simple then for some in the scientific community to dismiss reports of haunted houses and flying saucers as superstition or ignorance, thus sweeping them from the public conscious by means of imperial edict. However, beginning in the 1990s, new television programs dedicated to the paranormal began to bring documented, credible reports of such events into every living room in America. Although the bulk of these programs today are presented solely as sensationalized entertainment or for the telling of a good ghost story, others are the product of serious paranormal investigation accompanied by compelling audio and video evidence. Too, the ever-increasing number of video cameras in private hands have produced visual recordings that cannot be so easily disregarded.

Science's cynicism toward the subject of the paranormal is quite understandable. Most efforts to study paranormal activity under laboratory conditions have produced inconsistent and inconclusive results. On the face of it, there seems to be little in common between hard scientific data and things that go bump in the night. However, a truly objective person cannot simply brush aside the sheer volume of paranormal events reported by untold thousands of credible witnesses. This would be like the approach taken by ancient mapmakers who, after drafting all known areas of the world, painted images of scary sea serpents around the map's perimeter accompanied by the caption "Here Be Monsters."

If modern science sails off the edge of its own map by plying these uncharted waters, then so be it. Little progress will be made toward explaining the inexplicable until we can admit that our current worldview is far from complete. Discovering the hidden processes behind these bizarre events would answer important scientific riddles and significantly expand our understanding of the universe. No TOE could be complete without explaining the physical mechanisms underlying these mysterious events.

UNDERSTANDING THE PARANORMAL

The term *paranormal* has been tossed around for so long that it has become a sort of generic brand name for anything spooky and mysterious. It often gets misused by applying it to any activity or practice that delves into such mysteries. For instance, the use of Ouija or spirit boards, while perhaps an occult practice, is not in itself paranormal. The term is loosely defined even among serious investigators and researchers in this field.

Establishing a functional and consistent definition is the first step toward getting a handle on this bizarre subject.

Paranormal phenomena are usually interpreted as events that appear to operate outside normal scientific laws, hence the name *para*normal. But this is far too vague to be practical. The most important standard in determining whether or not a given event is paranormal is the scientific concept of *local causality*. This is the principle of cause and effect—for every event or effect in the universe, there must be a physical force or influence (i.e., matter or energy) directly in contact with or *local* to it to cause that effect.

Say, for example, you're going to pick up a sheet of paper from your desk. To perform this, you must first touch the paper with your hand. The force of your hand contacting the paper's surface is considered to be *localized*, or at the same location as the surface of the paper. The same hand movement performed several feet away will have no effect because your hand is not *local* to the paper. Now let's assume you try to be clever by moving the paper without touching it locally with your hand. You might open a window and allow an incoming breeze to blow the paper off the desk for you. But this method is just another example of local causality, since the effect causing the paper to move (in this case, the in-rushing air molecules) must still come in physical contact with it. Now what if you really got smart and tried to lift the paper using the magnetic properties of static electricity? You could hold a glass rod charged with static electricity directly above the paper and without touching it lift the paper off the desk. But even though the static charge is pure energy instead of a material like your hand or air molecules, it is still considered to be physical, and must still come in local contact with the paper to move it.

The challenge to science is that paranormal incidents operate by way of *non*-local causality in that no known material or energetic causes are in physical contact with the effects in question. It's like getting a dent in your car in Cleveland from an accident occurring in Atlanta! Take for example the paranormal phenomenon of telepathy, which is the act of one mind "reading" the thoughts of another. Decades of research have failed to detect any physical substance (matter or energy) connecting the two minds that is responsible for or even capable of conveying such mental information. The absence of a physical connection between the two minds means this phenomenon operates by way of non-local causality, a physical impossibility according to the standard model of the universe.

The absence of a local, physical cause is enough reason for many scientists to dismiss the whole idea of telepathy as fantasy. But there's more than enough evidence to show that the telepathic effect is real. All we can say for certain is that we do not currently possess the necessary understanding or technology to determine the means by which telepathic information is transmitted. Unfortunately, the materialism of scientific dogma demands that if it does not register on its measuring devices, then it cannot be real—except, of course, when the existence of such non-real things (like dark matter) are proclaimed by its own distinguished clergy.

The most likely reason for our inability to detect the cause behind paranormal activity is that it lies outside the four-dimensional space-time to which our measuring instruments are confined. Imagine a two-dimensional world like the surface of a sheet of paper, having length and width but no height or depth. Say it is populated by a race of people that are also two-dimensional, and so are completely confined to the length and width of the paper's surface. Let's single out an individual from this race and call her Toody (after 2-D). Toody can observe with her normal senses all the things in her two-dimensional world, but cannot perceive anything in the areas of the third dimension above and below the paper's surface. Author Edwin Abbott first described this kind of imaginary two-dimensional world in his famous work *Flatland: A Romance of Many Dimensions* published in 1884, so many readers will already be familiar with it.

His vision adapts well to our purpose here.

Now, what if some three-dimensional troublemakers (like ourselves) come along and decide to disturb Toody's world by taking a pencil and writing on the paper next to her? Toody can only see the very tip of the pencil contacting the paper. She can see the writing as it magically appears, but the rest of the pencil and the hand that directs it are hidden in the third dimension. What would happen if we were to lift the pencil off the paper to begin a new word? From Toody's perspective, the supernatural writing ceases abruptly with the pencil point vanishing into thin air. When we place the pencil back on the paper and begin writing the next word, Toody sees the point and the strange markings reappear at a different location on the surface of her world. This effect would be quite ordinary and easily understood from our higher perspective in the three-dimensional realm above the paper. But from Toody's perspective, she has just witnessed a series of paranormal events, namely materialization and teleportation. To her, the writing and the pencil tip spontaneously appear out of nowhere with no detectable local cause, then disappear just as suddenly, only to reappear again at a different location nearby.

Witnessing this event will change Toody's life, but not necessarily in a positive way. Were she a scientist, she might begin investigating this strange episode using tried-and-true scientific procedures. Unfortunately, she would soon find that her measuring devices are useless because they suffer from the same two-dimensional confinement as her bodily senses. She will not be able to trace either the movement of the pencil tip through the invisible third dimension nor the energy source driving it.

Toody would have to overcome other challenges that our own real-life paranormal investigators struggle against. For one, she cannot recreate the phenomenon on demand, an absolute necessity for scientific study. Also, since very few others have ever witnessed such an event themselves, few take her singular experience seriously. Toody's fellow scientists might consider her research to be a waste of time, and her observations the result of mistaken identity. They might even accuse her of fakery, quackery, or delusion. Her peers would certainly not accept her observations and research, and there would be little hope that her work might be published in any journal controlled by the scientific establishment.

In all fairness, Toody's fellow scientists have good cause to cling to their rigidly skeptical and materialistic methods. With them, they have made great progress toward understanding the nature of their universe. They discovered, for instance, that the surface of their world is composed primarily of cellulose fibers. But if Toody could only devise a means of catching a glimpse beyond her two-dimensional barrier into the third dimension of height, she could perhaps show her fellow scientists the very source of their reality. They might discover, for instance, a large cylindrical "force" (a tree) being broken down into a pulp to form the raw material of their world, then another cylindrical force (a roller in a paper mill) acting as a catalyst, shaping the raw material into the two-dimensional sheet on which they live.

At some future time when science makes the necessary theoretical and technological advances, we may fulfill Toody's dream by peering across our own space-time barrier and into the realm of the paranormal. In the meantime, we must use the power of reason and a keen imagination—the very same tools that served Einstein—to breach this barrier of materialism that imprisons both our sciences and our senses. And we must not reject or ignore the very body of evidence that points us in the direction of that breach.

PARNORMAL RESEARCH FOR THE 21st CENTURY

Be it ghosts, disembodied voices or floating objects, the incredible variety of bizarre events reported makes the study of paranormal activity quite perplexing. Paranormal investigators themselves unintentionally contribute to this confusion by often focusing only on those happenings that are of interest to them. Each one then devises a personal theory to explain their specific phenomenon of choice. For example, one researcher may believe that ghosts are mostly disembodied spirits, while another sees them as a replaying of images recorded in the past on the fabric of space-time (called a residual haunting). Some even consider them to be demons impersonating the dead. Decades of these diverse speculations have left us with a picture of the paranormal that is both chaotic and contradictory. Without a uniform set of definitions and principles, there is little hope that paranormal research will ever attain the status of an organized, unified and widely respected discipline.

This current state of affairs will not take us where we need to go. The search for Truth needs to be inclusionistic, embracing science, spiritual experience and paranormal evidence. It is challenging enough trying to reasonably correlate the first two without also having to deal with this kind of muddy perplexity as the third ingredient in the mix. We need to set aside the traditional archaic ways of looking at these events and re-examine them with a fresh perspective free from established dogma.

The first step toward this goal is to weed out the kinds of phenomena that are sometimes lumped in with the paranormal but properly belong to other categories of events. Of course, being now armed with a clear-cut and scientifically relevant definition for what is paranormal makes this a simple task. For example, there are many documented sightings from all across North America of a large biped commonly known as Bigfoot or Sasquatch. But the question of whether such biological species actually exist rightfully belongs to the field of cryptozoology. UFOs should probably fall under the heading of astrophysics or meteorology (although there may be a paranormal quality to some of their reported behavior that we'll discuss later in the book). Other examples include earthquake and "spook" lights, frog and fish falls, "mystery" areas like the Bermuda and Dover

Triangles, ancient astronauts and so on, all of which probably have local physical causes that are just not yet understood. We need to focus instead on those kinds of supernatural events that explicitly violate the known laws of physics by having no local physical causes. Confining ourselves to such events will greatly ease the burden of identifying, classifying and analyzing those types of phenomena that are truly paranormal.

This still leaves us with a vast body of supernatural evidence to consider. We can further reduce this list by purging duplicate entries, or in other words, events that go by multiple names but are essentially the very same phenomenon. A perfect example of this redundancy are reports of the mysterious appearance of objects seemingly out of thin air. Some investigators call these *materializations* while others use the terms *teleports* or *apports* for short. All three are the very same phenomenon—let's just all pick one name and go with it.

Another, more challenging simplification is to identify and cull out what we might call "compound" events, or those in which two or more individual phenomena usually occur together. For example, there are all kinds of molecular compounds in the universe that are assembled from simpler atomic elements. Common table salt or *sodium chloride* is a compound comprising the two base elements of sodium metal and chlorine gas. But it would be difficult to understand how these compounds are formed without having first established the periodic table of elements. We need to make this same kind of distinction in paranormal phenomena by first identifying and establishing a table of basic or elemental paranormal events, after which we can readily identify those occurrences that are actually paranormal "compounds" of two or more basic phenomena taking place simultaneously.

Here's what I mean by a compound phenomenon. Consider clairvoyance, which is the mind's ability to mentally receive information about remote persons, places or events. A common occurrence of simple clairvoyance is correctly "guessing" before answering the phone the identity of a caller whom you've not heard from in a long time (assuming, of course, that they called unexpectedly). Most would likely agree that this represents an "elementary" paranormal effect in its simplest form. A more complex form of this would be *remote viewing*, where a person attempts to paranormally receive information about a specific remote target. It's easy to see how remote viewing is a clairvoyant effect, even though it involves the additional complexity of focusing on a specific target at a specific time in a search for specific information. In other words, whatever force or process in the universe that allows the mind to pick up on the identity of the mystery caller is the very same process by which information about a remote location is conveyed. The more complex compound phenomenon of remote viewing has at its core the basic element of clairvoyance. If we can determine the means by which clairvoyance is conveyed, the vehicle behind remote viewing will also be revealed.

Not all instances of compound phenomena are that easily recognized. Take *astral travel* in which a person's consciousness temporarily leaves the body (usually in a sleep state or under anesthesia) and travels to a remote location where it observes objects and/or events that are later confirmed. It might appear at first that this is radically different than clairvoyance, since a fundamental aspect of the experience is the distinct feeling that the traveler personally visits the remote location. But is this feeling really sufficient to conclude that astral travel functions differently from basic clairvoyance? Remember that remote viewers also occasionally report this same uncanny feeling of having personally visited the remote site, even though they may not experience the same sense of journeying there as in astral travel. Even in cases of simple clairvoyance, some portion of our consciousness probably projects itself to the remote person or place being detected. After all, something in the clairvoyant's conscious proactively reaches out to this distant information in the same way as remote viewers and astral travelers. There is every indication that the underlying mechanism responsible for conveying remote information to a human mind outside normal space and time is at work in all three. So, in spite of the added depth and complexity of the experience, the essential elements of astral travel can be recognized as another form of clairvoyant communication.

What about those rare instances where an astral traveler apparently materializes in some form at the remote location and is seen by observers? One of the most famous and well documented example of this is the case of the Spanish Catholic nun Mary of Agreda, who reportedly made numerous astral voyages from her convent in Europe to the New World in the 1600s to minister to the conquered Indians in what is now western Texas (she even reported observing during her travels that the earth was a round globe, a heresy at the time). This is known as a case of *bilocation*, or literally being in two places at the same moment in time. That multiple phenomena like these can occur during astral travel is the strongest argument for it being a compound event, and so it's not one of the basic paranormal elements we seek to identify.

The following is a list of what I believe can be recognized as basic phenomena excluding duplicates and compound events—a periodic table of the paranormal:

Telepathy. Direct mind-to-mind communication.

Clairvoyance. Mentally receiving information pertaining to remote people, places or events. Closely related but much more infrequent is *clairaudience,* or the ability to hear remote sounds or disembodied voices beyond normal hearing. Clairvoyance differs from telepathy in that it is not exactly a form of two-way communication, but more a one-way receiving of information.

Precognition. Accurately predicting a future event by

means other than normal deduction (premonition or prophesy are included under this heading).

Telekinesis. The manipulation of matter or energy by means of mental power or "mind-over-matter."

Levitation. The movement of an object in defiance of gravity with no physical means of support or propulsion. It is distinct from telekinesis because there is no apparent human agent initiating the movement.

Apparition. Also called a ghost, it is a visible image of a material object (usually a person) without any material source being present.

Auditory Phenomena. Sounds without the presence of a physical mechanism to generate them, like footsteps heard where there is no living person walking. To my knowledge, this phenomenon has no special moniker associated with it.

Olfactory Phenomena. The detection of odors for which there is no physical source. Just as in the case of audible phenomena, there is no special name usually associated with it.

Electronic Voice Phenomena or EVP. The recording of sounds or voices on electronic media like a digital recorder or magnetic tape that were not heard by an observer at the time and place of its recording.

Spirit Photography. This is closely related to EVP except that it pertains to images captured on film or digital media that were not visible to the observer at the time and place of their capture.

Transformation. An event in which a physical substance undergoes a metamorphosis at the molecular level, thereby producing a change in its normal state and/or appearance. Also known as *transmutation* or *transfiguration.*

Dematerialization. The spontaneous disappearance of matter and/or energy.

Materialization. Conversely, the spontaneous appearance of matter and/or energy.

Teleportation. The spontaneous disappearance of an object from a given location, followed by its reappearance at a different location.

Bilocation. An event in which the same object (often a person) is located in two different spatial coordinates at the same moment or locus in time.

Synchronicity. A term coined by psychologist and parapsychologist Dr. Carl Jung to describe what he called *meaningful coincidence* beyond the probability of random chance.

This list could undoubtedly be simplified even further. For example, teleportation could be understood as a combination of dematerialization and rematerialization, the teleported object perhaps being guided to its destination by the same mechanism at work in clairvoyance. Telepathy appears to also be very closely linked to clairvoyance. But I believe we have a good starting point for getting accustomed to looking at the paranormal in this way, after which we can further simplify this list using a logical and meaningful approach.

The two compound phenomena of *hauntings* and *spirit*

possession are both ideal candidates for further simplification because of the sheer number of different paranormal events that tend to manifest together in these. For example, a house is said to be haunted when the occupants regularly observe multiple incidents like apparitions, strange sounds, doors that open and close by themselves, levitation, teleportation, and so on. In the case of spirit possession, it seems that individuals become haunted themselves, and the many happenings associated with a haunting occur in their immediate vicinity. Both of these are significant because they provide strong evidence that the causes behind all the various associated phenomena are very closely related. The process of unraveling these events in the attempt to simplify them could be very revealing.

I had originally planned to supplement this basic list of paranormal elements with documented cases of each. Except for a few instances where I felt the additional information would be helpful, I decided against it for several reasons. To do it justice would have easily occupied about twenty-five percent of the book. Plus, however well documented, the denier (and by this I don't mean the skeptic, because that's a very different mindset) will refuse to believe no matter what kind of evidence is offered, while the true believer at the other extreme doesn't require any hard evidence at all. For everyone else, the television programs previously mentioned, the hundreds of available books on the subject, and the wealth of information on the Internet will provide the serious inquirer with a quantity and quality of material far beyond what I could feasibly present in this single chapter.

There is one final thought regarding the validity of paranormal phenomena that I think any sincere skeptic needs to consider. Remember that the observation of only one meteorite is enough to confirm that rocks do indeed fall from the sky. Amid the staggering volume of strange experiences of perhaps millions of people over the entire course of history, there needs to be but one genuine supernatural occurrence among them to validate the reality of the paranormal. Only one.

A NEW SYSTEM OF PARANORMAL CLASSIFICATION

The effort to reduce paranormal phenomena to a list of elements still leaves us with a lengthy and diverse roster. One way
by which we can further simplify this collection is by grouping
similar phenomena under their own separate headings. But traditional paranormal terminology is too archaic and arbitrary to
provide a solid framework for re-classifying these phenomena
in a meaningful and beneficial way. Many of its headings were
originally devised in the latter part of the nineteenth century
when a heightened interest in spiritualism inspired the first
widespread investigation of the paranormal. The most common
approach at the time was to hold informal séances in an effort
to communicate with the dead or invoke some other ghostly
phenomena. These were frequently gathered more as a form of
entertainment than serious inquiry. Yet even in light of all the
subsequent advances in the field of paranormal research, the
primitive terminology derived from these early efforts is still in
common use, having been amended only by slight modifica-
tions or additions. The result has been a jumbled assemblage of
divergent ideas derived from a foundation that was sometimes
dubious if not outright fraudulent.

There's little sense in attempting to re-work this outworn
material. The stagnant state of paranormal theorizing in recent
years is proof enough that the old approach has outlived its
usefulness. I believe we need to discard a large portion of it, and
with a fresh outlook devise a more modern, consistent and sensible way to classify and understand these phenomena.

Another simplification that will prove absolutely essential
to scientific study is to defer for now any questions pertaining
to entities, either spiritual or carnal, that might be responsible
for initiating a paranormal episode. So much emphasis has been
placed by so many investigators on the possible identity and
motives of various spirit entities involved with paranormal occurrences that the study of the possible physics behind these

events has been sadly neglected. The result has been that many beliefs widely held within the paranormal community are based primarily on assumption and speculation without any sound scientific foundation. This traditional spirit-centric viewpoint has done little to uncover the mysteries behind the paranormal, while serving to dissuade serious scientists from participating. What does it matter if the creaking floorboards upstairs are the doings of dear old deceased Aunt Mary or even Mr. Beelzebub himself if we don't even understand the rudiments of how audible footsteps can occur without any physical cause? This is one of the reasons why paranormal investigators, even after many years in the field, remain in the rut of gathering more and more data from each successive investigation without ever arriving at more meaningful answers.

To make further scientific progress, we need to take a more agnostic approach to paranormal study. We need to shift our emphasis toward gaining insight into the physical laws and mechanisms that allow paranormal events to occur, rather than continuing to focus on what entity might initiate them and for what reason. In the case of a haunted house, for example, our focus needs to be on the physics of the actual phenomena, not on what spirit or spirits might be haunting the place or why. Such ethereal questions, however valid, should be assigned to a separate field of study led by those versed in spirituality, so that the physical investigation can be conducted without the blurry reasoning that has so plagued this discipline. If we were members of a police department investigating a murder committed with a handgun, we need to be the ballistics unit. We want to know about the gun—its construction and function, the bullet and its trajectory, and so on. In short, what physical processes actually caused the effect of the victim's death? The questions as to the identity of the murderer, why he killed the victim, why he chose that particular place and time, why he chose to use a gun and so on is a completely separate subject that's handled by the criminology unit. We want to know about the mechanism,

91

not the perpetrator or the motive.

Another way to look at this new approach is to liken it to the science of chemistry. Say we are discussing a simple chemical reaction where two clear liquids are combined together and heated, producing a red colored solution. It doesn't matter who did the mixing, be it a chemist, a cook, or by chance occurrence in nature. Neither is it of any consequence where the mixing was done, whether in a test tube, saucepan, or even a volcanic crater. Additionally, it makes no difference whether the source of the heat was a Bunsen burner, stove top or lava flow. These are all subjects of study by other disciplines. What is of primary importance here is the chemical process itself—that combining two liquids in the presence of heat produces a red color. The chemistry of this reaction will always be the same regardless to who or what mixed the ingredients, where they were mixed, or what may have served as the heat source. We must be like physicists who diligently study the nature and behavior of the creation itself, while leaving any questions as to what spirit or spirits may have created it and for what intent and purpose to the ecclesiastics and philosophers.

To include spiritualistic or religious overtones in our reckoning clouds our ability to observe and judge objectively, as it has done so for generations. Consider the volumes written on the appearances of apparitions. Everyone discusses points like who the specter might be (deceased person, demon, etc.), how it came to haunt such-and-such location, whether it's passive or interactive, and the like. All of these suppositions detour the inquirer's mind toward attempting to perceive who or what a given apparition might be as to a spiritual or even a personal sense. A mind so occupied with such spiritual matters is completely distracted from the more fundamental question of what an apparition actually is in a *physical* sense. It's almost like discussing the various parts of a flashlight and their function while neglecting to consider that the very light it projects is actually a beam of photons. Granted, it's much easier and safer to speculate on the spiritual because there are no established standards by which the value and accuracy of one's ideas might be judged. Theorizing on the hard physics of a phenomenon requires more accurate scientific knowledge, and exposes one's ideas to critical review against recognized scientific standards.

There is another important reason why we need to steer clear of the spirit-centric perspective. If we begin to consider whether a process was brought about by the deliberate act of some entity—be it human or spiritual, living or dead, divine or demonic—we become entangled in questions of religion involving things like spiritism, demonology and even the occult. Heated debate has been raging over such beliefs for millennia with no end in sight. It also drags us head-first into religious prejudices like those who might consider any discussion of the paranormal to be delving into witchcraft, divination, or sorcery, even though the Bible itself proclaims the supernatural from almost every page. Again, this is in no way implying that such beliefs are unimportant or without merit—it simply means that delving into these divisive and distracting religious contentions contributes nothing toward isolating the *physical* properties of paranormal phenomena.

With all this in mind, it's time to take a fresh look at the data and group similar types of paranormal events under their own categories. In most instances, it will quickly become clear how certain kinds of phenomena are very closely related, and so naturally fall into their own distinct groupings.

Mental Phenomena

Telepathy and clairvoyance involve the transmission of information about people, places, things and events directly to the mind in a manner that not only bypasses the usual external sensory paths to the brain, but also the normal limits of space. Precognition, the accurate foreseeing of future events, exhibits the same characteristics, but also hops over the barrier of time by peering into the future.

It's logical to conclude then that all three work similarly in that the remote information is transmitted by the very same unknown natural (or supernatural) mechanism, and is received in the same part of the brain. We can compare this to the way the mechanism of sight conveys images from the outside world into our eyes and to our brain. Regardless to the type of objects being viewed, the image is always transmitted via light waves to our eyes. Our eyes then always transmit that information to the singular part of the brain devoted to seeing. If we were to send signals from the eye directly to the brain stem instead of to the optic nerve, we would not have vision, just as wiring your optic nerves directly to your feet will not let you see with your toes (of course this sounds almost too simple, but when dealing with phenomena like the paranormal, sometimes we humans miss the obvious because our minds get lost in the wonderment of it all). In the same way, telepathic, clairvoyant and precognitive information appear to always come to us by traversing the same unknown cosmic medium to the very same part of the brain. It's hard to imagine that these three mental phenomena function differently from one another, or that each works on a different part of the mind. We should therefore classify them together in the same group of phenomena.

Although the traditional *extra-sensory perception* or ESP adequately represents the *receiving* of information by a means other than the five senses, it doesn't refer to the *transmission* of such information, which as we have already deduced functions according to the same principles. Another negative is that it's somewhat archaic, having fallen out of style in recent years in favor of *psychic* or *psi* for short. But even *psi* is unsuitable, because by indicating *any* phenomenon involving the mind, even things like telekinesis, it paints too broad a stroke. The name *psychic* has the added problem of being commonly used to refer to a person who practices divination and mediumship, which drags us again into religious issues.

After much thought, I settled on the term *Transmentation* to describe these phenomena. The term combines *trans* for the transporting of something from one location to another, and *mental* for what's being transported. Transmentation narrowly refers only to the sending and receiving of information, and so helps us to identify and discuss these particular paranormal phenomena more precisely. The term itself is also highly illustrative of the phenomenon associated with it. It further has the additional benefit of being religiously neutral, which allows us to apply it in all circumstances without any associated spiritual connotation.

The prefix *trans* lends itself very well for use in paranormal study, since it conveys a mental image of passing from one state to another. Since paranormal events behave in ways that bypass the normal physical laws of space, time, matter and energy, the source of these phenomena has to be *non-physical* in nature. The prefix *trans* implies not only a transporting between two locations, but also a transition between two states, in this case between the non-physical and physical. It is not only more linguistically precise, but also alludes to the processes behind the phenomenon in a way that existing terms simply fail to do.

Things That Go Bump in the Night

Next comes the phenomenon of objects that move with no apparent physical means. Levitations are one obvious example, such as books that fly off the shelf and float across the room. But we must also include telekinesis since the effect is identical. Traditionally, telekinesis has been classified as being a strictly mental phenomenon separate from levitation. But again, a part of our new approach is to focus on the effect itself, not on who or what initiates it. Accordingly, it doesn't matter if an object is moved telekinetically by a living person or levitated by a poltergeist or some other natural but misunderstood means. Both are the very same physical gravity-defying effect, and so both must operate according to the same physical principles.

Consider the many well-documented levitations reportedly performed by St. Joseph of Copertino in the 17th century. Most would attribute this strange talent to mind-over-matter. Why then isn't it called telekinesis instead of levitation? In cases like these, it's easy to see there is little distinction between the two. Levitation and telekinesis are the same effect, and should therefore be classified under the same category. This is a prime example of how focusing on the event itself can be a powerful tool in helping to re-organize the paranormal into a more useful and meaningful system.

What should we name this category? Both levitation and telekinesis are essentially the relocation of an object through space from point *A* to point *B* in a way that bypasses the known laws of physics. We're obviously not going to employ the word *relocation* because of its common usage. It also needs to be descriptive enough to represent the nature of the phenomenon in question while being sufficiently unique to avoid confusion.

Fortunately, a suitable term already exists. *Translocation* is a scientific term sometimes used to describe the transfer of genetic material from one chromosomal location to another. It is also used in referring to the transportation of molecules, flora and fauna, and even data. Since the term is application-neutral, its use is not intrinsically linked to any other specific discipline. Translocation is thus a perfect term for our needs—it's very descriptive of these phenomena, consistent in form and syntax with the other new term transmentation, easily conveys the intended meaning to the reader, and is sufficiently uncommon to minimize the chance of confusion with an alternative meaning or usage.

A Sound Idea

Here's an example where this new system really begins to show its superiority over the old way. Consider for a moment auditory phenomena like footsteps on a floor where no one is walking or hearing a disembodied voice. First, clear the mind of all thoughts concerning any spiritual or religious elements and concentrate instead on the physical phenomenon itself. Now we can clearly see that what we have here is nothing more or less than a sound with no physical cause. Just that, and nothing else. Now let's think about the physics of sound (remember, the mind's still cleared of the spiritual stuff). Sound is transmitted to our ears by the movement of air molecules as well as through other physical substances like water. The frequency and amplitude at which the air molecules are vibrated determine the type of sound we hear. In the case of disembodied voices, something non-physical displaces the molecules, causing them to vibrate at the right frequency and amplitude necessary to produce the sound of a voice in our ears.

Now recall that our definition of translocation is an event in which a physical thing is moved or displaced by non-physical means. Although very tiny, air molecules are physical things. Therefore, such voices are translocations of the surrounding air molecules. The physical air molecules are being displaced or vibrated by a non-physical source in the same way that a book levitating across a room is similarly displaced by a non-physical source. The translocated air molecules strike our eardrums, and we hear the sound of a voice, just as translocated floorboards carry to us the sound of footsteps.

Our new classification system reveals that the only difference between auditory phenomena and a levitated book is one of scale, not of quality—they are both translocations. This is a critical perceptual breakthrough.

A Ghostly Affair

What about apparitions? Apparitions are considered by many to be the 'holy grail' of paranormal investigation, so we should devote considerable attention to them. Based on all the available evidence, apparitions do not behave like hard physical objects. They appear and disappear, are often transparent, float or hover, fade away, or pass right through solid walls. Yet they are still visible to our eyes. This leads us to the same conclusion as with auditory phenomena in that an apparition must be understood as nothing more or less than a visual manifestation having no discernible physical source.

So let us now also look at the physics of vision as we did with sound. Vision is caused by light waves entering into our eyes. As with sound, the frequency and amplitude of the light waves determine what we see. To put it more accurately, we can't actually see an object itself, only the light reflected from its surface—without reflected light, we are quite blind (there's a brain teaser for you!). The difference, of course, is that in the case of an apparition, there is no physical person off which the local available light might reflect to cause the visual appearance of a figure. Keep in mind too that reflected light is a physical thing, even though it's pure energy. So in the case of an apparition, something non-physical displaces the available physical light waves, which then enter our eyes. The frequency and amplitude of these physical waves cause us to see a particular image, in this case the apparition. An apparition is therefore a translocation of available physical light waves, just like audible phenomenon is the translocation of physical air molecules, and levitation is the translocation of a physical material object. It's clear to see that this new approach enables us to understand phenomena like apparitions in a more informative, organized and revealing way.

Other Ghostly Matters

Because apparitions are the recipient of so much attention (and consequently all the more speculation), it's important to point out a few other common misconceptions surrounding them. Many researchers believe, for example, that apparitions are composed of pure energy. This view isn't entirely consistent with either the available evidence or the physics of energy. In almost every personal account, photo or video, apparitions display the visual characteristics of normal matter, even though they are not fully material. Their outward appearance is the same as what we would expect if we were viewing equivalent physical material in the same level of light at the same location —the dimmer the light source, the dimmer the apparition. In other words, they reflect the available ambient light in the same way as would a normal physical object similarly configured at that same location. Even when the apparition is misty and transparent, the overall appearance of the light it reflects is virtually identical to that of a normal misty substance like water vapor or smoke. An apparition is almost never seen in a pitch-black room where there is absolutely no available visible light to reflect off its surface, just as normal physical objects in the same total darkness are similarly invisible. This seems to hold true not only for light waves, but for other types of reflected radiation as well, like the wavelengths detected by night vision equipment. So whether it's an apparition or a normal object like a chair, nothing is visually detectable without specific wavelengths available in the vicinity to reflect off the subject's surface. Therefore, if we consider this in a strictly scientific way, we can only say with certainty that an apparition has but two components that cause it to be visible to the human eye—the reflected physical light that our eyes detect, and the non-physical surface which translocates that light into our eyes.

I See the Light

This more precise way of understanding apparitions calls into question the long-standing belief that they are composed of pure energy. It's easy to jump to this conclusion because they are obviously not solid matter, so the assumption is they must be energy. The ways in which they manifest also gives witnesses the impression that they are emitting light, which is indeed a form of energy. But just because an object reflects ambient light so we can see it does not mean it's an energy field (the page you are now looking at is a perfect example). We can only say for certain that the visible energy projected by most apparitions is that of reflected light, and that this invisible surface reflects light in a manner that appears identical to solid matter, even though it's not actually solid. We as yet have little idea what is taking place at the core of an apparition beneath its reflective surface. So to assume based on conventional reasoning that an apparition must comprise the same normal matter and energy with which we're familiar seems a bit presumptuous. After all, isn't an apparition a *para*normal object? If it weren't, why do we have these kinds of discussions over them? So, just because light is being directed to our eyes paranormally instead of normally, we cannot then get so excited that we completely forget that the light itself is still bound by *normal* physical laws.

So if apparitions are made visible by the available light energy that is reflected from their surfaces, we cannot just assume from this that an apparition's surface or even its core must be composed of energy as well. There is absolutely no scientific or observational foundation to conclude that visible light is somehow being reflected from the surface of some sort of dense energy wall as if it were a human-shaped force field, especially in the absence of any kind of mechanism that could generate such a field if it were even possible. Think about it.

Consider this: what kind of pure energy field could present a surface that reflects light in the identical manner as solid matter and in the identical shape, complete with all the visual details of a normal solid object? Think of a typical apparition like a lady dressed in 19th century clothing. If the apparition were a pure energy field, it would have to be sufficiently dense to reflect light in the same fashion as normal solid matter. The nearly solid wall of reflective energy would then also need to have an additional force to shape and sustain perhaps millions of geometric convolutions to configure its surface into the highly complex analog image of a distinct and recognizable ornately clothed woman. What kind of natural mechanism could bend and sustain an intense, concentrated energy field into the shape of such a complex figure? It's unlikely to be silent, and would in fact produce electromagnetic and atmospheric disturbances in its immediate vicinity far more intense than an EMF meter fluctuation or the passing of a slight breeze. Imagine the sound it might make, or the kind of scar it would leave upon passing through a wall. We can't ignore basic physics.

Think about a Star Wars light saber. Its "blade" is a beam of energy projected into empty space that is somehow sustained in a particular shape and length. When the beams of two light sabers make contact during a fight in the movie, they impact one another as if they were solid objects. Anyone who has read about or watched documentaries exploring the feasibility of such technology knows that this is one of the few Star Wars gadgets that is deemed almost certainly a physical impossibility. In the case of an apparition, shaping a field of energy by some unknown force or method into a perfect outline of a human being that can then physically interact with its surrounding environment and also float through a solid wall with no effect is similarly unrealistic. If it can't work for this simple cylindrical shape, how's it going to work for the shape of a Victorian lady? Paranormal investigators cannot simply disregard basic physics and hope to make any meaningful progress toward unraveling these mysteries, or to gain any credibility with the legitimate scientific community.

Those championing the idea that an apparition is made of energy also cite other types of specters as proof. A *shadow ghost* appears as a black silhouette having a blob-like or even human shape. But there's certainly nothing about a black form that would indicate it is pure energy. In the physical world, an object appears black when its surface absorbs the entire visible spectrum of light instead of reflecting it. Therefore, all we can say is that a shadow ghost merely presents a surface that absorbs the full spectrum of local light in much the same way as would a normal physical object painted black, or perhaps a thick black cloud of charcoal dust. This is entirely consistent with the normal properties of reflected or absorbed light, and so does not necessarily imply an energy field as the cause.

A Glowing Personality

Then there are the reports of apparitions that appear to be luminescent as if they were generating their own light instead of reflecting it. But bear in mind that photos like these (which comprise the bulk of evidence for these kinds of apparitions) are virtually all taken with a bright flash that reflects brilliantly off a white surface, thus giving the appearance that the subject is glowing. Based on the photographic evidence, these unusual phantoms seem merely to present a reflective surface like any other apparition, except that they reflect the entire spectrum of light (just as does a white painted object) so that they shine with a pure, almost glowing white in the camera's flash. So here too, there's nothing to refute the idea that the overwhelming majority of apparitions are made visible by presenting a surface that reflects or absorbs various wavelengths of available light, or in other words, a surface that *translocates* the light waves that are striking against it.

One certainly has a better argument for an apparition being composed of pure energy when considering mysterious lamp-like globes that appear to emit their own light. But one could also argue that these are not truly apparitions since they do not present the shape of a living creature. Some energy like charged plasma can indeed take round forms as in ball lightning, swamp lights, St. Elmo's fire, piezoelectric phenomena like earthquake lights, and so on. But not a Victorian lady.

Even in the extremely remote case of a genuinely luminous apparition, there are still other, more scientifically consistent explanations. When electrons in atoms are excited by a charge, the added energy propels them to a higher orbit around the nucleus. They soon drop back down to their original orbits and discharge this extra energy in the form of photons (this is how an LED works). Some process in the manifestation of certain paranormal phenomena may similarly excite the electrons of the surrounding air molecules in such a manner as to cause this kind of photon emission. Luminous phenomena would then be the result of a disturbance in—or again, *translocation* of—local matter and energy coming in contact with the phenomenon's surface without the need for the physical materialization of a phantom light bulb or oil lamp.

What about images recorded by thermal cameras? Aren't these an indication that apparitions are pure energy? Later I'll discuss this phenomenon in more detail, but for now, suffice it to say that a study of thermal imaged apparitions reveals they do not display the same kind of heat signatures emitted by real flesh-and-blood beings. The images tend to have a much more uniform heat signature across their entire surface as opposed to the extreme contrasts of warm and cool areas like cheeks, noses and clothing observed with living people. This indicates that an apparition's heat signature is actually being generated at its surface, not from its core. If it was generated in its core—if the entire apparition was a single large heat-generating field—the apparatus necessary to produce such a large, hot field, and the observable effect it would have on the surrounding environment would also have to be physically present at the location of the sighting, which of course they are not.

Energetic Immortality

Still another argument for an apparition being composed of pure energy is the belief that a person's spirit survives after death in the form of physical energy, and so there's an assumption that an apparition must be a visible manifestation of that spirit's energy field. Supporters of this supposition cite the laws of energy conservation, which state that matter/energy can neither be created nor destroyed. The argument is that the spirit in life is composed of normal, physical energy, but when we die, this energy is somehow preserved eternally by being converted to a different form.

Unfortunately, this is one of those wonderful-sounding and emotionally satisfying spiritual euphemisms that under closer examination proves to be without reasonable foundation in terms of either physics or traditional religion. In fact, religion teaches that souls persist in a *spiritual* form, not in a physical one. Since energy *is* physical, this concept would violate many a religious principle, be it Christian or otherwise. Furthermore, according to Christian teachings, the physical universe and all that is in it will someday be destroyed, leaving no way for a spirit composed of physical energy to survive eternally.

There's still other problems with this belief. A person's living spirit is supposed to possess certain characteristics that are unique to that individual. How are these embedded characteristics within a living person's "energy field" retained during its conversion to a different form of energy at death? And what about the spirits of all living creatures from the dawn of time? Where is all that energy being stored? Real energy is physical and therefore can be measured, and so this accumulating soul-field of energy should be measurable. Has there been a rise in background radiation over the course of the last century or even millennium that would account for all these extra spirits? And if they become part of the background radiation, by what mechanism do the energy fields from billions of souls maintain their unique characteristic shapes or patterns so that each is distinguishable from the others amid the enormous and homogenous background radiation field? And what process converts each unique energy pattern at the moment of death to another kind of energy having the exact same pattern? See what kind of trouble we can get into when we adopt a spirit-centric approach to the paranormal?

So, if apparitions were spirits of pure energy, what suddenly gives this manifesting energy field human form, where was this indestructible energy before it manifested as an apparition, and where does it go when the apparition vanishes? Physics.

The Bottom Line

All this is not to say that under any circumstance can a specter emit energy in the form of light, heat or EMF. The point I'm trying to make—a point that must be argued with enough weight and persistence to break through conventional thinking, traditional belief and spirit-centric preconception—is that the overwhelming majority of paranormal manifestations that take on a visible quality do so by reflecting the available ambient light in their vicinity. What this means is that whatever physical mechanism or process causes an apparition to present a visual, thermal or electromagnetic image of itself occurs at the apparition's *surface*, not at its core. In those very, very rare instances where an apparition appears to be emitting its own light, the nature of the apparition at its core is still the same as that of a reflective apparition. In either case, the process that renders it visible takes place at the surface of the apparition where it interacts with the surrounding environment, not at its core. So by these new criteria and definitions, *all* apparitions are trans-locational phenomena, since the visual effect is brought about by its surface interacting with its surroundings rather than the projecting outward of any of its core substance (no matter what substance that might be). A study of all available paranormal evidence leads to this as the only practical conclusion that is consistent with both established physics and the *entire* body of available data.

Understanding this fundamental aspect of the true physical nature of apparitions is essential toward accurately deciphering what physical laws are at work here. Too many well meaning paranormal investigators toss the term "energy" out at almost every opportunity, yet in a way that often reflects a complete misunderstanding or disregard for what energy really is. I can only imagine how many scientifically educated persons wince each time they hear this. Before we can have a real chance at deciphering the mysteries of the paranormal, our minds have to first arrive at an accurate comprehension of exactly what it is we are observing. And we have to discard those traditional notions that, however appealing they might seem, simply do not hold up to serious scrutiny.

Life in the Material World

If apparitions are not pure energy, could they then be composed of matter? Some investigators believe that apparitions are materializations, and so are material in nature. They often cite noticeable drops in temperature and the apparent draining of device batteries in the vicinity as evidence that a spirit is drawing energy from the surrounding area to use in "materializing" itself. We all know relativity theory states that matter and energy are two different forms of the same substance, and that one can be converted into the other, so it's easy to understand how one might conclude that a spirit draws surrounding energy to convert it into matter to become visible.

But here again, this spirit-centric view obscures the hard reality that the physics necessary to convert local heat or electrical energy into enough matter to manifest something like an apparition is simply not there. The biggest problem is when you consider how much energy would actually be required to physically materialize something like an apparition. Just as in an atomic blast, where a miniscule amount of matter yields a huge amount of energy, you'd need an incredible volume of energy to materialize even the thinnest wisp of matter, let alone something the size and shape of a human figure. We wouldn't be talking about "cold spots" of tens of degrees, but more like how many thousands of surrounding square miles would be reduced to absolute zero (minus 459 degrees Fahrenheit) in order to muster even a few molecules! According to physicists, the entire energy output of our sun would not yield even one ounce of matter. This single scientific fact alone is enough to kill the whole supposition.

Besides, researchers often detect a *rise* in electromagnetic fields in the presence of paranormal activity. If spirits do drain available energy from the surrounding area to manifest, why then doesn't the level of EMF *fall*? Or is there some "intelligent" transformer present that converts heat alone to electromagnetic emissions while retaining enough additional energy to physically manifest a visible human form? How? Where?

There's no doubt that fluctuations in energy levels like light, heat and EMF do indeed occur in areas local to a paranormal manifestation for some unknown reason. It's very understandable how researchers would feel compelled to come up with any kind of outwardly reasonable explanation for the many bizarre phenomena they encounter. And it certainly does appear by conventional reasoning that a spirit is drawing energy from the environment. But the real answer is not likely to be poor old deceased Uncle Ted who, upon passing on to the next world, magically acquires the uncanny ability to convert ridiculously small amounts of energy into material substance.

Smile for the Camera

Spirit photography and EVP are the last two audible and visible phenomena on our list of paranormal elements. These too are translocations, since they are also non-physical deflections of physical light waves and/or air molecules that are recorded on electro-mechanical devices instead of by our senses.

That cameras and recorders often record things that go undetected by human observers makes these phenomena quite perplexing. This is especially true with EVP, where disembodied voices are frequently recorded on the media that are not heard by the person with the recorder. At one time it was suspected that these phenomena escaped notice by imposing themselves directly onto the film or magnetic tape. But the advent of digital cameras and recorders makes this unlikely, since whatever produces these recordings would then have to "know" how to convert analog waves to the digital language of ones and zeros before placing them directly onto the devices' memory. It's also been found that the highest quality optics and microphones produce the best results. Keep in mind too that there are plenty of instances where observers actually do see and hear the evidence that gets recorded on their equipment. It's therefore logical to conclude that the recorded sights and sounds reach the media in the form of normal physical waves collected through the customary lens or microphone.

The most likely explanation then is that there is some quality to these phenomena that recording devices are more adept at capturing than the senses. Take for example a transparent apparition that is virtually invisible to the naked eye, and yet is sufficiently illuminated by the brief, intensely bright camera flash to be captured on film. In the case of audible phenomena like EVP, the translocation may directly affect the microphone diaphragm by way of sympathetic vibration, just as an inaudible vibration in your house might set your pots and pans audibly rattling. In any case, the fundamental mechanism behind spirit photography and EVP is still translocational, since in both cases the wave patterns are being manipulated into recordable sights and sounds by a non-physical source.

Those trained in traditional paranormal thought might find it bizarre to group audible and visual phenomena with events like levitation and telekinesis. But when we turn our minds away from concepts rooted in spiritualism and focus instead on the actual physics of the phenomena, it soon becomes apparent how all these events are just different examples of the same hidden mechanism.

So here's our list of phenomena that fall under the category of translocation, or events where physical matter and energy are moved, deflected or otherwise displaced by no detectable localized physical cause: levitation, telekinesis, apparitions, spirit photography, audible and olfactory phenomena, and EVP.

Now we're making progress.

Paranormal Chameleons

Transformations are those occurrences where the molecular structure of a physical substance is altered paranormally. In science, the conversion of one chemical element into another is called *transmutation*. The ancient alchemist's attempt to turn base metals into gold was also defined as transmutation. I'm hard pressed to find a better term for paranormal transformations, especially since it employs the prefix *trans* in a way that is completely consistent with the other new terms.

Transmutation goes one step further than translocational displacements by actually changing an object's basic makeup. The transmuted object undergoes a metamorphosis at the molecular level, resulting in a different physical appearance and/or state. Because of this, it's likely that both are merely different manifestations of the same process. If you think about it, any molecular changes caused by a non-physical influence would certainly be a translocational effect. The actual difference then would be one of degree or scale, transmutation being a more extreme translocational effect. In spite of this, it helps to group these extreme translocational events as a distinct class of phenomena to better isolate and analyze them. If the fundamental constituents of a physical thing can be non-locally transformed in this way, then a better understanding of the process responsible might provide valuable insights into other frustrating anomalies in fields like physics and evolution.

Documented examples of transmutation are extremely rare and frequently controversial. Changes to images on portraits or photographs, houseplants that seem to wither and die virtually overnight, or the spontaneous discoloration of materials are the kinds of transmutations sometimes reported during poltergeist activity. Images appearing on unexposed film or sounds recorded on magnetic tape without any microphone would be examples of direct transmutation of the recording media. The Bible is sprinkled liberally with instances of transmutations like Aaron's staff changing into a serpent and Lot's wife turning into a pillar of salt.

The most commonly reported transmutations are faith healings involving the apparent spontaneous regeneration of bone and tissue or the eradication of disease. But when such things are observed in the human body (as indeed they are on occasion), a debate always arises as to whether or not the cause may be due to some extraordinary but as-yet-misunderstood mechanism that enables the mind to physically change the body in dramatic ways. The mind is indeed a powerful force, and we do not yet fully know the extent to which it can exert its influence over the flesh of our bodies. It is still likely, though, that at least a few of these cases are bona fide transmutations.

Perhaps the most famous transmutations in modern times were those produced on Polaroid film by Ted Serios during the 1960s. A Chicago bellhop, Serios discovered after a severe illness that he could cause images to appear on film through mental focus alone. A typical session would have Serios point a Polaroid camera at his face while he concentrated. When he felt the moment was right he would snap a picture and then hand the camera off to wait for the print to develop. Though many shots showed nothing more than fuzzy images of his face, some bore images of buildings both famous and obscure and other structures such as ships and planes. He also occasionally produced images of subjects suggested by an observer. Sometimes the camera would yield prints that were either completely white or black (called "whities" and "blackies"), which in itself is very strange. Unfortunately, Serios' unusual abilities seem to have diminished significantly by the end of the decade. Dr. Jule Eisenbud, who worked closely with Serios in researching his abilities, published his findings in 1967 in the book *The World of Ted Serios: "Thoughtographic" Studies of an Extra-ordinary Mind.*

Serios was not without his detractors. As time went on, he began to increasingly employ a rolled up tube of plastic or paper he called a "gizmo" that he positioned over the camera lens to help him "focus" his energies. This of course drew lots of suspicion, and accusations of fraud were common. The denier James Randi and professional photographer Nile Root were able to produce similar photographs by concealing miniature images inside gizmo-like appliances. But they were unable to duplicate these results when the camera was at a distance or if the gizmos were not used, both circumstances under which Serios had successfully produced images. He generated images when the camera was placed as much as 66 feet away, when it was in another room, and even one time when the camera's lens had been removed. Many fail-safes were utilized during numerous tests including strip-search and being filmed continuously to detect trickery. On one occasion, he was sealed in a Faraday cage while an investigator outside the cage held and worked the camera with positive results. He even underwent controlled testing by researchers at the Division of Parapsychology of the University of Virginia Medical School, who failed to uncover any evidence of deceit. There's just too much documentation by credible observers to thoughtlessly dismiss all this as bunk.

After having studied the available material both pro and con, my own conclusion lies somewhere in between. It was attested to by many people that Serios was an emotionally unstable and troubled person. I personally believe that all the intense scrutiny and pressure to perform on demand led to the deterioration of his talent over time. He may have indeed developed some form of trick with the gizmo to help him get results when his normal methods failed. But I have also come away from my research convinced that, on occasion, Ted Serios indeed produced genuine transmutational phenomena.

Now You See It, Now You Don't

The next category of events are those phenomena in which matter and energy seem to appear, disappear, or transport from one location to another. These are *materialization* and *dematerialization, teleportation,* and *bilocation*. Unlike translocation, where matter and energy are moved across space, objects that undergo these kinds of shifts migrate to other spatial locations without actually traversing the physical path between. They pop in and out of physical existence in a way that bypasses normal space and time. In keeping with our established naming convention, an appropriate term for these kinds of phenomena is *transmigration*.

Dematerialization is the fading or complete disappearance of an object from our physical plane, while materialization is its spontaneous appearance. Just as in the case of transmutation, most of the evidence for these kinds of events is anecdotal. This is no surprise, since a dematerialized object leaves no physical artifact to study, and the inspection of a materialized object cannot reveal how it arrived at the location where it was found. During poltergeist episodes, persons who live in the affected home sometime report that objects go missing from secured areas or enclosures only to resurface at improbable locations in another part of the house. Objects are found in some instances that apparently originated from outside the home, since these are confirmed not to belong to any of the residents.

A few paranormal researchers cite the appearance and disappearance of apparitions as examples of materialization and dematerialization. But again, all we can say for certain about apparitions is that they present a surface that reflects energy. The available evidence suggests that apparitions themselves are not physical bodies, and therefore cannot possibly represent true materializations. In other words, since they are not mater-ial, they cannot be *material*-izations.

Anyone who has watched even a single episode of *Star Trek* knows what teleportation is. In the real world, the teleporting of an object from one location to another is a feat far beyond our current understanding. Now, you may have recently heard about a process known as "photon teleport" that has been suc-cessfully executed in laboratories since the 1990s. But the name scientists gave to this procedure (a decision that I believe was disingenuously made to be intentionally sensational) is very misleading, since it refers only to the spontaneous transmission of information about a given photon's state, and in no way in-volves the teleportation of anything physical from one location to another.

According to our current scientific understanding, to affect a genuine teleportation would first require the conversion of the object's physical structure into a pattern of energy that can then be transmitted out to a remote destination. Some kind of "receiving station" or other mechanism at the destination site would then have to collect the signal, recognize the pattern of energy for what it once was, and reconstitute it back into its original material form. We do not even possess the theoretical knowledge to fathom such a process, let alone the technology to perform it. That teleportation could occur by some naturally occurring mechanism is incomprehensible in light of the laws of physics as we know them. Yet documented cases of tele-portation do exist, like those that are occasionally reported in instances of poltergeists.

A famous account of teleportation comes from the Gospel of John when Jesus walked on water to reach a boat manned by his disciples. As soon as he entered the boat, they suddenly found themselves on the shore at their destination. There is also the incident in Acts where the apostle Philip was instantly whisked away to a distant city immediately after baptizing the eunuch with whom he was traveling.

Bilocation is a curious phenomenon that appears to defy the laws of mass and energy conservation. If matter and energy can neither be created nor destroyed, how can an object multiply itself so that it can be in two different places at once? The case of Mary of Agreda mentioned earlier is a well-documented example of this very strange kind of event. It's most likely that the mechanism behind bilocation is exactly the same as in teleportation, except that the process is for some reason suspended in midstream so that the duplicate is sufficiently materialized to be physically present at the second location, but not sufficiently dematerialized at the starting location to cause the original to completely vanish there.

French physiologist Charles Richet conducted considerable research into what we are calling translocational and transmigrational phenomena around the beginning of the 20th century. Working with a number of mediums, Richet devised controlled experiments and compiled volumes of compelling evidence for the authenticity of these kinds of occurrences. His findings are worthy of serious consideration primarily due to his impressive list of credentials. He was named Professor of Physiology at the Collège de France (1887), and was a member of both the French Academy of Medicine (1898) and the French Academy of Sciences (1914). Richet was also the winner of the 1913 Nobel Prize for Physiology and Medicine for his pioneering research into anaphylaxis, a term he himself coined. In 1905 he became President of the Society for Psychical Research in the United Kingdom, as well as President of the International Metapsychic Institute of Paris in 1929. His achievements include an impressive number of authoritative books on a variety of subjects such as history, philosophy, sociology, psychology, and of course, the paranormal. Richet was obviously no gullible or uneducated fool, but was a highly intelligent man, a keen observer, and meticulous at setting up experimental controls to eliminate the possibility of fraud. His book *Thirty Years of Psychical Research* is a must-read for anyone interested in this subject.

All Things are One

Last in our bastion of the bizarre is the phenomenon known as *synchronicity*, a term coined by psychologist Dr. Carl Jung to describe what he called "meaningful" coincidence. The difference between meaningful coincidence and simple coincidence is one of degree. For instance, on a given day, co-workers Sally and Kim both arrive to work wearing similar red dresses. This is simple coincidence, and except for vanity, most people would not give it a second thought. However, when Sally and Kim discuss the coincidence, they discover that both selected their respective dresses because each is meeting a new date immediately after work. This would now be a *meaningful* coincidence —the two women's independent decisions to select a red dress, coupled with both of them having a new date, and immediately after work, represent an unusual series of circumstantial events. The plot thickens when they discover that their dates are both named Scott. The ladies react to this unusual series of coincidences with words such as creepy, spooky, and so on. It almost seems their life paths are running parallel, or are *synchronized*. Most of us have experienced something like this at one time in our lives.

I personally experienced a minor instance of synchronicity while writing this book. I had been devoting so much time to it that I fell almost a week behind in my grocery shopping. That Saturday, my supplies ran too low for even a bachelor's tolerance, so I had to pull myself from the computer and go. Two seemingly unrelated and coincidental factors were to influence what I purchased, which in turn set into motion an unusual string of coincidences.

First, I had been looking several months for a certain type of rectangular 30-gallon trash container similar to the kind seen placed around the parking lots of fast food restaurants. Because of the time I was devoting to writing, I had confined my search to a small circle of stores within close proximity to my home.

Upon arriving at one of these stores on this particular Saturday in April, I found for the first time the receptacle I was looking for (keep in mind I had searched this store numerous times in the previous months without success). The containers were arranged in a row and stacked one inside the other, each stack being of a different sized unit, while the various size lids were piled at random on the shelf above. Both the containers and the lids were marked with a model number, so that one would have to rummage through the lids for the number corresponding to a particular size can. I quickly found the one that bore the same number as the receptacle I had selected, a model #102.

The second stage in this series of events was a notification from my employer that I was to receive a significant raise in salary. This was another unusual event because the company for which I worked always awarded raises at the end of the year, not in April. Seeing this as cause for celebration, and in view of my near-empty cabinets, I decided to give myself a special treat at the grocery store by purchasing a selection of choice seafood, the centerpiece of which was a sizable lobster.

Bear in mind that all these unrelated events were out of the ordinary—finding for the first time an item in a store I had frequented the previous several months without success, having received a raise in April from a company that always awarded raises at the end of the year, waiting so long after my normal shopping weekday to buy groceries, and finally purchasing a large lobster.

The above elements came together or "synchronized" when I arrived home. After putting away the groceries, I made myself a small snack and sat down to watch a few minutes of television. Turning to one of the public television channels, I caught the tail end of a cooking program. The host had a guest cook who was demonstrating a number of seafood dishes, the last of which (and the only segment I saw in its entirety) was the preparation of a *lobster*. As usual, a video of the program was offered for sale at the end of the broadcast. When ordering, they asked that you specify the program number shown on the screen. The number of this program was #102. The event left me with one of those eerie feelings that you get after experiencing a string of uncanny coincidences.

There is yet another peculiar angle to this account. The section of this book I was working on so diligently at the time—the one that delayed my grocery shopping and thus initiated this series of coincidences—was this very chapter on paranormal phenomena.

Synchronicity implies that there exists a greater pattern or matrix to which worldly events adhere. Since the beginning of recorded history, philosophers and spiritual sages have been telling us that some grand cosmic web interconnects all things and events in the universe. Coincidental patterns of events are evidence of a greater, universal "mind" that is somehow synchronized with the world at large. Our sense of fate or destiny probably stems from a subconscious awareness of this grand pattern. The concept brings to mind the age-old debate as to whether we truly have free will or whether we are merely pawns on some vast cosmic chessboard. The purpose here, however, is not to enter into a philosophical discussion of free will versus destiny, but merely to demonstrate that such a grand pattern exists.

By far the most famous instance of synchronicity is the long list of remarkable coincidences surrounding the assassinations of Presidents Abraham Lincoln and John F. Kennedy. The patterns set in motion by the death of Lincoln appear to have reverberated exactly 100 years later when they were replayed in Kennedy's death:

- Both Presidents served during times of great civil unrest in which African Americans played a major role, and both were seen as champions of black civil rights.
- The civil unrest during both men's respective terms came to be known by very similar names (Civil War and

117

Civil Rights).

- Both Presidents sent Federal troops into the South.
- Both had premonitions of their assassinations. On the day he died, Lincoln said to a guard that there were "men who want to take my life.... And I have no doubt that they will do it.... If it is to be done, it is impossible to prevent it." Kennedy declared on the day of his assassination, "If somebody wants to shoot me from a window with a rifle, nobody can stop it, so why worry about it?"
- Both were elected to the presidency 100 years apart.
- Both were first elected to Congress exactly 100 years apart (1846 and 1946).
- Both Vice-Presidents—Andrew Johnson and Lyndon Johnson—were also born 100 years apart (1808 and 1908).
- The birth dates of the assassins John Wilkes Booth and Lee Harvey Oswald closely follow the above century marks, being born 101 years apart.
- Lincoln had a personal secretary named Kennedy, while Kennedy had a personal secretary named Lincoln.
- Both had Vice-Presidents named Johnson.
- Both Lincoln and Kennedy were shot on a Friday.
- Both were shot in the back of the head.
- Both were shot in the presence of their wives.
- Lincoln was shot in Ford's Theater. Kennedy was shot in a car made by Ford Motor Co.
- The model of the car in which Kennedy was shot was a Lincoln.
- Booth shot Lincoln in a theater, then fled to a ware-house. Oswald shot Kennedy while in a warehouse, then fled to a theater.
- Both assassins received injuries during their escape— Booth broke his leg, and Oswald was badly beaten by police while resisting arrest.

- Both assassins were killed before they could be brought to trial.

For those inclined to numerology, there are even more parallels:

- The names Kennedy, Lincoln, and Johnson all contain seven letters each.
- All three of the above names contain two pairs of double letters, and all three possess a double N:
  Kennedy = two E's and two N's
  Lincoln = two L's and two N's
  Johnson = two O's and two N's
- The names John Wilkes Booth and Lee Harvey Oswald both contain fifteen letters each.
- If each of the twenty-six letters in the alphabet are substituted with their numerical equivalent (1-26), the numbers of the initials of both assassins add up to thirty-five:
  John Wilkes Booth = JWB (10th, 23rd, and 2nd)
  [10+23+2=35]
  Lee Harvey Oswald = LHO (12th, 8th, and 15th)
  [12+8+15=35]
- With respect to the above, John Kennedy was our 35th President.

Any one of these parallels viewed individually is an interesting coincidence. But when all are considered together, the evidence for synchronicity is overwhelming. The mathematical odds of all these parallels being the result of mere random chance are almost incalculable.

Jung's term *synchronicity* is so well suited as a label for these kinds of phenomena that there really is no need for us to seek another.

The Completed List

Here's the final list of our new classifications. Virtually all supernatural phenomena resulting from non-local causality can be placed under one of these categories:

1. *Transmentation.* Events in which a human mind transmits and/or receives information about people, places, or events by non-physical means.

2. *Translocation.* Events in which physical things are moved or displaced by non-physical means.

3. *Transmutation.* Events in which the appearance or structure of a physical thing is altered by non-physical means.

4. *Transmigration.* Events in which physical objects spontaneously pass in and out of space-time, appearing, disappearing, or teleporting from one place to another by non-physical means.

5. *Synchronicity.* Meaningful coincidences beyond statistical probability, in which apparently unrelated events are connected in unique and purposeful ways.

These new classifications, which I simply call the *Revised System*, provide several advantages over the old. The Revised System sorts each phenomenon according to its primary characteristic regardless to whether the event occurs by itself or in combination with others. It makes no distinction as to who or what initiates the occurrence, nor when and where. It steers clear of spiritual and religious connotations. In addition, the names of the new categories are more consistent with each other both in form and in the concepts they convey, and are even suggestive of the underlying processes involved. These improvements and simplifications are invaluable in helping to isolate and analyze every type of event with greater clarity and exactitude.

MAKING SENSE OF IT ALL

One of the benefits to this Revised System is how well it illustrates the idea of a non-physical aspect to reality as being an intrinsic element in paranormal phenomena. This is a very old concept—the belief in an invisible spiritual universe is perhaps as old as humanity itself. But too often in the field of paranormal research, proponents speak of it in vague terms like "another realm" or a "parallel dimension" or "the spirit world." These impressive-sounding but outmoded terms are too ambiguous to be of much use, and often contribute to the kind of misunderstanding that characterizes such discussions. At best they serve to indicate that the speaker has little idea of what is really going on. If we're to make progress defining this realm, we need to be a bit more exact and scientific with our approach.

Our physical universe is contained within four dimensions. The first three are the spatial dimensions of height, width, and depth. The fourth dimension is time, or what's known as the temporal dimension. Einstein demonstrated that these four are inseparably bound together, and coined the collective term *space-time*. By definition, everything that is physical is measurable. Everything that is measurable is by its very nature dimensional. Everything that is dimensional—every single bit of matter and energy in our universe—is measurable not only by its spatial dimensions, but also the moment of time it occupies. To accurately measure and place anything in the universe, one must not only determine the exact spatial coordinates it occupies, but also at what precise moment it occupies that space.

It then stands to reason that a realm outside space-time would not be confined to the dimensions of space-time. That means this outer realm would not be "another dimension" at all as is commonly said. Instead, such a non-physical realm would be *a*-dimensional, or more specifically, *super*-dimensional. An even better set of terms are *superphysical* or *paraphysical* (i.e., extra-physical or beyond physical), both of which could be used interchangeably. Whatever resides in this non-dimensional, superphysical realm is not subject to the normal physical dimensions of space-time, and therefore cannot be defined or measured in normal terms of length, width and height. Since it exists outside dimensional space, it also exists outside normal time, and so cannot be "timed" in the same way as with normal reality.

With this in mind, we can identify four distinct superphysical or paraphysical principles from the Revised System's five classifications:

1. There exists a means by which information can be gathered, stored, and transmitted outside normal space-time. [Transmentation]

2. Matter and energy can be influenced and manipulated by some unknown mechanism, the source of which is non-physical and which originates outside normal space-time. [Translocation and Transmutation]

3. Matter and energy can pass in and out of normal space-time. During this passage, the original pattern of matter and energy is maintained. [Transmigration]

4. There exists a non-physical pattern or matrix on a grand scale. Seemingly unrelated physical things and/or events are in fact related through their alignment and resonance with this non-physical matrix. The existence of this matrix can be recognized by the occurrence of meaningful coincidences. [Synchronicity]

These four fundamental paraphysical concepts are the result of the reduction or simplification process begun with the earlier reclassification of paranormal phenomena according to their physical characteristics. They represent the very essence of what is paranormal. With them, we can now begin to construct a very generalized theoretical model of the mechanism behind paranormal events.

Admittedly, this is no easy task. The subject is deep and complex. Let's face it—if the answers were close to the surface, the world would already have a good idea as to what's behind these phenomena. We should anticipate that certain characteristics are naturally going to be counter-intuitive (like the wind being *pulled* along). Because of this, we need to take care not to fall into the same old traps of conventional thinking and preconception. Like Sherlock Holmes, we need to eliminate the impossible—whatever remains, no matter how improbable, has to be the truth.

1. There exists a means by which information can be gathered, stored, and transmitted outside normal space-time. Although thought itself cannot be measured, science has studied the physical processes of thought that take place in the brain. This research indicates that the hard, physical components of thought are electro-chemical in nature. Our thought processes are physically manifested in both the sequence of electrical impulses across the neurons of the brain and the chemicals that are produced and stored there. Remove either the electrical or chemical element, and human thought ceases to be.

The phenomenon of transmentation, however, proves that this definition is incomplete. For transmentation to operate, thought must also have a superphysical component. Experiments conducted with the use of a shielding Faraday cage confirm that in the case of transmental phenomena, the mental images received are not carried by any known physical medium

123

like energy waves or particles. Even if one could demonstrate the ability to transmit the electrical component in the form of "thought patterns" uncorrupted across a physical energy wave, the other essential component of the transmitted thought—the brain chemicals—would still be missing. As far as it is known, chemicals cannot be transported by an energy wave through space (that would be teleportation!). It is impossible then for conventional physical methods of signal transmission to be the means by which thought is directly conveyed transmentally.

Another strong argument for a superphysical component to thought is that transmentation operates outside the boundaries of established physical law. Physical law demands that the transmission of information from one place to another must be conducted through some physical substance connecting (or local to) both transmitter and receiver. The conductor can be almost anything like a beam of light, energy wave, copper wire or other physical medium. But no such physical link exists between two minds in telepathic communication. All efforts to detect a substance through which telepathic signals travel from one mind to another have consistently turned up nothing. Too, every attempt to shield or block telepathic signals by methods used to interrupt other known forms of energy have absolutely no effect on transmental transmissions. This, along with the absence of any transfer of the chemical component of thought, leaves us to conclude that the process behind transmentation lies outside the realm where our normal physical laws apply.

The transmental phenomenon of precognition—the mind's ability to receive information from the future—performs even more "illegal" acts. According to science, the future does not yet physically exist, and therefore cannot possibly serve as a source of information from which a prediction can be made. Even if science were to concede that perhaps the future does exist in some parallel plane with the present, there is still no physical law that would allow a human mind to peer into it. A signal bearing information from the future has no physical means to travel backward into the past, even if it were moving at the speed of light. Furthermore, physicists insist that the future is determined by random events only, and is therefore by its very nature unpredictable. Yet, in spite of violating every known physical law, precognition still occurs, which tells us that the cause of this and other transmental phenomena must reside outside the realm of those physical laws.

There must be a superphysical component to thought that exists independent of the brain's physical system of electrical impulses, chemicals, and neurons in the form of a blueprint that can be stored, transmitted and received outside of space-time. Because of the clarity and precision with which some telepathic images are conveyed, these superphysical blueprints must contain within their matrices every piece of information pertaining to the original thought. From this blueprint, the human mind can perfectly replicate the original physical thought down to its minutest detail.

It would be a mistake, however, to assume that these super-physical blueprints are limited to human thought. For example, it can be argued that telepathy is merely the synchronicity of two minds. The idea is quite attractive, and would provide a simple and satisfying explanation for telepathy. But what about clairvoyance, which often involves the remote viewing of inanimate places and things? Do places and things also have "minds" with which to synchronize, or "thoughts" which can be transmitted telepathically?

That the mind can receive lucid images telepathically from other minds *and* clairvoyantly from inanimate objects, loca-tions, and events shows that the transmental process for both are likely the same. Telepathy, clairvoyance, and precognition must all function in the same way, whether the remote source of information is a person, place, or thing. The process also appears identical whether the source of information is remote in terms of space (distance) or time (past, present, or future). If that is so, then *all* physical sources of information, whether people, places, things, events, and even thoughts themselves, must also have a corresponding superphysical component with which the mind can synchronize. We should then define trans-mentation as the human mind's ability to synchronize with any remote, superphysical source of information, whether person, place or thing. Furthermore, since the mind can use this super-physical aspect of reality to re-create in its "inner vision" such precise images of thoughts, places and events, these ethereal blueprints that the mind picks up on must contain all the information pertaining to the physical things to which they are connected.

The following example illustrates this idea well. Consider an instance where a clairvoyant "sees" the image of a car parked at a remote location and correctly identifies its make and color. Such details are part of an object's *physical* attributes—the style of that make and model is determined by its physical geometry, and its color by the particular spectrum of light waves reflected by its painted surface. In order to transmit a signal containing all this precise physical information to a remote location (such as a television screen), some physical medium like a radio wave or a beam of light is required. But in the case of the clairvoyant, this information is being received *super*physically—there is no medium (i.e., no matter or energy) connecting clairvoyant to car by which such physical information can be conveyed. Since the detailed knowledge about the car is coming to the clairvoyant through a superphysical means, the information being received then must *also* be superphysical in nature. Therefore, all information concerning all things in the universe has both a physical and superphysical constituent.

Recall for a moment the principle of local causality. In the above example, we could easily capture the information con-veyed through reflected light about the car's design and color with a television camera. The signal containing this information is then transmitted from the camera over a broadcasted wave to a remote receiving station where it is re-assembled as an image on a television screen. This method of transmission is simply a series of localized causes—the light waves reflecting off the car contact the camera lens, the camera then transmits the signal over a broadcasted wave, the wave then contacts the receiving station, etc. Each time the information containing the image of the car is transferred from one medium to the next, there is a local, physical connection or causality through which the transference takes place, whether that connection is in the form of matter or energy. Without these physical connections, there is no conduit by which the physical information can travel from one location to the next. Transmentally conveyed information, on the other hand, has no such physical connection, no series of localized causes between source and recipient. Therefore, since the clairvoyant receives the information about the car without any physical connection to the object, the information being conveyed cannot be physical either. Moreover, since the clairvoyant sees the shape and color of the car, the superphysical information also contains physical details like its geometry and the chemistry of its paint from which an accurate image can be reconstructed.

The only conclusion must then be once again that not only thought, but also *all* physical things—all objects, events, and places—have their own superphysical patterns that can serve as a blueprint from which a human mind can reconstruct a complete image of the original.

2. Matter and energy can be influenced and manipulated by some unknown mechanism, the source of which is non-physical and which originates outside normal space-time. For any physical effect to occur, the force or influence causing it must be local to the effected matter and energy. Of course, the problem with paranormal events is that there is no local physical cause. So what can it be? I believe our first paraphysical principle provides the key. What if the superphysical patterns or blueprints previously discussed are not just reflections of physical reality, but are a fundamental part of it? Every physical thing would then have its own superphysical pattern connected to it that might serve as a local cause.

Can these ethereal, superphysical patterns affect changes to physical reality? We've already concluded that these patterns contain all the information needed to enable a human mind to reconstruct the original object in all its detail. We've also suggested that the creative mechanism in the human brain (i.e., the ability to convert invisible thought into visible reality) is almost certainly a microcosm in flesh and blood of the larger macrocosmic mechanism responsible for the creation of the physical universe itself out of nothingness. So, if the mind can reconstruct an exact, detailed image of the original object from that object's superphysical matrix, could it be that these superphysical patterns are actually the very source of physical reality itself?

As strange as this notion may seem, it is by no means a new concept, nor is it some wacky fringe fantasy far removed from any legitimate scientific consideration. Physicist John Wheeler (whose ideas we will visit again later) also believes that such non-physical patterns exist and coined the term *pre-geometry* to describe them. According to Wheeler, the physical structure of everything in the universe, as well as the very fabric of dimensional space and time, emerge from these pre-geometric patterns.

Instead of the ambiguous nothingness suggested by the term *non-physical*, Wheeler's pre-geometry indicates that there is indeed something tangible in this realm beyond space-time. It implies that this "*some*-thing" is not-quite-yet physical and not-quite-yet dimensional, but is in the process of becoming physical and dimensional—it is actually *pre*-physical and *pre*-dimensional. This would be consistent with our assertion that something outside the normal world of physical cause and effect is indeed responsible for paranormal effects.

A point has now been reached in this investigation where

existing terminology is failing us. Since these superphysical patterns will become increasingly important to this discussion, a new term is needed to identify them that not only conveys a sense of what these patterns truly represent, but will also be free from existing conventions. Although Wheeler's term *pre-geometry* is a good one, it does have a few shortcomings. For one, it implies that this pre-physical realm is a sub-layer of physical reality, and so holds an inferior position to it. Instead, what is suggested by both Wheeler's pre-geometry and our own paraphysical principles is that these pre-physical blueprints are actually the *source* of physical reality, and therefore hold a *superior* position over it.

The tendency to visualize the pre-physical as an underlying reality rather than an overlaying reality is one of mistaken perspective brought about by conventional thinking. We tend to judge all things in relation to ourselves, and so automatically assume that the physical world we perceive and interact with almost exclusively must be primary reality, while everything else is secondary. Admittedly, it would be unnerving for most to entertain the thought that everything we see and experience around us emanates from some invisible universe we cannot perceive or touch. But if our premises are correct, then the world of the pre-physical is the overlaying *primary* reality, while our physical world is instead the underlying *secondary* reality. The physical universe is actually the consequence or after-effect of superphysical reality. In light of this, the term *pre-geometry* seems a bit inadequate.

Furthermore, if all physical reality rises from this pre-physical matrix (or to put it more perceptually accurate, *descends* from it), then the master blueprint must be enormous in scale. Here too, the term pre-geometry is too pale to paint such a grand picture.

In light of all this, the term *superphysical* seems preferable to either *pre-physical* or *paraphysical*, as it specifically implies the superior placement of this realm over the physical. Even so, the lofty goals of this book seem to demand a term that's even more specific, sufficiently unique to easily recall, and perhaps even a bit spectacular. The term *supergeometry* seems to fit all these criteria well. It implies a superiorly positioned, pre-physical superstructure on a cosmic scale from which emerges the fabric of space-time, universal order and all physical structures contained within.

Every dimensional structure in the physical universe—be it car, tree, electron, even thought—has its own corresponding supergeometric pattern containing all the information necessary to reproduce or assemble its material form in the physical world. It is this superphysical blueprint that the clairvoyant "sees" during transmental phenomena, and from which the mind can recreate an accurate and precise image of the original physical form or thought.

It's difficult to devise a simple model to illustrate the principle of supergeometry. Any such visible representation would have to be drawn using the spatial dimensions of length, width and height, whereas true supergeometry exists outside those dimensions. We must accept that any physical rendering is going to be incomplete and inaccurate. With this in mind, we might try comparing it to the effect of a magnet on iron filings. As a child I had a toy that made novel use of this effect. On a thin sheet of cardboard was printed the cartoon face of a man. A clear plastic bubble-like cover was glued over the printed face, much like the blister packs used to package small items for retail. A small amount of iron filings were trapped under the plastic cover. When the magnet was placed underneath the cardboard, the filings stood on end and aligned themselves to the magnetic field. You could then use the magnet to move and deposit the filings on various parts of the face to form a mustache, beard, sideburns, etc.

Imagine that the iron filings represent the basic building blocks of a physical object—matter, energy, space and time. When the magnet is held beneath them (below the surface of the cardboard where an observer cannot see it), the iron filings stand on end in alignment with the magnetic field. The magnetic field acts like a supergeometric pattern, providing the framework around which the physical elements adhere and conform. The shaped filings represent the completed object in the physical world, its geometry and other characteristics being established by the invisible pattern of the magnetic field. The cardboard sheet represents the space-time barrier, which separates the physical from the pre-physical. The visible topside of the board represents the physical universe, while the hidden underside with the magnet is the pre-physical realm of supergeometry. Our physical senses and measuring instruments are confined to the upper side, and cannot penetrate the barrier to detect what is below. [Figure 3.1, next page]

Now let's look at the phenomenon of translocation, where something physical is moved or deflected. If we were to slide the magnet across the bottom of the board, the physical object above (the iron filings) will follow, appearing to move on its own from one place to another as if by magic. An observer standing in the physical world (on the top surface of the cardboard) cannot detect the manipulation of the object's supergeometry (the moving of the magnet) beneath the cardboard. The movement of the object would be a paranormal event—in this case, a translocation of the object from one place to another by some unknown and undetectable means. [see diagrams, next two pages]

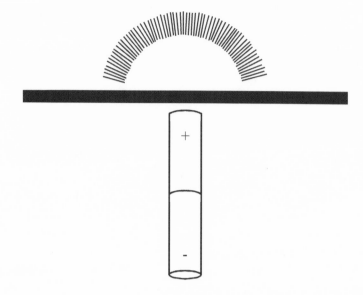

Figure 3.1 — A Simple Model of Supergeometry. Iron filings on a sheet of cardboard are aligned to the field of a magnet placed below. The filings represent a physical object in the world of space-time, while the magnet represents a superphysical influence outside the physical universe. The invisible magnetic field acts like a supergeometric pattern, establishing the geometric structure of the physical object in space-time.

A variation of this same model can be used to demonstrate transmutation. Let's say we introduce a second, much smaller magnet under the cardboard, placing it at an angle next to the first. The second magnet slightly alters the existing magnetic field, resulting in a somewhat different supergeometric pattern. In response to this altered pattern, the filings now shift their position, producing a modified physical geometric shape. From our perspective on this side of the space-time barrier, we would see the object's appearance or shape spontaneously change in a way consistent with paranormal transmutation. [Figure 3.2, next page]

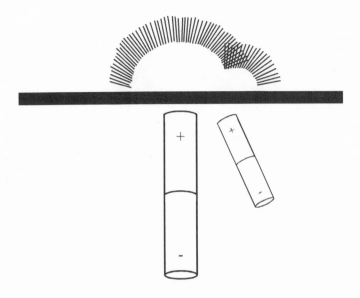

Figure 3.2 — A Model of Transmutation. The addition of a second magnetic field changes the overall supergeometric pattern. The shape of the iron filings changes accordingly, producing the effect of a paranormal transmutation.

This model neatly portrays how a transmutation like psychic photography might work, where images mysteriously appear on photographic film. If a copy of the target object's supergeometric pattern were somehow discerned by the mind and then superimposed over the supergeometric pattern of the film, we would expect an image of that object to appear on it. Since the human mind is apparently capable of "broadcasting" such images to another location as in telepathy, there's no reason why it could not transmit such an image to film under the right circumstances.

3. Matter and energy can pass in and out of normal space-time. During this passage, the original pattern of matter and energy is maintained. This principle, which describes transmigrational phenomena, can also be illustrated with our magnet-and-iron-filings model. Physical matter and energy are composed of atomic particles like protons, neutrons, electrons and photons. These in turn are assembled from smaller sub-atomic particles, the smallest of which are called quarks. Being the smallest of particles, they are the fundamental building blocks of the physical universe. We can liken the iron filings in our model to the quarks from which a physical object is constructed.

Quarks are classified according to the direction of their spin. Let's assume for the moment that the spin of quarks is in part determined by their supergeometry in the same way as the magnetic field in our model determines the orientation of all the iron filings. The spinning quarks coalesce into the required neutrons, protons, atoms, molecules and so on according to the greater supergeometric pattern of the final physical object.

Now let's go back to our model and pull the magnet away from the board so that its magnetic field no longer exerts an influence over the iron filings. As the magnetic pattern is removed, the filings lose their cohesive shape and collapse in a random pile on the cardboard's surface. This would be like causing the object's quarks to lose their mutual cohesiveness and dissipate into the cosmic background. An observer viewing the top of the cardboard would see the equivalent to what we'd call a paranormal dematerialization. If we were to bring the magnet once again to the same location on the underside of the cardboard, the iron filings would stand up and take shape as they did before, and so we would have a paranormal materialization. Now repeat this process, but this time bring the magnet up to a different location under the cardboard. The filings rush to this new location and re-assemble themselves there. We on the upper side of the cardboard would then witness an example of teleportation.

It's important to remember that this model not only offers a reasonably digestible explanation for the processes governing paranormal events, but also illustrates how an exact blueprint of a physical object might be faithfully preserved even after it disappears from dimensional space-time. It also indicates how the exact original object might be re-created in dimensional space from its pre-physical supergeometric blueprint.

This model of teleportation at first seems too weird, since it suggests that physical particles could simply dissolve into space. After all, the laws of conservation state that matter can neither be created nor destroyed. But the truth is that particles as tiny as quarks don't follow the same rules as the large, solid objects assembled from them, just as the micro-universe of quantum physics behaves quite differently than the macro-universe of relativity. A quark doesn't even take the form of a distinct particle until a device is used to observe it. Until that moment, its real nature is perhaps best expressed as a wave of mathematical probability. And no one can say for certain how quarks came into being, just as we are still trying to determine how the universe at large was created. So no one can say with absolute, positive certainty that quarks cannot coalesce and dissipate in the way our model suggests they might.

What about bilocation? Say we were to split the end of the bar magnet into two separate, smaller branches. Even though the divided bars would now each have half the strength, each would still emit the exact identical electromagnetic pattern as the original whole. Now let's touch the cardboard with our divided magnet so that each branch contacts at a different location. Just as in a real magnet, splitting it in two does not alter the characteristic pattern of its electromagnetic field. The two branches are like identical twins, each emitting the very same pattern, or in this case, the same supergeometry. The filings now rally around the separated patterns and form the exact same physical object in both locations at the same point in time as in a paranormal bilocation. [Figure 3.3, next page]

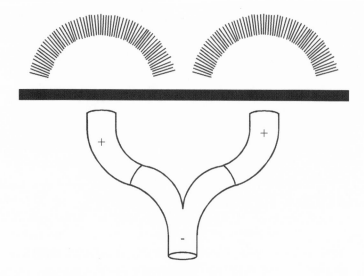

Figure 3.3 — A Model of Bilocation. The same supergeometric pattern presented at different locations causes the object to appear in two places at the same moment in time.

Let's look at how our iron filings model might be used to illustrate the translocational phenomenon of levitation. When the magnet is right up against the cardboard where its influence is strongest, the filings are firmly held in place so that our imaginary object is fully materialized. But when the magnet is pulled away, the filings collapse and the object fully dematerializes. We can think about these two different states in terms of physical *presence*—when fully materialized, the object has its greatest physical presence within dimensional space, but when fully dematerialized has no presence at all.

During this process, we can see there are intermediate stages of *partial* presence as the object transitions from being fully materialized to complete dissolution. Were we to slowly draw the magnet away from the cardboard, the field that holds the filings in place would gradually diminish. The structure in the iron filings would not collapse immediately because they are still under the retreating magnet's influence for a time, even though they are no longer held in place with the same rigidity as when the magnet was touching the cardboard. Eventually, a point will be reached where the magnet still holds the filings in their original shape, but its influence is so weak that even the gentlest of breeze could easily sweep them off the cardboard. The object would still be fully recognizable in its original shape, but its presence in dimensional space would be greatly reduced.

Such a reduction in physical presence would have some interesting effects. For one, we'd expect that the influence of normal physical law over the object would also diminish as its presence recedes. Since gravity is one of these laws, the object gradually loses weight (this might explain the weight loss of participants documented in Carl Jung's experiments following manifestations of psychic phenomena). Eventually, the object could become so light that it may begin to float or levitate. As its presence recedes almost to the point of dematerialization, the object would even become somewhat transparent, and could likely drift right through other, more solid objects like a wall. Picture a translucent object floating around a room in apparent defiance of gravity, and then passing through a closed door. Sounds an awful lot like an apparition, doesn't it?

I must re-emphasize that our three-dimensional model of the iron filings and magnet cannot truly serve as a precise representation of extra-dimensional mechanics. Like Einstein's impossible "thought experiments" where trains fly at the speed of light, its purpose is not to exactly replicate reality, but to help guide the mind to envision these concepts in a way that can be digested and understood with our dimensional reasoning.

4. There exists a non-physical pattern or matrix on a grand scale. Seemingly unrelated physical things and/or events are in fact related though their alignment and resonance with this non-physical matrix. The existence of this matrix can be recognized by the occurrence of meaningful coincidences. We've discussed at length the idea that all physical objects have their corresponding supergeometric patterns. Yet synchronicity implies that there are supergeometric patterns on a grand scale that encompass and influence the patterns of the lesser objects contained within them. These grand patterns help determine not only the structure and behavior of individual physical objects, but also the ways in which they interact. In the case of the parallels between Lincoln and Kennedy, the greater supergeometry of the Lincoln assassination containing all the lesser people, places, and actions somehow returned a century later to re-impose itself on the fabric of space-time like some sort of superphysical cosmic echo, causing events to once again closely conform to its fateful patterns.

For any location in space-time (such as our planet Earth), there exists a grand supergeometry containing a myriad of smaller, interrelated supergeometries, each one bearing some portion of the greater image. Many philosophers and even some progressively minded scientists have long maintained that all things and events are somehow interconnected. The concept of grand supergeometry provides a model for the actual structure and nature of this interconnectedness.

Ultimately, the grandest of all supergeometric patterns is that of the universe itself, a colossal organism in which all its constituents are distinct, yet all dance in harmony to the same universal cosmic melody.

CONCLUSION

Quite a lot has been accomplished in this chapter. We've identified non-local causality as the universal, scientific description for what defines a paranormal event, established a new classification system having numerous advantages over traditional methods, derived four paraphysical principles from this new system that cover all aspects of the supernatural, and presented a model of paranormal mechanics that illustrates in a reasonable way the processes responsible for such events while being consistent with real-world paranormal observations.

Earlier, I mentioned hauntings because of the many different classes of events that occur simultaneously. That all these various happenings appear together is strong evidence that the underlying mechanics for each are very similar. It's far less likely that levitations, disembodied sounds, apparitions and the rest are each caused by a fundamentally different process. Our model of supergeometry provides such a single, uniform system that can give rise to all these diverse phenomena.

Because of the imperfections in this model (i.e., depicting a superdimensional process with a dimensional representation), certain aspects of it can be misleading if taken too literally. For example, the model suggests there is a hard, distinct separation between the realms of the physical and superphysical. Although such a distinction exists, it is very subtle—perhaps more like the distinction between different layers of density in the atmosphere. One might also mistakenly conclude from this model that the superphysical is an independent realm that supernaturally manipulates our physical environment from a distance like a cosmic puppet on a string so that any sense of physical cause-and-effect or even free will is an illusion. This is not the case. The superphysical and physical would have to be two levels of the exact same reality that are intrinsically connected to each other. The transition from superphysical to physical would then be continuous, the latter gradually and perpetually unfolding from the former.

Say you were to pick up a cup from a table. The thought in your mind, the movements of your arm, as well as the cup itself, are all present and active in the superphysical at the same moment, even though we may not be consciously aware of it. Your superphysical brain is moving your superphysical arm at the same instant your physical brain is moving your physical arm. These are two different levels of the same, continuous whole. This is hard to envision because of our typically linear thinking. But if it were easy to see, we would have cracked this mystery a long time ago.

Furthermore, the progression of things from superphysical to physical appears to be persistent and unvarying. This process is a very stable part of the continuous mechanical workings of the universe. To break this connection or to reverse its effect might be like trying to walk against the current of a mighty, raging river. But paranormal events indicate that given the right conditions, these natural processes can indeed be altered or interrupted. Perhaps it is like the occasional genetic malfunction that produces birth defects. Certain environmental factors increase the frequency and severity of genetic defects, just like a certain few locations might be very haunted because of the unusual conditions there, while elsewhere dwells in peaceful neutrality. What's most tantalizing about this is that the occurrence of such natural "accidents" implies that the same effect might be reproduced *intentionally* by artificial means (we will explore this fantastic notion in a later chapter).

The scientific method has a fixed procedure to formulate a theory. First, questions are asked about the nature of a given body of data. Next, hypotheses are formulated in an attempt to answer those questions in a consistent and uniform way. When a single hypothetical model seems to answer all the questions posed to it while remaining consistent with itself (i.e., without having to make exceptions to its rules), then the hypothesis is elevated to a theory. This chapter has endeavored to do just that. The concepts presented here and the mechanical models derived from them provide the foundation of a bona fide superphysical theory that describes the processes behind all paranormal phenomena using a single set of principles.

The skeletal framework for a fascinating TOE is now in place—let's see if we can add some flesh to its bones.

4

Science and the Paranormal

Consummating Unlikely Bedfellows:
The First Step Toward Unification

*I believe that if we are to make any
real progress in psychic investigation,
we must do it with scientific apparatus
and in a scientific manner.*
                                    —Thomas Edison

Paranormal phenomena challenge the very foundation of
the conventional worldview. Clairvoyance, ghosts, teleports,
and their freaky associates are unwelcome guests amid those
who champion the dull but steady predictability of the corpore-
al. Although scientific peer pressure begrudgingly tolerates a
certain amount of scholarly speculation, it is still somewhat
heretical for a member of the scientific community to embrace
the paranormal with too much enthusiasm. Yet the evidence for
the paranormal is there, and the day is soon coming when
science will be forced to reckon with it.

In the last chapter, we forged a superphysical theory of
reality that suggests how paranormal events take place. This
theoretical model of supergeometry is very compelling because
of the consistent, logical and simple way in which it illustrates

the mechanism behind supernatural phenomena. But however fascinating or provocative, it's of little value if we can't find evidence for it in objective reality.

Tons of books have been written on the subject of science and the paranormal. Many cite scientific studies validating its existence—the sheer number of books presenting evidence for transmentation alone can provide many months of reading. I, on the other hand, have but a single chapter to devote. So rather than traveling the same outworn road of trying to prove that the paranormal is scientific, I'm going to take the opposite and perhaps the more sound approach of demonstrating that science itself is paranormal! Remember, the definition of what is paranormal is that which operates by non-local causality, or what Einstein called "spooky action at a distance." According to this definition, certain aspects of science are very paranormal indeed. Cutting edge scientific thought along with scientifically established examples of non-local causality are in my opinion the strongest validation for the paranormal.

Science has historically rejected the paranormal as fantasy because no local materialistic cause can be found for such events. This archaic position is gradually eroding in the face of increasing instances of non-local causality being discovered in the field of particle physics. The paranormal nature of subatomic behavior has encouraged some modern scientific minds to be more open to the investigation of the supernatural.

A number of scientists have formulated their own novel theories of reality based on the study of non-local anomalies. Several bear such a striking resemblance to our own super-geometric model that they are worth examining because they show that scientific authorities can sometimes arrive at the very same kinds of ideas when attempting to explain these anomalies. Their theories add to our own voice in suggesting there is more in common between the worlds of the photon and the poltergeist than was formally believed.

The Two-Slit Experiments

One of the earliest examples of non-local causality was displayed in Young's two-slit experiment described in Chapter Two where a beam of light projected through two separated slits produced a wave-interference pattern. Remember that at the time of this experiment, the physical laws established by Isaac Newton governed the way scientists perceived the world. The idea of energy wave fields was not understood. Particles were not supposed to act as waves because they were thought to be infinitesimal spheres of hard matter. Because of this, early researchers assumed that the photon particles flowing in steams through the two slits were interfering with one another like two rivers of tiny spheres converging, and so it was this mutual interference that produced an effect resembling a wave pattern.

To test this hypothesis, a variation of the original experiment was tried. Rather than projecting a full beam of photons at the slits, they fired single photons in succession and then recorded each impact. A single photon having no others to interfere with should travel straight through one of the slits and onto the screen beyond without deviating. Random chance would dictate a 50/50 probability that a photon might pass through one slit or the other. The accumulation of all these individual random impacts on the screen should then result in a homogenous field of light as dictated by Newtonian physics.

The new results were even more mystifying than before. Instead of the anticipated random homogeny, the individually fired particles collectively traced the very same interference pattern as did the full beams of light! To understand how strange this must have seemed, imagine pouring out sand from a bucket at chest height and having it trace an image of the Eiffel Tower as it hit the ground. There was absolutely nothing in local contact with the experiment that could force individually fired photons to collectively bend into any kind of wave pattern, let alone one that was identical to that caused by the full beams. No matter how the experiment was re-configured, it always generated these same peculiar results.

Physicists struggling to place this highly paranormal (yes, *paranormal*) anomaly within the framework of known physical law were faced with two weird possibilities. The first was that each photon somehow split itself into two before entering the slits, after which the two halves interfered with one another to produce the wave pattern. But the force needed to split a photon was simply not present in the experiment. Because only one hit was recorded for each photon fired, the severed particle would have also somehow fused itself back together before making contact with the detector. Even if this were somehow possible, it still wouldn't explain why the resulting cumulative pattern of many thousands of hits was identical to that produced by the full beams. The second possibility was even more bizarre in that each photon must somehow "know" in advance its exact position within the final pattern so it could arrive at its proper place on the screen. This would also require the individual photon to know in advance the exact paths of *all* the other photons released both before *and* after it so that it could take its proper place in the cumulative pattern.

Both possibilities were ultimately rejected as too fantastic to be true. Only a single, incredible possibility remained—whatever caused the photons to form these wave patterns was not in local physical contact with any part of the experiment.

Even today, with our advanced physical theories of relativity and quantum mechanics, we do not have a viable solution for the non-local causality demonstrated in the two-slit experiment. Physicist Dr. Richard P. Feynman, Nobel Prize winner and one of the developers of the atomic bomb, stated that no physicist yet understands this experiment. In his opinion, it represents the only mystery—as well as the *entire* mystery—of quantum mechanics. For now, scientists simply accept this behavior as a fundamental property of elementary particles without being able to adequately explain it.

It may seem surprising that the discipline of science can actually accept experimental results like this as truth without being able to provide an explanation. But scientists need not be omniscient to ply their trade. All that is required for a finding to be embraced as a scientific fact is for it to be predictable and repeatable, so that each experiment or measurement conducted under similar circumstances yield similar results. Science needs only to know *how* the universe works, not necessarily *why*. This not only illustrates science's greatest strength, but also defines its limitations. There are numerous facts that are accepted as scientific truth without the knowledge as to exactly why it is so.

"Psychic" Photons

Another amazing anomaly of non-local causality can be observed in the odd behavior of correlated or entangled photons. A single photon can be divided into what is called an *entangled* pair. Each of the halves function like a complete photon but at a lower energy level. One of the effects of splitting a photon is that each of the resulting lesser photons will become oppositely polarized. This polarity is not like a magnet or battery, but is defined by the way in which a particle spins. Physicists identify the various polarized spins with labels like up, down, left or right. In the case of split photon pairs, each partner spins in opposite direction, counterbalancing one another to maintain an inner harmony within the pair.

The bond between entangled photons is so strong that a change in the polarity of one will immediately produce an equal and opposite effect in the other. Say we have an entangled pair of photons with photon *A* having an up spin and photon *B* a down spin. If we force photon A to change its spin, photon *B* is so tightly bound to its partner that it will instantly respond by reversing its own, thereby restoring the balance within the pair.

What if we were to sever this bond by smashing the pair apart and sending each of them hurdling away from the other in opposite directions? Because they are photons, they will travel away from each other at the speed of light, each still with its original direction of spin. Unless something interferes with them, they will continue to spin this way no matter how far apart they journey, whether inches, miles, or light years.

Here's where it gets strange. What if we were to change the spin of one of the separated photons in mid-flight—particle *A* for example—from an up spin to a down spin by having it pass through a polarizing filter? According to the standard model of the universe, this action will have no effect on particle *B*. Were you to drive a golf ball down range, for example, a second ball still in your golf bag isn't going to suddenly leap into the air just because both were previously stored together in the same bag. Yet this is exactly what entangled photons do. In experiment after experiment, a change in the spin of particle *A* instantly produces an equal and opposite change in the spin of particle *B*. In defiance of known laws, these behave as if they were still tightly paired together even though there is no longer any physical connection between the two. No matter how much distance separates the particles, they continue to react to one another, displaying Einstein's spooky action at a distance.

There's absolutely no doubt that *A* somehow transmits the information about its changed state to *B*, otherwise *B* could not possibly react as if they were still connected. But how can this happen when a local physical connection no longer exists between the two? What's even weirder is that because these photons are traveling apart at the speed of light, any signal passing between the two would have to be going twice that fast. It's like two cars moving apart in opposite directions at 50 mph each (don't worry, this isn't one of those tricky word problems). A message sent from one car would need to be moving at least twice that, or 100 mph, for it to ever reach the other. The problem here is that nothing in the physical universe travels faster than light—Einstein issued this dictum many decades ago and it's been upheld since. It's not possible to have a faster-than-light signal between the two photons—two times lightspeed just isn't on the cosmic speedometer. So, how does the information from one photon ever reach the other?

That the reaction of *B* to *A* is virtually instantaneous is another clue that something paranormal is taking place. Even if it were possible for them to be connected by a twice-as-fast-as-light signal, there would still be a measurable delay, especially if separated by vast distance. For both cause and effect to happen simultaneously over light years of space would require a signal to travel at *infinite* velocity. Simply put, something traveling at infinite velocity is so fast that it would be in every possible location in the universe at the exact same instant. At the precise moment *A* changes, that information would spontaneously be everywhere throughout the entire cosmos. The implications of this are almost mystical, belonging more to the realm of the spiritual than the physical. It's as if the information about our photon ascends immediately to a grand cosmic consciousness that permeates and encompasses every corner of creation. Could it be, in observing this phenomenon, that we catch a tiny glimpse into the Mind of God?

Physicists have been working on ways to use this feature of photon entanglement as a means to transmit data across vast distances of space instantaneously, say between earth and an interstellar spacecraft. Some of them have taken up the habit of calling this a "photon teleport." As mentioned before, this is an unfortunate choice of words in light of our culture's vernacular, which is based on how teleportation is depicted in *Star Trek*. I have seen comments written by obviously educated people who have been fooled by this phrase into believing that science has actually succeeded in physically transporting a photon from one location to another. I believe this misleading and intellectually dishonest term was coined to be intentionally sensational by researchers trying to glorify themselves before a dazzled public eye. In truth, no one has ever teleported a physical particle in the *Star Trek* sense, or has even the first clue about how to do it. The only thing being instantly "transported" between these separated photons is information about a particle's state, not anything physical. And, according to our vernacular, that isn't teleporting. So, if you ever happen upon this term, you'll now know the real story.

In view of all this, we can only conclude that whatever connects entangled photons dwells outside the physical universe of matter and energy. It must therefore be recognized as a genuine example of non-local causality. And so by definition it must also be classified along with the two-slit experiment as a genuine example of paranormal phenomena.

OTHER EVENTS OUTSIDE SPACE-TIME

Entangled photons and the two-slit experiment are not the only indicators of a world above space-time. Although some physicists believe these two are already sufficient hard evidence for such a superlight realm, numerous other scientific data and hypotheses also give support to the existence of this superphysical, non-local domain.

Theodore Kalusa and His "Five-Fold" Unification

Einstein theorized that at the instant of the Big Bang, all elemental forces were joined together into a single, unified field of primordial energy. As the cloud of particles and energy of the newly created universe expanded and cooled, this field separated into the four elemental forces of electromagnetism, gravity, and the strong and weak nuclear forces.

Without the technology to demonstrate that all these forces were once unified, Einstein attempted a mathematical proof. Although his efforts met with some success, he was never able to produce an equation that unified gravity with electromagnetism. Theodore Kalusa, a German physicist, was also working at the time toward perfecting Einstein's equations. One day in 1919, while mulling over the problem, he came upon a novel solution. Einstein's calculations relied upon establishing a numerical expression of gravity in four dimensions (three spatial and one temporal). Kalusa added a fifth co-ordinate—a fifth dimension, if you will—to the equations. Suddenly, all the formulas balanced! After working out all the calculations, then removing the fifth co-ordinate, Kalusa was left with an equation demonstrating the unification of electromagnetism and gravity.

Since space-time is limited to only four dimensions (which were already fully represented in Einstein's original equations), Kalusa's new fifth co-ordinate had to be located someplace outside space and time. In later years, when Kalusa further developed and refined his theories, he came to the conclusion that the cause of gravity itself was non-local and originated from outside space-time. Again, this very paranormal conclusion fits well with our own supergeometric model, which also proposes the virtually identical concept.

It's important to note that Theodore Kalusa's ideas still garner much respect and serious consideration in the scientific community.

Matter and Energy Across the Space-Time Barrier

According to classical physics, matter and energy cannot simply pop in and out of space-time. But once again the weird world of subatomic particles indicates they might. Take for example the strange ability of electrons to emit and absorb photons. These photons spontaneously materialize from within the electron itself. Imagine a single electron. Suddenly a photon emerges from the electron and appears beside it. The electron's mass and charge does not diminish in the process, nor does it draw energy from an outside source to generate the new particle. It simply produces the photon out of literally nothing.

The materialization of this photon is in direct violation of

149

the conservation laws of thermodynamics, which state that the total amount of mass and energy in the universe always remains constant. The offending photon seems to "know" this, and as if embarrassed by being caught in its law-breaking act, immediately jumps back into the electron. The photon hangs around for only one thousand trillionth (10^{-15}) of a second before vanishing. Physicists have labeled these *virtual* photons since they are not sustained as independent particles beyond this extremely brief moment. These particles only come close to being real, appearing and vanishing within a mysterious level of reality that is not quite fully physical.

Because virtual photons stop short of being fully realized particles, physicists have declared that their brief forays in and out of quasi-reality do not disturb the laws of mass-energy conservation. This however is essentially a whitewash to defend the faith of classical physics, since it fails to answer the most important question—how can an electron give birth to a photon (a distinctly different particle with its own unique qualities) while not being itself altered in any way?

If science can accept the notion of "unreal" particles that mystically appear and disappear without explanation, then it cannot reject paranormal events like transmigrational phenomena simply because it is "unscientific" to believe that things can of themselves paranormally slip in and out of our physical reality.

The Supergeometric Universe of Carl Jung

The notion of a superphysical supergeometry outside space-time is by no means new to scientific thought. Psychologist Carl Jung proposed this very same idea early in the 20th century. His many years of research into parapsychology convinced him there was a part of reality beyond the classical cause-and-effect world of matter and energy. He believed this outer domain was occupied by ethereal structures that were precursors to the physical world. These precursive structures, which he called *archetypes*, were a kind of primordial cosmic language that consisted of images and symbols the human psyche could discern at a subconscious level. He offered these non-physical archetypes as the reason why many of humanity's traditional legends, symbols, morals, and fantasies are remarkably similar between individuals and even entire cultures widely separated by time and geographic location.

Admittedly, Jung imagined these archetypes as being purely psychological in form, like thought images embedded in some deep cosmic consciousness. However, he further theorized that beneath these archetypes dwelt an even deeper elemental layer of structures he called *psychoid entities*. Unlike archetypes, psychoid entities had a tangible equivalent in every physical structure of the universe from electrons to galaxies, each which was configured according to the pattern of its respective entity. They served the identical function as supergeometry by providing a sort of scaffolding around which the material components of our physical world are shaped.

Quantum Topology

When physicists peer into the micro-universe of elementary particles, they witness events that defy all known laws governing the macro-universe. Their efforts at explaining these weird phenomena have given rise to a number of theories uncannily similar to the supergeometric model. One such theory proposed by physicist David Finkelstein is called *quantum topology*. It is based on the idea that the primary building block of the universe is not an actual physical particle like a quark, but an elementary process or event. A group of these events combine to form a simple pattern or web. The simple webs then interact to form larger, more complex webs. Eventually, areas of distinct organization begin to materialize within this growing prephysical matrix. These areas, or *coherent superpositions*, possess

151

their own distinct patterns that distinguish them from the surrounding random-like background of web strands. A photon, for example, is a coherent superposition possessing a specific recognizable pattern that is both highly organized and distinct from all others.

Finkelstein believes his theory of coherent superposition offers a satisfactory explanation for many of the strange events observed in particle physics. Take for example our entangled photons. According to Finkelstein's theory, the physical separation of particles *A* and *B* is only an illusion resulting from the limitations of our measuring instruments. The photons are in fact still interconnected through the underlying substrate of superimposed webs. It is this interwoven connection that allows the two particles to "communicate" with each other beneath the physical plane in apparent violation of classical laws.

Most interesting is Finkelstein's view that the fundamental events giving rise to these coherent superpositional patterns occur *outside* space-time. They are *prior* to space-time and as such are not part of our observable physical reality. According to the theory, the universe of matter and energy, space and time is not primary reality but only *secondary* reality. Physical reality is the result or after-effect of a greater fundamental reality of pre-physical processes and mechanisms. Except for terminology and depth of mechanical descriptions, Finkelstein's paranormal vision of reality is virtually identical to supergeometry.

The Pre-Geometry of John Wheeler

In order to explain the results of certain experiments like those involving quantum entangled particles, physicist John Wheeler has served up his own vision of reality outside of space-time. Wheeler believes that below the atomic level, the geometry of space-time disintegrates. There exists instead a subliminal realm with a bubbling, foamy structure. Patterns begin to emerge from this chaotic frothing that eventually give rise to the fabric of space-time. The patterns in this foam are expressions of an even deeper underlying pre-physical structure or order acting as a cosmic blueprint for the universe that directs and shapes this foam into recognizable structures.

Wheeler was the first to devise the term *pre-geometry* to describe such pre-physical (or in his case, sub-physical) structures. His hypothesis states that all events in the physical universe are a reflection of the primary reality of pre-geometry. In a universal picture echoing Finkelstein's quantum topology and our own supergeometry, Wheeler's theory contends that the structure and behavior of all elementary particles, as well as the fabric of space-time itself, is determined by these pre-physical, pre-geometric patterns.

Morphogenesis

Biologist Dr. Rupert Sheldrake asserts that traditional biology and genetics, while providing valuable insights into many natural processes, cannot fully explain the method by which an assemblage of non-specific cells we call an embryo forms into complete differentiated individuals like ducks, daffodils, daisies and dogs through cell multiplication alone.

To demonstrate his point, Sheldrake posed six basic questions to which genetics alone could not provide definitive and verifiable answers:

1. *How does an acorn grow into a giant oak tree?* An acorn is a type of embryonic structure. It doesn't just get bigger as it grows, but sprouts into a myriad of other structures such as roots, limbs, leaves, veins, bark, flowers, and seeds. All the cells in these various structures carry a slightly different genetic code that tells one cell to form part of a leaf, another to form part of a flower, and so on. But in its earliest stage of development, the embryo is just a bundle of identical non-differentiated cells, *all containing the exact same genetic code.* Suddenly, certain cells

153

in the embryo mutate into specialized cells, each bearing a slightly different genetic code than their nonspecific cellular "parent," which then migrate to specific areas. Biologists believe that the instructions for this cellular activity are encoded in the original genome, but have yet to demonstrate a definitive linear path between each segment of the original non-specialized genes, nor from the minor variations that occur in the initial stages of differentiation within the embryo.

2. *How does an embryo regulate its development?* An embryo begins as a single fertilized egg cell. Its first division results in a two-cell embryo. If one of these two cells is destroyed, the remaining cell does not grow into half an organism but goes on to form a whole creature. If two fertilized egg cells are placed together, they do not grow into twins but combine to again form a single complete organism. How do these cells regulate themselves so that a complete creature develops in spite of these exceptional circumstances?

3. *How do certain organisms regenerate?* Many lizards and amphibians have the ability to regenerate a tail lost to a predator grabbing hold of it. Biologists propose that this ability evolved as a defensive mechanism. In an experiment to test whether this regenerative ability is truly the result of evolution, the lens from a newt's eye was removed surgically in such a way so that it would be virtually impossible to occur in nature, thereby precluding genetic conditioning. In spite of this, the newt regenerated a perfect new lens. What makes this even more remarkable is the startling contrast between the way in which the lens forms in normal embryonic development and the method of regeneration in the experiment. In the embryonic stage, the lens develops from a fold in the skin, then detaches and migrates away so that lens and skin are no longer in contact. But in the experiment, the lens regenerated *from the edge of the iris*, a structure having nothing to do with the skin from which the lens originated. How can a body part regenerate out of tissues totally different than those from which it originally formed? And from where does the blueprint for the new lens come?

4. How do sperm and egg combine to form a whole that is completely different from its parts? Sperm and egg both have their own genetic blueprints that dictate their shape. How these two can combine to form a shape different than their cellular parents is not yet fully explained (I believe this mystery is likely related to the question of how life began on earth).

5. What causes living things to behave as they do? Although genes play a major role in passing on the physical character-istics of an organism, their possible role in the inheritance of behavior is uncertain. For example, biologists generally agree that an individual bee has no concept of how its own duties and actions contribute to the greater scheme of the hive. Collective-ly they behave more as a single large organism than a group of individuals. The same peculiar trait can be observed in weaver ants during nest building, where some individuals act as living clamps to hold the edges of leaves together while other, gen-etically identical workers pick up larvae in their jaws and glue the edges of the leaves together with a sticky substance secreted by them. Although genes may account for the larvae's secret-ions, can they also be responsible for the workers' habit of using the larvae as living glue guns? Such highly specialized and intertwined social behavior is difficult to attribute to genetic inheritance alone. If it is true that each of these individuals do not themselves possess the master blueprint for their collective duties, who or what does?

6. Why doesn't evolution explain all inherited physical characteristics of living things? There are many physical traits found in living things that cannot be fully accounted for by the gradual random changes proposed by evolution. Evolutionary "leaps" appear to take place between one living form and the next. Sometimes an entirely new system of interdependent structures appears simultaneously within a single life form. What causes these radical evolutionary leaps? How can multiple organs like heart, lung or brain suddenly transmute together in an interrelated and synchronized way within a single organism?

Sheldrake is not alone in posing such questions about the nature of life. Speaking on similar mysteries involving humanity, Geneticist Francis S. Collins, who at the time of this writing heads the famous Human Genome Project, recently stated that "DNA sequence alone, even if accompanied by a vast trove of data on biological function, will never explain certain special human attributes, such as the knowledge of Moral Law and the universal search for God."

To explain these anomalies, Sheldrake proposes a system he calls *morphogenesis* in which he contends that there must be pre-physical blueprints or *life fields* from which life forms are derived. These life fields possess distinct patterns that determine the physical structure and characteristic behavior of each organism. Additionally, each species has its own larger life field called a *species field* that establishes it as a separate life form distinct from all others.

The way in which individual life fields relate to their greater species field can be compared to a holographic image. Unlike a regular flat photographic plate that records only a single image of reflected light from a subject, a holographic plate is engraved with thousands of concentric rings, each of which records a slightly different angle of interference pattern reflecting off the subject. A laser beam projected into the developed holographic plate splits and bends along the different rings, collectively reproducing the identical pattern of light reflected from the original subject. The result is a three-dimensional image of the subject projected into space.

Since each ring records a complete image of the subject, and since these rings overlap across the entire surface of the holographic plate, any portion of the plate will produce a complete image. If you cut the plate into one hundred pieces, you'll have one hundred complete holographic images of the subject. In a similar way, a species field can consist of millions of individual life fields, each containing within it a complete image of the original species field pattern.

Life fields supply the pattern along which the multiplying cells of an embryo align themselves as they grow. A single cell of a two-cell embryo can develop into a complete organism because the blueprint of its life field remains unaffected and undivided. The newt can regenerate its missing lens in defiance of conventional genetics because the newly reproducing cells conform to the original pattern or blueprint of the lens still contained in its life field.

Morphogenesis offers solutions to a number of evolutionary anomalies. Traditional evolution asserts that organisms undergo change through random mutations or drifts in their genetic code, but does not offer a convincing explanation as to how or why these changes take place. Random mutations we observe today in living creatures virtually all result in an inferior creature with physiological deformities and abnormalities, which hardly represents an improved adaptation. Nor is it true that a minor variation would accrue such a significant advantage for the modified organism that it would begin to supplant its perfectly functioning predecessor. Morphogenesis suggests instead that subtle changes in the genetic DNA may occur in response to a change in an organism's life field. Assuming that these life fields tend to have symmetrical patterns like other types of fields, minor changes or fluctuations would be propagated throughout the field's entire matrix in a harmonious way. Corresponding changes in the organism will then be reflected throughout the entire creature in an equally harmonious way. This would explain how different subsystems like a giraffe's longer neck and the circulatory system needed to support it could co-evolve in a balanced way. Such synchronous system-wide changes are typical of what we find in the fossil record rather than the crippling abnormalities normally resulting from random individual changes.

According to Sheldrake, morphogenesis also plays a role in the emergence of new species. He proposes there are instances when two life fields from different species somehow become superimposed over one another like a double exposure on a photographic negative. In a manner similar to Finkelstein's coherent superpositions, these combined life fields form an entirely new pattern separate and distinct from its "parents." When such a *morphic resonance* produces a pattern that is both coherent and stable, a new species is born. Instead of a series of incremental changes, the newly morphed life field produces multiple changes at once throughout the strands of DNA. If the pattern of the new life field is stable, the various changes within the physical creature will function together in harmony, and the newly evolved organism will become a viable species. This explains how several interdependent changes can occur simul-taneously in an evolving life form. Both fins and blowhole can appear concurrently in an evolving whale, while a longer neck and a specialized vascular system can both develop together in an evolving giraffe. In this manner morphic resonance provides a reasonable answer for the sudden leaps of evolution so often found in the fossil record.

Sheldrake's species fields also offer insights into the be-havior of certain social organisms. Schools of fish and flocks of birds often behave as a single creature, collectively changing speed and direction in a synchronized flowing motion that is a thing of wonder and beauty. A nest of weaver ants also seem to work together as if they were a collection of specialized cells within a single organism. The species fields of these groups provide a common set of instructions to all members, thereby enabling them to coordinate their behavior like parts a single, larger entity. According to this model, there is no need for each individual to be consciously aware of the master plan.

Like many theoretical abstractions, there is no practical way to prove the soundness of Sheldrake's theory of morphogenesis. We currently have no devices capable of detecting elements residing beyond space-time. Nevertheless, his superphysical life fields provide valuable insights into a number of biological and evolutionary anomalies that continue to escape conventional explanation.

Kirlian Photography

Some researchers might argue that the empirical evidence for the morphogenesis theory already exists. A photographic technique known as *Kirlian photography* produces images that appear very much like "snapshots" of Sheldrake's life fields.

The technique bears the names of the Russian couple responsible for its development as a practical research tool. While monitoring a high-frequency electrotherapy device during use, Semyon Davidovich Kirlian noticed strange flashes emanating from the space between the patient's skin and one of the electrodes, and wondered if he could capture these on film. He and his wife Valentina constructed a device that projected an electrical field across a glass plate so that a subject placed on the glass was in direct contact with the field. The tiny flashes produced by the interplay between subject and electrical field were then recorded through the glass plate onto an exposed photographic film. Since this technique produced only still images, an improved method was later developed that allowed researchers to observe the phenomenon in motion. [see images, next two pages]

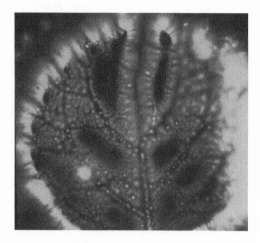

Figure 4.1 — Kirlian Photograph of a Living Coleus Leaf. Science is still in the midst of a debate as to what forces or energies are actually being captured in these strange and wonderful images. [Photograph courtesy of Dr. Thelma Moss]

The remarkable images recorded by the Kirlian technique are truly a thing of beauty and wonder. Inanimate objects like a coin or a stone display a surrounding luminescent halo that is even and unchanging. But living things like a leaf or a hand are immersed in a complex dazzling exhibition of flashing lights, glowing clouds and multi-colored flares. [Figure 4.1]

Some startling facts have been discovered about the flashes seen emanating from living tissues. Locations on the human body that consistently emit prominent flares correspond exactly to the 741 acupuncture points described by ancient Chinese medicine. Various emotional states are also evidenced in these images. A calm peaceful state is characterized by a warm, even glow, while an angry state produces wildly fluctuating flares accompanied by reddish "auras" of energy. Intoxication by drugs or alcohol is similarly marked by a corresponding change in the energy field. [Figures 4.2 and 4.3, next page]

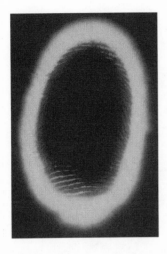 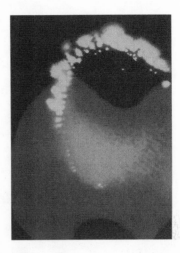

Figures 4.2 and 4.3 — Kirlian Photographs Displaying Different Emotional States. Figure 4.2 shows the fingertip of a person who is calm and peaceful. Figure 4.3 is of the same person in an angry state. The even glow shown in the "calm" photo has changed to fluctuating bursts and stabbing flares in the "angry" photo (the irregularly-shaped cloud at the lower center of 4.3 is a reddish-orange color). [Photographs courtesy of Dr. Thelma Moss]

The strangest of these Kirlian phenomena—and therefore the one of greatest interest to us—is called the "phantom leaf" effect. Researchers wondering how damaged living tissue might appear in a Kirlian image removed a portion of a leaf before photographing it. To their astonishment, several photographs continued to show the entire image of the original leaf intact! Although this "ghost" is typically darker than the rest of the image, the outline of the missing section is distinct and unmistakable. [Figure 4.4, next page]

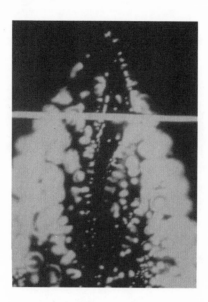

Figure 4.4 — The Phantom Leaf Effect. This Kirlian photograph of a tomato plant leaf shows the "phantom leaf" effect. The tip of the leaf above the white horizontal line was removed before this photo was taken. Are we looking at an actual photograph of Rupert Sheldrake's life fields? [Photograph courtesy of Dr. Thelma Moss]

Much more than a mere curiosity, the phantom leaf effect has far-reaching implications. The very presence of these phantoms demonstrates the existence of a mirror image or blueprint that is not only identical to the physical subject, but exists *independently* of it. The image of the missing portion remains intact in spite of the destruction of its physical counterpart. This evidence (when coupled with the fact that changes are observed in Kirlian patterns *before* they can be detected in their physical counterparts) is a strong indication that these Kirlian patterns are a reflection of *primary* reality. In other words, the structure of physical matter is determined by whatever produces the Kirlian image, rather than the image being produced by the physical matter. To put it another way, it is the physical subject that actually emanates from the Kirlian pattern rather than the pattern emanating from the physical subject.

The phantom leaf effect also sheds new light on a phenomenon reported by amputees who frequently complain they can still feel the presence of the removed limb. They often report sensations of being able to move the missing limb as if it were still there. They continue to have feelings of warmth, cold, pain, and occasionally even touch. The medical profession calls this a *phantom limb*, and has always considered the sensation to be purely psychological. But the phantom leaf effect implies that there's more to the phantom limbs of amputees than just imagination.

There is yet another fascinating aspect to the phantom leaf effect. Not only does the main section of leaf continue to show the pattern of the removed section, but the severed piece also displays the same pattern as well. This means that severing the leaf produces two identical patterns in two different places for the same portion of leaf. The study of this curiosity may lead to a deeper understanding of the workings behind phenomena such as bilocation and teleportation.

No one knows for certain exactly what is being depicted in Kirlian photographs. Those inclined to spiritualism see Kirlian images as evidence for the existence of spiritual auras. Others feel that this *bioplasma* as its called represents a second spiritual body that co-exists alongside the physical one. The Kirlian effect has been likened to the stylized halos depicted around the heads of religious figures, complete with the twinkling stars and projections of energy rays.

Mainstream science attempts to understand these strange images in terms of traditional physics. One belief is that the emanation is a "corona discharge" produced by the ionization of air molecules being excited from the interaction between the charged plate and electrons emitted by the subject. Others believe that moisture from the surface of the subject becomes charged by the plate and then transferred to the emulsion on the film. But none of these conventional views are satisfactory because they fail to explain certain paranormal characteristics displayed in these Kirlian images. The phantom leaf effect is a particularly prickly puzzle for conventional explanation. The removed material leaves behind no physical matter to emit the particles or moisture necessary for their theories. No physical source has yet been found to explain the appearance of these mysterious phantoms.

Because of the seemingly supernatural quality to certain aspects of this phenomenon, the images recorded by Kirlian photography may provide the best physical evidence to date for Jung's psychoid entities, Finkelstein's coherent superpositions, Sheldrake's life fields, and Wheeler's pre-geometry.

Synchronicity and de Broglie Guide Waves

It seems unlikely to find a bedfellow amid the prudish ranks of establishment science for a symptom as outrageous as synchronicity. The notion that seemingly random events carry with them some unseen pattern having the power to impose itself onto other segments of reality across both space and time is a pill even the most open-minded of pragmatists might have trouble swallowing.

Nevertheless, such a parallel to synchronicity can be found in a theory originally proposed by physicist Louis de Broglie in 1927, and later published jointly with noted physicist David Bohm. The theory seeks to reconcile the differences between the predictability of relativity and the uncertainty of quantum mechanics, and in doing so also lends support to the idea that synchronicity is a real effect.

Recall that the difficulties encountered while trying to determine both the momentum and location of a given electron led physicists to formulate the uncertainty principle of quantum mechanics, which states that it is impossible to ascertain both the momentum and location of a particle at the same time. All that can be determined is the probability of a particle to be at a given location or to have a certain momentum, but not both at once, and not with absolute certainty. The uncertainty principle further states that the observer (i.e., physicists and their measuring equipment) becomes an integral part of any experiment. Without the participation of an observer, nothing in the subatomic world can be concluded with absolute certainty.

This scenario is much like the well-known philosophical question, "If a tree falls in a forest without anyone present to hear it, does it still make a sound?" Quantum mechanics takes the position that no sound is made without the participation of an observer. Moreover, it is *impossible* for the sound to actualize *without* the actions of the observer.

This uncertainty principle has given rise to a picture of the atom quite unlike the miniature solar system first proposed by classical physics. Instead of an electron orbiting the nucleus like a tiny satellite, it is now seen as a cloud-like structure enveloping the nucleus. Both the electron cloud and the particle are actually two forms of the same thing. In this new model, an electron is not at any location at any given time within the cloud-ring, but is in a sense *everywhere* in the cloud at the same time. It is impossible to say precisely where an electron might actually be until an observational measurement is taken. The cloud-ring then collapses at the exact moment of measurement, and the electron materializes at the location where it first made contact with the measuring medium. What is difficult to grasp because it is so alien to what we observe in our daily lives is that until the intervention of an observer, the electron *cannot* exist as an actualized particle. It remains in the form of a nebulous cloud of probability until an observer collapses the cloud by the act of observing it, which then causes the electron to leave its uncertain world of probability and solidify as a definite physical particle at a definite physical location.

Picture a hummingbird hovering in mid-air. Its wings beat

so fast that they appear to us as a blur. We may even notice the appearance of oscillating "probability" waves within the blur of the beating wings. It is impossible to determine from this fuzzy image exactly where the wings might be at any given moment or even how fast they are beating. The area of blurriness surrounding the hummingbird can be compared with the electron cloud surrounding the nucleus of an atom. Now imagine taking a photograph of the bird using high-speed film and a fast shutter speed. The resulting picture would show precisely where the wings were at the exact moment it was taken. However, once "frozen" in time by the photograph, there is no way to tell what speed the wings might have been previously traveling or in what direction. The act of photographing the bird can be compared to the act of observing an electron—the act of observing "collapses" the fuzzy cloud, and a clear image of a solid object materializes. But now that its location is known, the ability to measure its momentum and trajectory is lost.

This picture of subatomic uncertainty (and the associated quantum probability equations) is perfect for describing what takes place in the micro-world. The only problem is that the classical physics which accurately describes the macro-world also requires that an electron *must* have an objective reality independent of the observer. According to the standard model of the universe, a falling tree always makes a sound regardless of whether or not an observer is present to hear it. The classical model of an electron as a real materialized particle with a definite location and momentum is the foundation for our understanding of all chemical and electrical processes in the universe. These processes occur at the subatomic level everywhere and at all times without being dependent on the participation of an observer, and were operating long before the first human observer appeared. If the electron were merely a cloud of probability instead of a definite localized particle, chemical and electrical processes would still be the mysteries they once were, and our understanding of the universe would once again be plunged into the murky waters of medieval ignorance. This continues to be one of the biggest conundrums in theoretical physics today.

de Broglie offered a compromise between the two opposing views. He said that the apparent unpredictability of the location of a particle at any given moment is an illusion based on a mistake in perception. The entire experimental array—physicist, apparatus, and environment—must all be viewed as elements of a greater whole. The individual actions of these elements each generate unseen "waves" that combine to form a *total potential guide wave* for the entire experimental system. These guide waves exist outside space-time and so are not physical, which is why they cannot be directly observed. Every component of the experiment contributes in some complex way to the overall pattern of the total potential guide wave of the entire system. The guide wave also synchronizes with the electron itself, guiding or piloting the particle to a definite location at any given moment, just as a laser is used today to guide a missile to its target. Theoretically, the precise location of the particle *is* predictable because it has been established in advance by the sum total of all the guide waves in the greater whole of the system. This theory was also offered as a sensible explanation for the mystery of the two-slit experiment.

I have yet to see—either from a scientific theorist or paranormal researcher—a more precise description of both the phenomenon of synchronicity and the behavior of pre-physical supergeometry. The one significant difference is that de Broglie perceived the physical elements of the experimental system to be the source that generated these guide waves, whereas supergeometry contends that it is instead the guide waves themselves that generate the physical experiment.

Although de Broglie focused on the confines of a laboratory experiment, his guide waves imply even higher levels of supergeometric systems, each becoming increasingly more elaborate as the number of elements increase. For example, de Broglie's interrelationship of all elements in an experiment represents a small, localized supergeometric system comprising only the combination of the experimental elements. The biosphere of the earth that contains the experiment, the experimenters, and their laboratory, represents a much larger guide wave or super-geometry that incorporates within its matrix all smaller or subsidiary supergeometric systems on the planet. This localized planetary supergeometry is itself contained within the greater supergeometry of the solar system, which in turn is contained within the even larger supergeometry of our galaxy. Clusters of galaxies represent the next supergeometric level. Finally, we reach the ultimate superphysical level comprising the entire universe, or the *grand* supergeometry of the creation itself. All localized or subsidiary supergeometric systems are contained within and determined by this primary, grand supergeometry, or from a de Broglian perspective, the fundamental guide wave of the cosmos.

SUMMARY

Modern scientific thought has much in common with the world of the paranormal. In fact, given the nature of particle physics, it is a wonder why scientists sometimes look disdainfully upon paranormal phenomena. Physicists observe and accept without question many bizarre phenomena. Particles appear and disappear, transmute from one form to another, communicate with each other as if by telepathy, and generally break every physical law in the book—phenomena *precisely* like those seen in paranormal events. In fact, the paranormal may offer theoretical physicists an important opportunity to observe a one-to-one relationship between the quantum mechanics of the subatomic micro-world and events in the everyday macro-world of classical physics.

It is time to return to the four paraphysical principles introduced in the last chapter and briefly review how closely they are related to modern physical concepts.

1. There exists a means by which information can be gathered, stored, and transmitted outside of normal space-time. It has been said that all things in the universe are expressions of processed information. For the formation of particles, planets and galaxies, a database of the information that defines their constituent elements and structures must exist somewhere. Within each atom is stored the information necessary to construct all its components, just as genes contain the information required to assemble each organism. The scaffold of space-time itself is erected from a collection of information that determines its geometry.

A number of modern scientific ideas support the notion that this information is stored and transmitted superphysically:

- Kalusa successfully balanced Einstein's equations with the assumption that there was an additional source of information (i.e., a fifth value or co-ordinate) beside the four dimensions of space-time;
- Finkelstein's coherent superpositional patterns store information about the nature and behavior of all particles in a non-physical form;
- Wheeler's pre-geometry contains the information that establishes the order of physical space-time;
- Sheldrake's superphysical life fields likewise store all information on the physical structure and behavior of living organisms;
- The Kirlian phantom leaf effect indicates that all the information needed to manufacture the geometry of a living thing is stored separately from its physical counterpart;
- The experiments involving entangled particles demonstrate that information can indeed be transmitted from

one place to another outside space-time;

- Information as to the exact location of an electron at any precise moment is contained within and conveyed to the physical world by de Broglie's superphysical guide waves.

2. Matter and energy can be influenced and manipulated by some unknown mechanism, the source of which is non-physical and which originates outside normal space-time. The scientific ideas presented in this chapter not only support the existence of a superphysical realm, but that the processes taking place there establish the very nature of physical reality:

- Finkelstein's coherent superpositional patterns determine the nature and behavior of all physical particles from outside space-time;
- Wheeler's superphysical pre-geometry defines the fabric of space-time, thereby establishing universal physical order;
- Sheldrake's superphysical life fields influence the physical geometry, behavior, and growth patterns of living organisms, even causing them to sometimes transmute into new and different species;
- Changes are observed in Kirlian patterns before they become evident in their physical counterparts, indicating there is a superphysical cause behind the physical effect;
- The experiments involving entangled particles demonstrate that information from a superphysical source can directly influence the behavior of physical matter and energy;
- de Broglie's superphysical guide waves determine the processes that take place in all physical systems.

3. Matter and energy can pass in and out of normal space-

time. During this passage, the original pattern of matter and energy is maintained. If this superphysical realm is indeed "primary" reality, then it can stand as a separate and independent entity from the "secondary" or consequential realm of physical space and time:

- Virtual photons pass in and out of space-time when they are emitted and absorbed by electrons. The superphysical blueprint from which these photons are created is not contained within the electron, but is stored independently of it in a realm where the integrity of its pattern is maintained throughout the process of materializing and dematerializing;
- The geometry of space-time unfolds directly into physical reality from Wheeler's pre-geometry. Matter and energy spontaneously materialize from the pre-material "foam" that is generated by these pre-geometric patterns.

4. There exists a non-physical pattern or matrix on a grand scale. Seemingly unrelated physical things and/or events are in fact related though their alignment and resonance with this non-physical matrix. The existence of this matrix can be recognized by the occurrence of meaningful coincidences. The superphysical realm contains the grand supergeometric pattern from which all physical reality is designed. This pattern possesses a deep, inner cohesion and harmony through which the whole of creation is interconnected:

- Finkelstein's coherent superpositions are supported by an underlying matrix of pre-physical webs through which all physical things are interrelated and interconnected;
- All things within the boundaries of space-time are interrelated through the pre-material foam (from which

171

all space-time emerges) produced by Wheeler's pre-geometry;

- All individuals of a given species are interconnected through Sheldrake's pre-physical species fields;
- All seemingly unrelated elements within a given system are in fact interrelated or synchronized through de Broglie's superphysical guide waves, which determine the outcome of future events;
- The concept of grand supergeometry with its localized, subsidiary supergeometric systems demonstrates the synchronization of all things.

CONCLUSION

If we are to seek an all-encompassing TOE that incorporates the scientific, spiritual and supernatural disciplines, we need to do more than just explore the aspects of each. We need to find those places where they intersect in a sensible way so that we can build solid bridges between them. Considerable progress toward that end has been made in this chapter by correlating the mechanics of paranormal phenomena with the principles of modern scientific theory and the evidence presented by scientific anomalies. We now have a firm foundation from which we can begin to look at the third, most challenging, volatile and controversial element in our three-fold unification—the body of Biblical principles.

5

The Challenge of the Scriptures

Sorting Fact from Fantasy in a Sea of Spiritual Speculation

> For every person, in whatever walk of life, both in an application to study and in all forms of occupation, arrives at the same conclusions by the three worst arguments, namely, this is a pattern set by our elders, this is the custom, this is the popular belief: therefore, it should be held.
>
> —Roger Bacon

[Until now we've dealt mainly with scientific facts, observable evidence and objective logical argument. The remaining chapters in this book will more or less follow the same approach. This chapter, however, diverges from this pragmatic path by addressing the firestorm of religion and religious beliefs. The arguments here are subjective, doctrinal, and deeply personal. The flavor shifts so much that its pages will seem to be from another book, and in a sense, they are. As a Christian, I cannot simply go prancing through the most Holy of books irreverently extracting from it what some will view as novel interpretations that may profoundly contradict certain established denominational traditions without taking the time to respectfully and with heart-felt sincerity justify through sound religious argument and persuasion both my approach and my conclusions. I feel it is also necessary

for the sake of scholastic integrity to show that the interpretat-ions relevant to this book are based on solid reasoning and are not arbitrary or skewed by denominational prejudice. If I am to include Biblical principles in my reckoning, I must boldly go where more prudent and perhaps wiser souls fear to tread—play-ing it safe by avoiding controversy rarely leads one to Truth. I realize that embarking on such an in-depth religious disser-tation will not be to everyone's taste—an agnostic reader could easily skip over this chapter without missing anything critical to the theme of this book. But I hope that even those who have no interest in what appears to be little more than interdenom-inational disputing at times will find this debate interesting, and the discussion on Biblical interpretation enlightening. Those who read the Bible will find these insights useful in arriving at a deeper and more precise understanding of its ancient authors' worldview.]

It has been said that the Bible is the all-time bestseller. Con-tained within its covers are some the most powerful words ever written. Many have attributed miracles to it, devoted their en-tire lives to it, and have willingly gone to their deaths rather than renounce their faith in it.

But however impressive its credentials, the Bible is still a work devoted almost entirely to spiritual matters. Why should we even consider it in our cauldron of cosmic theorizing?

We've already established that the processes behind certain psychic phenomena like telekinesis and telepathy must operate outside normal space-time. Current scientific measuring instru-ments designed to detect only those things contained within the physical cannot guide us in probing the landscape of this superphysical realm. Yet the human psyche can occasionally break into the superdimensional and perceive certain aspects of its ethereal nature. These kinds of experiences would certainly be understood by most as religious or spiritual in nature. If one of these personal revelations was particularly profound, it might even be interpreted as divine inspiration. A person having such an experience who is able to communicate it to others in an orderly, meaningful and authoritative way would be recognized as a spiritual sage. I believe that these kind of experiences can contain profound insights into the nature of reality if translated correctly, and so should be considered in any search for Truth.

The Biblical authors could indeed be seen as spiritual sages. The spiritual concepts they put forth bear a strong resemblance to our emerging picture of the superphysical. It's therefore logical to conclude that the Scriptures might contain relevant information to our search, filling in the gaps where our measuring instruments fail. Its pages are filled with accounts of both paranormal occurrences and inspired revelations, along with descriptions detailing the nature of God's invisible domain. The power displayed by some who have adhered to its principles is strong evidence that the Bible contains accurate information about supergeometric elements and how they directly influence physical reality. What is derived through spiritual inspiration can at times accurately reflect what is observed in the physical world, albeit from a very different perspective and with very different language.

But justifying why we should examine the Bible for hard evidence of the superphysical is only part of the challenge. The greater task by far is wading through the myriad of contradictory religious and denominational interpretations piled over it through the centuries to arrive at the original meanings behind these ancient authors' writings. The difficulties in overcoming these traditional viewpoints are so formidable that few even attempt it.

Prominent among these traditions is the gradual movement by Christianity in recent centuries away from a physical interpretation of the Bible to one that is exclusively humanistic. It's apparent from their writings that the ancient Biblical authors understood the principles of God to be "all in all" in that they applied uniformly to the entire creation, not just to humanity.

But after the unfortunate incident involving Galileo, it became increasingly difficult for the Church to maintain this traditional teaching. Each new scientific discovery brought with it the appearance of a direct challenge to Biblical integrity. It soon became clear that if the Church was to retain its position of prominence and respect, it should shy away from physical law and confine itself to purely spiritual matters, and so gradually withdrew the all-in-all principle from its lay teachings. Christianity subsequently drifted so far from this original all-in-all understanding that the idea of deriving physical principles from the Scriptures seems quite strange today.

Of course, few would suggest we return to the times when the earth was seen as the center of the universe. But in removing the ancient all-in-all principle from its lay teaching, the baby went out with the bath water. The real problem was not with this ancient principle itself but a lack of sound scientific data by which it could be effectively applied. Basing church doctrine on the flawed earth-centered cosmology of Aristotle was bound to fail at some point.

It is difficult to appreciate the full extent to how abandoning the all-in-all principle has affected Biblical interpretation among modern Christians. Once the connection to the natural world was broken, there was no longer any hard physical reference on which to anchor Biblical teaching. If the substance of its words were now strictly personal, then one could interpret the Scriptures in almost any way that seemed right to the individual. There was no longer any compelling need to adhere to the Church's interpretation of Biblical meaning, since all was now subjective and introspective.

This shift in philosophy helped give rise to an almost dizzying array of Biblical interpretations as diverse as the uniqueness of each person, especially among Protestantism. While many of these private interpretations arose from a sincere search for truth, others were put forth with the intent to promote a particular preconceived doctrinal or political agenda. The latter are a far more difficult group to address, since a challenge to their interpretation also threatens their agendas, which all too often have grown to be of greater importance than the actual pursuit of truth itself.

It's not easy to cut through this modern interpretative static and arrive at a pure Scriptural signal. Such a multitude of Biblical conventions have emerged over the centuries that even the keenest of minds might stumble over them into erroneous assumptions. To accurately decipher the underlying principles of the Scriptures relevant to the workings of creation, certain conventional edifices must fall. Biblical texts must be examined objectively at their face value without preconceived notions and denominational dogma. Post-Biblical conventional traditions handed down to us—most of which emerged either from the oversimplifications of well-meaning clergy or from the efforts of leaders to promote their particular denominational agendas— must be set aside. We must also endeavor in our reading to be ever mindful of both the times and the culture in which the Biblical texts were written by resisting the natural inclination to interpret these ancient writings according to our 21st century worldview.

Choosing a Translation

The first step is to select the most appropriate translation of the Bible from which to work. While no translation is perfect or without contention, the Revised Standard Version (RSV) holds a distinct advantage over all other English translations. It is considered by many scholars to adhere most faithfully to the earliest and best witnesses (i.e., the ancient manuscripts) while still being very readable in the modern tongue. For these reasons, it is the only English translation that is recognized as authoritative by both the Catholic Church and most Protestant denominations. When speaking to the entire body of Christianity and its many factions, the use of such a translation is almost

177

compulsory. Even though a number of other translations could have equally served the requirements of this book, I believe the widespread consensus throughout the Christian community as to the integrity of the RSV is a necessary step toward satisfying the sincere spiritual and doctrinal concerns of the majority of Christians.

Denominational Tradition

Every Christian denomination has its own set of traditional views based on its unique interpretation of the Scriptures. In light of the fact that centuries of ecumenical effort has failed to reconcile these differences, I'd be a fool to think my current discourse will fare any better. Fortunately for us, these contentions focus primarily with issues of worship and church politics, and so have little to do with physics or cosmology. Yet there are still instances where denominational dogma fails to take into account the long-forsaken all-in-all viewpoint that is vital to accurate interpretation, and so some clashing is unavoidable. We should therefore set aside such traditions as best we can and focus exclusively on the *precise* wording of the original Biblical authors, whose writings were rendered long before any of these factions and their theological controversies came to be.

Creationism

A typical conventional assumption is the view that any attempt to interpret the Bible as science must be in some way related to fundamentalist creationism. Recall that creationism asserts the Bible is literal and inerrant truth and as such serves as the incontrovertible model for how the world came into being. Any scientific data appearing to conflict with the Bible must therefore be erroneous or misinterpreted. Rigid adherence to this dogma has served to perpetuate the perennial conflict between science and religion, thereby re-enforcing another modern convention that religion should best confine itself to spiritual matters.

This book has nothing to do with creationism as it is commonly represented. Although I too believe that many Biblical principles are scientifically relevant, my approach is quite different. By embracing an inclusionistic overview, I am seeking areas of *agreement* between scientific data and the Bible. The purpose is not to place scientific data on trial in the courtroom of religious dogma—scientific data, if sound, requires no such validation regardless to how one might interpret that data. Nor do I seek to refute Biblical precepts with science, since the nature of the Creator is beyond the scope of scientific materialism. The goal instead is to attain a more extensive and all-encompassing interpretation of the Scriptures with the *support* of scientific ideas. This writer believes—as did Kepler, Newton, and Einstein—that God created a universe of order, and that all observable phenomena are a reflection of that Divine Order. This writer also believes—as do many other Christians—that the Scriptures too are a reflection of that same Order. Neither modern science nor the Bible alone have proven sufficient to draw a *complete* picture of everything that we experience and observe in the creation. By combining the scientific with the spiritual, a more comprehensive model of the universe can be arrived at that should provide deeper insights into both.

The Original All-in-All Principle of the Bible

As mentioned before, one of the most common modern Biblical conventions is the view that its theology applies only to humanity by addressing matters strictly psychological, moral, or spiritual. Yet the ancient authors perceived the Word of God as applying not only to the spiritual, but to the entire physical creation as well. The early Christian churches embraced this all-in-all interpretation of Scripture and taught it as part of their

179

fundamental belief system. An excellent example of this principle is found in Romans 8:20-23;

> For the creation was subjected to futility, not of its
> own will but by the will of him who subjected it in
> hope; because the creation itself will be set free from
> its bondage to decay and obtain the glorious liberty
> of the children of God. We know that the whole
> creation has been groaning in travail together until
> now; and not only the creation, but we ourselves,
> who have the first fruits of the Spirit, groan inwardly
> as we wait for adoption as sons, the redemption of
> our bodies.

Even without delving into the deeper religious implications
of this passage, it's clear the apostle Paul believed the struggle
within us between good and evil (or between the physical flesh
and the spiritual self) extended also to the entire creation, and
that the resurrection of our bodies that will free us from this
turmoil was to likewise occur with the entire physical universe.
Most Christians are very familiar with the first part of this
teaching, but often fail to notice the part involving the physical
world, even though Paul gives both equal press. This all-inclu-
sive approach to understanding the Scriptures was a universally
recognized and accepted principle in early Christianity.

Stepping out of our modern mindset to assume this archaic
view can be very challenging. It's almost like looking up at the
night sky and interpreting what you see as a crystal firmament.
It's quite a mind-twisting exercise. Take for example the notion
of good and evil. Today we view this concept as a human standard by which we judge the moral quality of our thoughts and
deeds. Yet in Biblical times, especially in the early Christian era,
good and evil were seen instead as powerful opposing forces,
permeating and affecting everything in the physical world. Both
good and evil found expression through human behavior, not
just because we were spiritual beings, but also because humans

were an integral part of the overall moral conflict in the greater physical creation. What distinguished us from all the other elements in this universal, primal battle was our unique position in it as creatures made in the image of the Creator, and with this came the ability to choose good over evil, a quality that the rest of creation lacked.

Modern conventionalism just doesn't allow for this ancient mindset. It's easy to see how our personal actions might be labeled as either good or evil. But what about a stone or a blade of grass? Can a stone be good, or blade of grass evil? It simply doesn't make sense to our 21st century reason. Yet the Scriptures assert that the forces of good and evil extend to all things. God sheds his goodness on the entire world (not just humanity), while the whole world (again, not just humanity) is in the power of the evil one. Our difficulty in grasping this paradox is due to our modern thinking, which forbids our projecting human morality onto inanimate objects. But if we apply this contemporary notion to a reading of the Bible as most of us do unconsciously, we blindfold ourselves to an important aspect of its authors' deeper meaning. Rather than the ancient writers projecting human morality onto the creation, they perceived the battle between good and evil as being primarily waged in the spiritual realms, the turmoil of that conflict then spilling out from those realms onto the entire creation, including us. The primary guiding principle was not one of opposing morality within humans, but of opposing *forces* in the greater physical world of which we were only a part. Morality narrowly referred to the challenges facing human beings living within a world caught in the crossfire between these two great opposing spiritual camps, so we might learn to recognize and choose out of this fray that which is good.

Churches today focus exclusively on the human moralism of good versus evil. Yet a careful study of the Bible text reveals a conflict between these two forces on a cosmic scale, extending far beyond humanity to encompass both the entire physical and spiritual realms. To uncover its cosmology, we must look beyond the confines of its human relevance in order to also grasp its authors' greater cosmological perspective.

The "Human" God

The idea of a human God is a very old convention, the classical representation of which is the distinguished, white-haired, bearded patriarch seated upon His throne. Of course, we all know that the Creator of the heavens and earth is not an elderly human male, even though He has often been depicted in this way. In reality, no one knows what God looks like. To speak as if He were a visible flesh-and-blood being is really not Biblically accurate. No one has ever seen God (John 1:18). Neither is God a physical being, but is a spirit (John 4:24). According to the Scriptures, were anyone to actually hear God's voice or see His face as it actually is, they would perish from the experience (Exodus 20:19, Judges 13:22). The true nature of God is not bound by the human frailties of our fleshy bodies and minds, and is far beyond anything we mortals can reasonably comprehend.

Yet we seem to have a real need for a human image with which to relate both our inner being and outer flesh. Our visual depiction of a human God is a simple way to satisfy that need as it relates to our bodily form. But relating to God with our psychological part is a bit more complex. The different areas of our psyche—emotional, spiritual and rational—each speak their own language. What makes perfect sense to our hearts can be completely irrational to our minds, and vice versa. For instance, when I consider with my mind the Big Bang and the formation of elementary particles and forces, I envision the Creator as a huge, dynamic ethereal spirit. When I practice my faith, however, I am calling upon my emotional and spiritual centers, neither which relate very well with a creative force of electrons and light waves. I find both my emotional and spiritual selves require instead a humanized image with which to bond and interact.

I accept this apparent paradox without any philosophical debate because I know my intellectual, emotional, and spiritual selves each reckon differently. My heart cannot relate with, nor can it lovingly embrace, a Creator of particle waves and gravity fields whose expression is that of a mathematical equation or scientific law. On the other hand, my rational mind cannot relate with the archaic image of the Grand Old Man. Yet without the human characterization of "Father" with which to connect, my faith would not be the wondrous and enriching experience that it is. I find I must include both the personal *and* the intellectual to have a more complete experience of the Almighty. This is one of the purposes for the coming of Jesus Christ according to the Christian faith. He provided us with a living, breathing image of the invisible God with which each of the parts of our inner human being, as well as our outer form, could identify and interact.

But the entirety of that which is God the Father Creator is so much bigger than what is reflected in human beings. His superdimensional nature cannot possibly be grasped by peering through this narrow singular lens. If we want to have any chance at truly perceiving His eternal power and deity—the power and deity that shaped the cosmos—we must reach above the human notion of *God* (without abandoning it) so that we can also embrace the super-human notion of *Universal Creative Power*.

The Ancient Worldview

The instinctive tendency to interpret the Bible through our twenty-first century mindset is a significant obstacle to understanding the ancient authors. The almost obsessive inclination to force Biblical concepts into our modern way of thinking sometimes leads to gross distortion of the original meaning.

Few stop to realize how radically different our mindset is today when compared to that in Biblical times. Only by reading the Bible within the context of the old worldview can anyone hope to really understand what its authors are trying to convey.

Here's an example of what I mean. Consider the contrast between today's world and that of just two centuries ago. There was no modern technology to fall back on when some external force came along to threaten our way of life. If a child fell ill, there were no miracle cures easily obtainable at the local drug store. If a person suffered serious injury, there was no modern operating room in which to be anesthetized and stitched back together. If we were unable to work due to sickness or injury, there was no private insurance or state-sponsored financial assistance. If a farmer planted a crop and the rains did not come, there were no irrigation systems to prevent the crop from failing. If a swarm of locusts descended on the crop, there were no insecticides to eradicate them. If robbers broke into your home, there were no telephones with which to call the police. Anyone who puts their mind to it could easily cite dozens more examples of the ancients' helplessness when compared to our own modern empowerment. Today we carry on our lives without giving a second thought to our incredible technologies and the miraculous remedies they afford.

The point is that the kinds of troubles to which we give little thought today weighed heavily on the ancient mind. They had good reason to fear such calamities. Just a single occurrence could easily result in disaster or death. This ever-present vigilance to guard themselves carefully in every place they went and in everything they did was a fundamental part of their day-to-day mindset that we can barely imagine today.

Of course, we know that no one can long endure such a state of constant apprehension. To combat this fear and have some measure of peace, the ancients turned to religion. There were perhaps hundreds of religions of almost every imaginable description being practiced within the Roman Empire alone.

Everyone had their own idol to guard their home, a talisman to guard their person, and prayers to guide their actions and ward off misfortune. This religious/faith-based way of looking at virtually every aspect of life permeated everything they said and did.

This mindset deeply influenced their spoken and written language. The conceptualizations and imagery that erupt from our inner conscious out to the shaping of words in our mouths determine the semantics of our language. The intensely mystical and deeply religious worldview of the ancients produced a vocabulary and manner of speaking that were far different than the materialistic, casual and sometimes shallow nature of contemporary tongues. Much of the subtle meaning and "between-the-lines" inferences inherent in Biblical writings is lost with a reading that does not take this into account.

Computer owners who dial a technical support number and are connected to someone in another country experience a modern example of this kind of cultural communication gap. Although the people manning the overseas call center speak your language and understand the basic definitions of most words, they often cannot *communicate* effectively in it—the cultural background and the subtleties of meaning are just too different. Likewise, one cannot meaningfully communicate with the ancient authors from a modern mindset.

Speaking of phone calls, consider the common phase *on the phone*. We all understand the meaning because the telephone is an integral part of our culture. When we speak these words, it immediately conjures a mental image of using the device. But think about how this would translate to people from Biblical times. Even if they understood that it was some sort of remote communication device, how would they translate or interpret the idea of being *on* the phone during its use without further explanation? Wouldn't it make more sense for the user to be *off* the device so that it was accessible? Why would you be sitting, laying or standing on it anyway? A translator might add a footnote speculating how the application of bodily weight on the device may have contributed to its function. Another scholar might even see it as an error in transcription, and change the wording according to his or her best guess as to what the original author might have really meant. There are numerous such phrases in the Bible, like Paul's mention of a "third" heaven, for which no supportive explanation is provided because the ancient audience was already familiar with the cultural vernacular of the day.

Here's another example. Consider the contrast between the archaic and modern usage of the word *about*. Today, the sentence "Let's talk *about* this tree" is understood as "Let's have a conversation regarding this tree." But in earlier times, the word *about* in this context conveyed a meaning of greater depth and complexity. Today we see the world around us through the eyes of modern science and understand the elements of creation as assemblies of matter and energy defined by physical laws and scientific principles. But this kind of modern analytical perception was almost completely foreign to the ancient Jews and Christians who viewed the world with mystical awe. They saw every created thing as a materialization of a creational facet of God. A tree, for instance, was a direct physical emanation from God that reflected a specific aspect of His creative Wisdom. As mere mortals, we could never fully understand the true nature of the tree, since its essence lay beyond our limited perception. Thus, to have a conversation regarding a tree, we would be forced to talk "about" it or *around* it, since it would be impossible for us to actually conceptualize the tree's true essence or speak it with our lips.

Cast within the framework of this earlier worldview, the sentence "Let's talk *about* this tree" conjures a mental image in the speaker's mind of both a gesture of movement around the subject ("about" the tree) and an implicit sense of wonderment toward the incomprehensibility of God's creation (one cannot pronounce with human lips the tree's true essence). There is simply no single word in our present-day vocabulary to convey this subtle mental imagery that was an integral part of the ancient mindset. Our 21st century worldview from which arises the meaning and usage of our words is based on the fundamental belief that *all* things are ultimately knowable. The peoples of Biblical times believed virtually the opposite.

A very common phrase from the New Testament illustrates how this ancient worldview must be applied to a reading of the Scriptures in order to fully comprehend its intended meaning. There are numerous instances where afflicted people approached Christ with the words, "Have mercy on me." The modern mindset typically interprets this as begging Jesus to show compassion because of their misery so that He would be willing to heal them. Yet if you stop to think about it, "mercy" is an odd choice of word. It's as if Jesus was about to levy some penalty against them, and they in turn were asking for leniency.

The reason behind these pleadings for mercy lies in the ancient worldview. It was believed at the time that many maladies like disfiguring diseases, injuries, deforming birth defects and even barren wombs were inflicted by God as punishment for sins committed by themselves or their ancestors. Now recall that Jesus was seen by many as a direct emissary from God, and thus carried in Him that same Divine authority. Therefore, He also had the power to judge innocence or guilt, to absolve or convict the accused, and to reward or punish. The request for mercy was therefore not so much a plea for compassion, but a petition to this Divine Judge to commute or even vacate the sentence imposed by God as a punishment for whatever sin had been committed that led to their affliction.

Thus the words *have mercy on me* actually represents an image in the petitioners' minds of Jesus as a Divine Judge and themselves as miserable sinners. It was much more a begging for forgiveness through pity rather than for a healing through compassion. They believed that once their sins were divinely forgiven, the sentence would be lifted, and the spontaneous

187

healing would automatically follow. This is why, on the occasion when Jesus healed the paralytic, He first spoke the words *your sins are forgiven*. The scribes accused Him of blasphemy, not because He was healing, but because He was forgiving sin, which only the Divine Judge can do.

A reader approaching these verses from a modern viewpoint would mistakenly conclude that the passages merely attest to Christ being a great spiritual healer, while completely missing the true meaning behind them. The accounts of these miracles were offered by the ancient authors as proof of the divinity of Christ as God incarnate in the flesh, not so much as attested by His power to heal, but instead by His authority to forgive the sin that originally caused the affliction.

If you missed this important concept in your reading (and let's be honest, lots of us have), how many more subtleties have been overlooked or misinterpreted by failing to consider the worldview of the times? Some mistaken Biblical concepts circulating today are due to this one simple but terribly important misstep. But take heart—instances like these do not require you to be a Biblical scholar who can translate directly from the ancient tongue. Any conscientious reader can derive such in-depth interpretation by merely cross-referencing with other passages. You just have to keep it in mind when reading.

It's clear we cannot hope to extract a complete picture of the ancient authors' intended meanings by interpreting their words and phrases according to modern usage. The casual reader may understand what the ancient author is saying, but can completely miss what the ancient author is trying to *communicate*. Since the elements of a language depend largely on the culture in which it is spoken, it's easy to see how applying a 21st century interpretation to a reading of the Scriptures while disregarding both the ancient worldview and the old all-in-all principle virtually guarantees failure to grasp its full meaning. Yet the Bible is read like this all the time. This is not to say that our modern pragmatism or our scientific knowledge should be abandoned, for without them we would not recognize the true significance of the hidden Biblical principles we'll identify in a later chapter. But we must also read with first century eyes, for without them we cannot see what the Biblical authors were really trying to convey to us.

The Legend of the Fallen Lucifer

Perhaps no single conventional concept has had a greater impact on Scriptural interpretation than the legend of the fallen Lucifer. For those not familiar with this, it is the belief that Satan or "Lucifer" was at first a glorified angel in Heaven who then rebelled against God and was subsequently cast out and down to the earth. The concept is often used as an explanation for the age-old philosophical question, "If God is so good, why is there sickness and evil in the world?" The fallen Lucifer story is typically employed as a means to deflect the blame away from an all-good, all-loving God and onto another being of power who circumvents the good intention of God by rebelling against Him. Of course, this in itself doesn't really provide a suitable answer, since it begs the follow-up question, "Why would an all-benevolent God afflict us so by even allowing such a creature to exist, let alone letting it run loose in our world." It's this very issue that is most cited by non-believers against the faith. Yet despite the awkwardness of this solution, it's still the view held by many Christian denominations.

Even though this controversy seems strictly theological, the issue of Satan's origins is important to any examination of the Scriptures for principles that are relevant to the nature of physical reality. Any Biblical subject having as much influence on the nature of reality as Satan must be factored into consideration. This requires we also address religious conventions that might obscure the literal meaning behind the ancient authors' writings on this subject.

So what does a being like Satan have to do with creation?

189

Isn't there only one Creator? Isn't Satan just a rebellious, fallen angel who tempts humanity and spreads evil around the world? According to the traditions of many Christian denominations, yes. But if we set aside these church traditions and instead focus exclusively on the actual wording of Biblical content composed centuries before these traditions came into being, we find no passages that clearly state Satan was once a glorified angel who of his own free will turned evil and rebelled against God out of jealousy. Instead, we find clear, concise statements defending the minority Christian view, namely that God created Satan as an adversarial force, and that his opposition to God is fundamental to his very created nature. This minority view—and the only view fully supported by the Biblical text—is vital to deciphering the hidden cosmological picture held by the Biblical authors.

The idea that an all-good, all-loving God intentionally created evil is so contrary to conventional thinking that many have difficulty contemplating it for even a brief moment. The need for Christians to provide a reasonable explanation for this apparent religious paradox has given rise over the centuries to a number of complex solutions. One of the earliest and more extreme was a belief held by a Christian heretical sect known as Gnosticism that flourished in the second and third centuries (this was long before the "fallen Lucifer" solution achieved widespread acclaim). According to the Gnostics, the God of the Old Testament was actually a different deity than the Father of Jesus Christ. The ancient Jewish God was seen as an evil creator who took eternal light and trapped it inside corruptible matter. It was this same evil God that ordered the Israelites to sacrifice animals and slaughter entire towns. The good God came to earth in the form of Jesus Christ to reveal this truth to us and to free us spiritually from this bondage to the flesh and the world of the physical. This early explanation at least had a certain appearance of consistency with the Old Testament texts.

It would be impractical here for me to launch into a full-blown, chapter-length debate extolling the virtues of the Satan-Created-As-Such interpretation over the more popular Once-Glorified-Satan-Turned-Evil view. But the issue is sufficiently important to deserve at least some serious attention, not just for the purposes of this book, but also out of spiritual concerns. On the occasions when I have shared the "minority view" with other believers, most have granted me a fair hearing (which is all one could ask). But some are so entrenched in church tradition that any idea in seeming contrast to what they've been taught draws a "here be monsters" reaction as if I were speaking unconscionable blasphemies. It's been suggested I should not worry about this, but concern myself with how to present my case in the most reasonable way and let the chips fall where they may. But I believe the subject is too important, not only toward understanding the Biblical description of creation, but to the Christian faith itself. I can't in good conscience abandon those who in their hearts righteously defend what they believe is true without at least offering up hard evidence from the very Scriptures on which the faith is supposed to be based. When all is said and done, the real solution to this paradox is not only doctrinally sound and spiritually satisfying, but is also far more sensible than the traditional explanation that was originally taken from non-canonical Hebrew mythology and then Christianized in the post-Biblical era.

Let's first take a look at the most frequently quoted Bible passages from the fourteenth chapter of Isaiah defending the traditional mythology of Satan having once been a glorified angel in Heaven who subsequently rebelled against God. If one examines these passages with both care and sincerity, it quickly becomes apparent that the ideas being presented are simply not consistent with this interpretation:

> [12] How you are fallen from heaven, O Morning Star [Lucifer], son of Dawn! How you are cut down to the ground, you who laid the nations low!
> [13] You said in your heart, "I will ascend to heaven;

191

above the stars of God I will set my throne on high; I will sit on the mount of assembly in the far north [according to Syrian legend, the earthly abode of God];
[14] I will ascend above the heights of the clouds, I will make myself like the Most High."
[15] But you are brought down to Sheol, to the depths of the Pit.
[16] Those who see you will stare at you, and ponder over you: "Is this the man who made the earth tremble, who shook kingdoms,
[17] who made the world like a desert and overthrew its cities, who did not let his prisoners go home?"
[18] All the kings of the nations lie in glory, each in his own tomb;
[19] but you are cast out, away from your sepulchre, like a loathed untimely birth; clothed with the slain, those pierced by the sword, who go down to the stones of the Pit, like a dead body trodden under foot.
[20] You will not be joined with them in burial, because you have destroyed your land, you have slain your people.

First, we need to recognize that these passages were written as part of a larger prophecy or "taunt song" against the reigning king of Babylon. Anyone championing an alternative, satanic interpretation should at least acknowledge this was the original context.

Next, let's take a closer look at the name *Lucifer*, which I added to the text in brackets. This has been tossed around as a name for Satan for so many centuries that most people assume it has always been so. But no book of the Bible—including any by the New Testament authors—ever used this as a name for the devil. In fact, the name never appears in any ancient copy of Isaiah or in any ancient manuscript of other Biblical books. Instead, in every instance, the term *morning star* or *day star* is applied.

To understand how this name came to be, we need to first

look at the intent behind the original use of "morning star" in the text. Here's an instance where being mindful of the ancient worldview helps clarify the purpose and meaning behind the use of this Biblical metaphor. It was very common in ancient times to compare people or nations with elements in the natural world. Perhaps the most common example in the Bible is that of comparing a person or nation having great stature, authority or power with the giant cedar trees of Lebanon. The cedars of Lebanon were by far the tallest of all the known trees and so the persons or nations being compared to them were among the most powerful, most wealthy, and so on. In the case of these passages, the ancient author chose the relative magnitude of the stars in the sky as his metaphor. He thus compares Babylon, the most powerful nation in the world of the ancient Jews, to the brightest of all the stars. Of course, the brightest visible "star" is the planet Venus when it appears in the morning sky, hence the name *morning star*. The morning star was a common metaphor for greatness in Biblical times since there are several other occurrences of it in the Scriptures. Yet none of these other instances even remotely relate to Satan. In fact, Revelation 22:16 also calls Jesus the morning star. Scholars universally accept without debate that the ancient authors were indeed referring to the planet Venus with these metaphors. It's the only interpretation that is both historically accurate and contextually consistent.

So when did this term *Lucifer* first appear, and how did it come to be interpreted as a name for Satan? The name first shows up in Jerome's fourth century translation of the Bible into Latin known as the *Latin Vulgate*. The Latin language had two different proper names for the planet Venus—when it appeared in the morning sky it was called *Lucifer*, or the Morning Star, while its evening appearance was known as *Hesperus*, the Evening Star. Jerome simply applied the Latin word *Lucifer* for this astronomical body as any good translator would. It's that simple. This is just a documented, historical fact, and there's really nothing more to it. No deep mystical meaning or deistic title was ever intended. Even the translators of the original King James Version, who carried over the name Lucifer directly from the Latin Vulgate, acknowledged in a footnote that the term meant "*day starre*" and nothing more. The author never, ever intended it as a proper name for a deity. Virtually every objective authority is in complete agreement on this point. While there's certainly nothing wrong with using it as another name for Satan, it should not be done so in the erroneous belief that there is any foundation for it in the original Hebrew or Greek Biblical texts.

What about the rest of the passages? Don't they describe a fallen Satan? Take a look at verses 13 and 14. According to the Lucifer legend, Satan was once a glorified angel who resided in heaven with God at the time of his rebellion, after which he was then cast down to earth. But these passages in Isaiah tell the *exact opposite* story. The subject of these verses is *already down on earth* at the time of his rebellion, and then aspires to ascend up into heaven to the same height as the throne of God. Of course, if we were speaking of a human, earth-bound king who in his arrogance dared to believe he could equate himself with the Most High God, these two passages make perfect sense. But the passages make absolutely no sense in relation to the fallen Lucifer story. The contrast is so pronounced that it's difficult to conceive how anyone might confuse the two. Remember, we are seeking the ancient authors' meanings from their *precise* wording, not from a "similar to" or "sounds something like" approach. Otherwise, we will fare no better than the early Spanish explorers of the New World who, upon having first sighted the Florida manatee, reported they had seen the elusive mermaid of legend.

Finally, the traditional legend tells that Satan became the prince of Hell (or Sheol in the ancient tongue) after his fall. But the remaining passages in Isaiah tell a very different story, in that there were already people in Hell when this troubled individual arrives. According to the legend, wasn't Satan Hell's first inhabitant? Wasn't he cast to the earth *before* there were any descendents of Adam and Eve to occupy hell? How then did these souls get there before Satan's arrival? And what imprisoned, tortured souls would dare taunt the very prince of Hell with such words as attested to in these passages when Satan had the power to torment those souls eternally in any manner he chose? Think about it.

As for the reference in verses 18-20 about the king not receiving an honorable burial, what kind of immortal deity has any care about an earthly tomb?

None of this makes any sense at all as a reference to Satan. But it makes complete sense in reference to the human, earthly king of Babylon against which this prophecy was levied.

The second set of Biblical passages often cited as referring to a fallen Lucifer is from Ezekiel 28:12-19. At first glance, these seem a more convincing parallel to the traditional legend. But, just as in the case with the Isaiah passages, when taken in its intended context as a prophecy against a worldly king, and the precise wording carefully examined, it too falls short:

> [12] Son of man, raise a lamentation over the king of Tyre, and say to him, Thus says the Lord God: "You were the signet of perfection, full of wisdom and perfect in beauty.
> [13] You were in Eden, the garden of God; every precious stone was your covering.... and wrought in gold were your settings and your engravings. On the day that you were created they were prepared.
> [14] With an anointed guardian cherub I placed you; you were on the holy mountain of God; in the midst of the stones of fire you walked.
> [15] You were blameless in your ways from the day that you were created, until iniquity was found in you.
> [16] In the abundance of your trade you were filled with violence, and you sinned; so I cast you as a profane thing from the mountain of God, and the guardian

195

cherub drove you out from the midst of the stones of fire.

[17] Your heart was proud because of your beauty; you corrupted your wisdom for the sake of your splendor. I cast you to the ground; I exposed you before kings, to feast their eyes on you.

[18] By the multitude of your iniquities, in the unrighteousness of your trade you profaned your sanctuaries; so I brought forth fire from the midst of you; it consumed you, and I turned you to ashes upon the earth in the sight of all who saw you.

[19] All who know you among the peoples are appalled at you; you have come to a dreadful end and shall be no more forever.

Admittedly, verses 12-14 might be reasonably interpreted as a description of what a glorified angel might look like. But if you go back and read the account of the Garden of Eden in Genesis, you'll find no mention of any such being. There's no way this wording bears any resemblance to Satan in the Garden, who is depicted in Genesis as a cunning snake, being one of the many "wild creatures" of the field (*beasts* in older translations—hardly a glorified being) that the Lord had made, none of which were so adorned. So, where did the idea come from that this is a description of Satan? Certainly not from an accurate reading of the text. Of course, someone holding the preconceived notion would find these passages "similar to" or "sounds something like" a glorified Lucifer. But there is no direct description of Satan anywhere in the Bible itself that even remotely resembles this imagery.

Verses 15-16 tell that the person in question was cast from Eden once he committed his transgression. But in the Genesis account, only Adam and Eve were cast out, not Satan.

Verse 14 mentions a guardian cherub. Nowhere in the account of Eden is a cherub associated with the serpent.

Verse 17 does speak of this person being cast to the ground, as was the serpent in Genesis. But there were no human kings to "feast their eyes on" the fallen serpent at the time of this cast-ing down. In fact, by the time these words were written, Satan was not understood as a visible being at all in a physical sense, but a spiritual being. And he was never publicly burned to ashes as a city might be. So the "casting down" speaks in metaphor of the king of Tyre.

However, it's also clear the ancient author is making a con-nection between these passages and the Genesis account of Eden. Who then is he referring to? The only person in the story of Eden that even comes close to fitting *all* the criteria laid out in these passages is Adam. God made Adam in His image, so before the fall this first man must have been a creature of beauty and splendor (not a common beast like a snake), just as Ezekiel depicts. Additional references in apocryphal works like the *Book of Adam and Eve* attest to the ancient view that Adam was indeed a glorified being before being cast out of the Garden. Such imagery was no doubt commonly understood at the time, so there would have been no reason for Ezekiel to elaborate further as to whom he was alluding. It is only we moderns who might be confused.

As for the transgression, the Genesis text clearly indicates the serpent was merely behaving according to his God-given nature when he deceived Eve—in other words, Satan was just being Satan. It was instead Adam who violated his perfection when he sinned. It was Adam who was cast out of the lofty Gar-den down "to the ground" of common earth, and only against him did God set the guardian cherub to prevent him from re-entering.

If you lay down the post-Biblical man-made traditions and look objectively at the actual wording of Ezekiel, the only viable answer is that the prophet was comparing the fall of the king of Tyre to the fall of Adam, not to any fall of the serpent. It tells that the king was corrupted by the acquiring of material riches, just as Adam was corrupted by the acquiring of the knowledge of good and evil. According the Genesis, Satan was already corrupt—he was in fact the corrupter, not the one being corrupted. Besides, wasn't Satan's corruption supposed to be through the envy of God? How then is it now suddenly because of earthly riches that he didn't even possess yet? Do you see what I mean? When you stop and really think carefully about these passages, a parallel to a fallen Satan—at least, the Satan described in the Scriptures—is shaky at best.

Although there are several other often-quoted passages scattered throughout the Bible that refer to fallen angels, a careful reader will find that none of them specifically mention Satan, although it's implied that these rebelling angels became followers of him. A good example is Jude 1:6;

> And the angels that did not keep their own position
> but left their proper dwelling have been kept by him
> in eternal chains in the nether gloom.... (Jude 1:6a)

Note that these passage makes no direct reference to Satan (again, we're going by the precise wording, not assumption). More importantly, these fallen angels are described as being chained, whereas according to Scriptural doctrine, Satan currently runs loose, destined to be chained only *after* the second coming of Christ. For a Christian to believe that Satan is among these currently chained angels would be heretical, since it would not only serve to diminish the significance of Christ's return, but also deny the role that Satan currently plays in exerting his evil influence over the world—which of course is why Jude doesn't mention him.

If no Scriptural passages clearly describe a once-good Satan turned evil by an act of free will, are there any that indicate Satan was purposely created by the will of God as an opposing, evil adversary from the very beginning? There are indeed several such passages. And unlike the ambiguous and weak references used to defend a fallen Lucifer, those that describe the intentional creation of evil are both clear and concise. As strange as this concept might seem to some, it is quite simply the only position that is wholly supported by the actual Scriptural texts.

From the first Biblical book of Genesis, the Scriptures bear witness to God having intentionally created not only an evil adversity, but also evil itself [italics and brackets added]:

> Now the serpent was more subtle [i.e., cunning and crafty] than any other wild creature *that the Lord God had made.* (Genesis 3:1) [This serpent is identified as Satan in the book of Revelation]

The following passages unmistakably demonstrate the Biblical principle that the origin of evil came directly from God [italics and brackets added]:

> The Lord said to him, "Who gave man his mouth? *Who makes him deaf or mute?* Who gives him sight or *makes him blind*? Is it not I, the Lord? (Exodus 4:11)

> Now the Spirit of the LORD departed from Saul, and *an evil spirit from the LORD* tormented him. (1 Samuel 16:14)

> The next day *an evil spirit from God* came forcefully upon Saul. (1 Samuel 18:10)

> Consider the work of God; who can make straight what *he has made crooked*? (Ecclesiastes 7:13)

> Good things and *bad*, life and *death*, *poverty* and wealth, *are from the Lord.* (Sirach 11:14)

> I am the Lord, and there is no other. I form the light and *create darkness*, I make weal and *create woe....* (Isaiah 45:6-7a)

> *The Lord kills* and brings to life; *he brings down to Sheol* and raises up. (1 Samuel 2:6)

> And the devil took him [Jesus] up, and showed him all the kingdoms of the world in a moment of time, and said to him, "To you I will give all this authority and their glory, for *it has been delivered to me*, and I give it to whom I will." [Satan has power over worldly things, not because he seized such power, but that it was given to him. Only God would have the authority to grant Satan this power.](Luke 4:5-7)

The following three passages must be examined together in order to grasp their full meaning [italics and brackets added]:

> Put on the whole armor of God, that you may be able to stand against the wiles of the devil. For we are not contending against flesh and blood [as in physical combat], but against *the principalities*, against *the powers*.... against the spiritual hosts of wickedness in the heavenly places. (Ephesians 6:11)

> .... For in him [Christ/God] *all* things were created, in heaven and on earth, visible or invisible, whether thrones or dominions or *principalities or authorities* [i.e., powers].... (Colossians 1:16a)

> He [Christ/God] disarmed the *principalities and powers* and made a public example of them, triumphing over them.... (Colossians 2:15a)

The principalities, powers and authorities are classified as being of an evil spiritual nature in Ephesians. Furthermore, in Colossians 2:15, these evil principalities were "disarmed" and "triumphed over" by Jesus Christ. Yet Colossians 1:16 clearly states that these same evil principalities and powers were actually created by God through Christ.

That God intentionally imposed evil on the world is evident from a remarkable passage in Romans [italics added]:

> .... For the creation was subjected to futility, not of its

200

own will but *by the will of him who subjected it in hope*, because creation itself will [one day] be set free from its bondage to decay.... (Romans 8:20-21*a*)

Futility in this instance is a reference to the corruptible and perishable nature of the creation, which is attributed in the Bible to the forces of evil. This passage asserts that the world was intentionally subjected to this futility. The phrase "by the will of him who subjected it in hope" is clearly referring to God. Only God has the power to impose such futility over the whole of creation. Remember that in Luke 4:5-7, Satan was *given* the authority over the kingdoms of the world., The passage *he who made it subject* cannot therefore refer to Satan, since that would mean he granted these things to himself. The passage emphatically states that the futility of the creation is due *not of its own will*, but by God's design. The words *in hope* also convey a Divine origin, since Satan is instead the father of hopelessness. The evil nature of the physical world has nothing to do with the issue of free will, be it Satan's or otherwise, but with God's hidden purpose.

The real "clincher" comes from the words of Christ Himself:

> He [Satan] was *a murderer from the beginning*, and has nothing to do with the truth, because there is no truth in him. When he lies, *he speaks according to his own nature, for he is a liar and the father of lies.* (John 8:44)

If Satan was a murderer from the beginning, and is a liar, not by free-will choice, but by his very nature, how could he have ever been a glorified angel? How could Almighty God glorify a murderer and liar? And remember, these are words from the mouth of Christ Himself. Clearly, these words were written well before the now-familiar Lucifer legend began circulating.

On the occasions I have spoken with a believer in a fallen Lucifer about this hard Scriptural evidence, I've gotten a variety of responses from surprise to acceptance, even shock. Sadly, some actually continue, "I don't know why it says all that, and I don't care. All I know is that Satan was once good; the passages in Isaiah refer to Satan..." and so on. You must forgive me, but what credibility is there in clinging to a myth that is in direct contradiction to the very Scriptures we claim are sacred? How can it be that a non-believer, reading without prejudice, could make perfect sense of all these passages while we cannot? When the words are read and received precisely as they are written, there is no mythology hidden in these passages, and no incongruities in its spiritual message.

Whether one believes that Satan was evil from the beginning (as Christ taught), or instead later turned evil by his own will, his nature would still be as the Bible describes. Everything we know about the nature and behavior of Satan would be precisely the same for either scenario. But the conclusions that can be drawn about the greater order of creation—and the nature of its Creator—are very different from one than from the other. And it is the original Judeo-Christian view of this greater creational order that this book is seeking.

The Wisdom Books of the Apocrypha

The *Apocrypha* is the name given to a collection of books found in the Greek version of the Old Testament (called the Greek Septuagint) but not in the Hebrew canonical Scriptures. An additional book (2 Esdras), although not in the Septuagint, appears in the Old Latin translations made from the Greek, and therefore has traditionally been included with the others. They are as follows:

1 Esdras
2 Esdras (also known as *Nehemiah*)
Tobit
Judith

Esther (certain later additions—the rest is canonical)
The Wisdom of Solomon (also known as *Wisdom*)
Ecclesiasticus (also known as *Sirach*, or *Wisdom of Jesus the son of Sirach*)
Baruch
The Letter of Jeremiah (attached as the last chapter of *Baruch* in the Latin version)
The Prayer of Azariah and The Song of the Three Young Men (additions to *Daniel*)
Susanna (also an addition to *Daniel*)
Bel and the Dragon (also an addition to *Daniel*)
The Prayer of Manasseh
The First Book of Maccabees (also known as *1 Maccabees*)
The Second Book of Maccabees (also known as *2 Maccabees*)

All these books were originally embodied in the Latin Vulgate, the first "official" bible sanctioned and approved by the Church, since its compilation by Jerome in the fourth century AD. Because these were not found in the Hebrew canon, Jerome considered them to be of lesser spiritual significance than the other Old Testament books, and he prefaced them accordingly. However, many of the subsequent copyists excluded Jerome's comments, so that most readers received the Apocrypha in a form that made it appear equal in stature to the other books. By the Middle Ages, these books were generally accepted as Holy Scripture.

During the sixteenth century, disputes arose again over the spiritual significance of the Apocryphal books. In an unprecedented move, the Roman Church officially declared most of the Apocrypha as canonical at the Council of Trent in 1546, while members of the Protestant Reformation tended to reject them as such. These opposing viewpoints have been retained by their respective dogmas into modern times.

Two of these books, *Wisdom* and *Sirach*, are relevant to this work because of how well they represent the ancient Biblical concept of the *Wisdom of God*. According to the Old Testament, God shaped all things in the creation by means of His Wisdom, which contained His Divine Order. Any principle so fundamental to the structure and workings of the physical cosmos will naturally be of great interest to us. Wisdom and Sirach delve into the characteristics of this Divine Wisdom to a much greater depth than the canonical Biblical books. Whatever one may opine concerning their canonical merits, they unquestionably reflect the predominant Jewish beliefs of the time about the nature of God's Wisdom. Because these books address this subject in such detail and scope, passages from them shed significant light on certain references in other parts of the Bible that would be otherwise ambiguous or incomplete.

Since a percentage of Protestants still reject these books, I once again find myself obligated to my Christian brethren to offer a meaningful argument defending my position, in this case for my choice to make use of passages from these two books. As was the case with the Lucifer controversy, I cannot devote the time and space here to a full-blown ecclesiastical dissertation on the subject. Nor am I arguing for inclusion of these books in the Canon. I will, however, offer the following intriguing facts to show that the concepts cited in Wisdom and Sirach should be considered as a valid and accurate reflection of what the ancient Judeo-Christian community believed concerning the Wisdom of God (most of the following historical information can be referenced in the very scholarly work, *The Oxford Annotated Apocrypha*).

Although most Protestant Bibles today omit the books of the Apocrypha, this was not always the practice. These were included in most Protestant Bibles as an independent section or as an integral part of the text as early as Martin Luther's German translation of 1534. The first English translation, made in the fourteenth century by John Wycliffe, also contained all the disputed books. Additionally, all English translations of the sixteenth century included the Apocrypha. They were even included in the venerated King James Version of 1611.

Many of the early founders of the Protestant Reformation embraced these books as being useful for spiritual guidance and enlightenment. George Abbott, the Archbishop of Canterbury and one of the original translators of the King James Bible, strongly agreed, decreeing in 1615 that anyone guilty of binding and selling Bibles without including the Apocrypha would be subject to one year in prison!

The primary dispute over these books involved certain Catholic rituals (like holding Masses for the dead) that the Protestants wished to eliminate. Since many of these practices were rooted in the books of the Apocrypha, discrediting them would not only legitimize the Protestant position, but also 'legalize' their rebellion against what they sincerely perceived as a corrupt and oppressive Catholic Church, and by doing so remove the stigma of excommunication. These motivations were more political than spiritual.

The first known instance of an English Bible being published without the Apocrypha was not apparently for religious reasons, but is believed to have been a business decision made at the bindery to save on the cost of paper to better facilitate the increasing demand for inexpensive Bibles. A few Geneva Bibles published in 1599, as well as certain editions of the King James Bible dated 1616 to 1633, are missing the pages of the Apocrypha even though the books are listed in the table of contents, a clear indication that these were meant to be included. This practice of omission proliferated to the point that almost all English Bibles today (save Catholic versions) exclude the Apocrypha.

There were two main legal arguments lodged against these books at the time. First, it was claimed that their authorship could not be confirmed, and therefore were likely ancient forgeries. For example, the approximate dating for the *Wisdom of Solomon* (also known as *Wisdom* for short) makes it highly unlikely to have been penned by that king. Secondly, none of these books were included in the Jewish Canon, which is why Jerome originally segregated them in the Vulgate. These two reasons provided the needed justification for some Protestants to reject the Apocrypha, and with it the associated rituals, practices, and beliefs.

These arguments are far less persuasive in light of current knowledge. We now know it was a common practice in ancient times to attribute a literary work to a famous individual to help gain its widespread acceptance. Biblical scholars understand that significant portions of the Canon were similarly "forged" like the *Song of Solomon* written long after Solomon's death. Other Old Testament examples of such pseudonymous text are Chapters 40-55 of *Isaiah* (also known as *Deutero-Isaiah*), the book of *Malachi*, and Chapter 52 of *Jeremiah*. The New Testament has many works, including the Gospels themselves, that scholars generally consider pseudonymous. This by no means takes anything away from the spiritual significance and merits of these writings. It just means that significant portions of the Canon meet the same criteria used to justify the rejection of the Apocrypha.

With regard to the second argument, recent discoveries of ancient manuscripts including the Dead Sea Scrolls have confirmed both the antiquity and authenticity of Wisdom and Sirach. As for the requirement of being included in the original Hebrew Canon, I might humbly observe that neither are any of the New Testament writings.

Since the original arguments against the Apocrypha have today been largely discredited, these books must be rightfully judged not by archaic legal dispute, but by examining the spiritual integrity of their content.

Internal evidence from the Biblical writings bears witness that the New Testament authors were very familiar with both Wisdom and Sirach. The qualities assigned to Divine Wisdom in these two books were embraced and upheld by the early Christians, who expressed this concept as the Word of God, of which Jesus Christ was the physical personification. Many New Testament passages bear an uncanny similarity to those of the apocryphal wisdom books:

> For the Word of God is living and active, sharper than any two-edged sword, piercing to the division of soul and spirit, of joints and marrow, and discerning the thoughts and intentions of the heart. (Hebrews 5:12)
> *For Wisdom is more mobile than any motion; because of her pureness she pervades and penetrates all things. (Wisdom 7:24)*

> I tell you this brethren: flesh and blood cannot inherit the kingdom of God, nor does the perishable inherit the imperishable. (1 Corinthians 15:50)
> *.... Nothing defiled gains entrance into her. (Wisdom 7:25b)*

> The Son can do nothing of his own accord, but only what he sees the Father doing; for whatever he does, the Son does likewise. (John 5:19) [the Son, who, according to John 1:14 is Wisdom personified, "mirrors" the working of God].
> *For she is.... a spotless mirror of the working of God.... (Wisdom 7:26a)*

> He [Christ, the Word] is the image of the invisible God.... (Colossians 1:15a)
> *.... An image of his goodness. (Wisdom 7:26b)*

> .... All things were created in him and for him. He is before all things, and in him all things hold together. (Colossians 1:17b)
> *Though she is but one she can do all things, and while remaining in herself, she renews all things.... (Wisdom 7:27a)*

Here are more correlations to consider:

207

Will what is molded say to the molder "Why have you made me thus?" Has the potter no right over the clay, to make out of the same lump one vessel for beauty and another for menial use? (Romans 9:20-21)
For when a potter kneads the soft earth.... he fashions out of the same clay both the vessels that serve clean uses and those for contrary uses.... but which shall be the use of each of these, the worker in clay decides. (Wisdom 15:7)

For while we are still in this tent, we sigh with anxiety.... (2 Corinthians 5:4a)
.... For a perishable body weighs down the soul, and this earthly tent burdens the thoughtful mind. (Wisdom 9:15b)

But the wisdom from above is first pure, then peaceable, gentle, open to reason, full of mercy and good fruits, without uncertainty or insincerity. (James 3:17)
For in her there is a spirit that is intelligent, holy, unique, manifold, subtle, mobile, clear, unpolluted, distinct, invulnerable, loving the good, keen, irresistible, beneficent, humane, steadfast, sure, free from anxiety, all-powerful, overseeing all, and penetrating through all spirits that are intelligent and pure and most subtle. (Wisdom 7:22)

The same relationships are found in the book of Sirach:

And I will say to my soul, Soul, you have ample goods laid up for many years; take your ease, eat, drink, and be merry. "Fool! This night your soul is required of you; and the things you have prepared, whose will they be?" So is he who lays up treasure for himself, and is not rich toward God. (Luke 12:19-21)
Do not delay to turn to the Lord, nor postpone it from day to day; for suddenly the wrath of the Lord will go forth, and at the time of the punishment you will perish. Do not depend on dishonest wealth, for it will not

benefit you on the day of calamity. (Sirach 5:7-9)

And in praying do not heap up empty phrases as the Gentiles do; for they think that they will be heard for their many words. (Matthew 6:7)
Do not prattle in the assembly of the elders, nor repeat yourself in your prayer [i.e., adding extra words through repetition]. (Sirach 7:14)

Rejoice with those who rejoice, weep with those who weep. (Romans 12:15)
Do not fail those who weep, but mourn with those who mourn. (Sirach 7:34)

Do not be mismatched with unbelievers. For what partnership have righteousness and iniquity? Or what fellowship has light with darkness? What accord has Christ with Be'lial? Or what has a believer in common with an unbeliever? (2 Corinthians 6:14-15)
.... All living beings associate by species, and a man clings to one like himself. What fellowship has a wolf with a lamb? No more has a sinner with a godly man. What peace is there between a hyena and a dog? (Sirach 13:16-18)

Let no one say when he is tempted, "I am tempted by God"; for God cannot be tempted with evil and he himself tempts no one. (James 1:13)
Do not say, "Because of the Lord I left the right way"; for he will not do what he hates. Do not say "It was he who led me astray"; for he has no need of a sinful man. (Sirach 15:11-12)

For if you forgive men their trespasses, your heavenly Father also will forgive you.... (Matthew 6:14a)
Forgive your neighbor the wrong he has done, and then your sins will be pardoned when you pray. (Sirach 28:2)

I chose to list a multitude of examples to show indisputably that one of two things must be true—either the ancient New Testament authors drew directly from these books, or the above Apocrypha verses were derived through the same source of spiritual inspiration as those found in the Canon. I believe any reasonable Christian would see this as spiritually relevant.

One of the criteria cited to prove that the Holy Spirit guided the Old Testament authors is the appearance in their writings of *prefigures* of Christ. These prefigures so precisely and prophetically echo various aspects of the nature and life of the coming Messiah that it is believed they could only have been received through the Holy Spirit. There are many such prefigures in the Old Testament. Here is one well-known example:

> Yea, dogs are all around me; a company of evildoers encircle me; they have pierced my hands and feet—I can count all my bones—they stare and gloat over me; they divide my garments among them, and for my raiment they cast lots.

These remarkable words from Psalms 22:16-18 are a dramatic prefigure of Christ. When Jesus was crucified, they indeed pierced his hands and feet. In the hanging position of crucifixion, the skin of the chest is stretched over the rib cage, causing the bones to protrude so as to be visible enough to count each rib. At the site of the crucifixion, the crowd encircled him, gloating and shouting insults. The soldiers took his clothing from him, and divided them among themselves by casting lots.

Consider also the following verses:

> Let us lie in wait for the righteous man, because he is inconvenient to us and opposes our actions; he reproaches us for sins against the law, and accuses us of sins against our training. He professes to have knowledge of God, and calls himself a child of the Lord. He became to us a reproof of our thoughts; the very sight of him is a burden to us, because his manner of life is unlike that of others, and his ways are strange. We

are considered by him as something base, and he avoids our ways as unclean; he calls the last end of the righteous happy, and boasts that God is his father. Let us see if his words are true, and let us test what will happen at the end of his life; for if the righteous man is God's son, he will help him, and will deliver him from the hand of his adversaries. Let us test him with insult and torture, that we may find out how gentle he is, and make a trial of his forbearance. Let us condemn him to a shameful death, for, according to what he says, he will be protected.

The above is one of the most detailed and remarkable prefigures to be found in the ancient writings. It is a very accurate portrayal of the attitude of the Jewish religious authorities toward Jesus. They despised him for openly criticizing their ways in public. The priests plotted against him to have him crucified, indeed a shameful death. Jesus referred to God as his father. As he hung on the cross, people challenged him, taunting, "If you are the Son of God, save yourself." There can be little doubt as to whom these passages might be associated with. Its prophetic accuracy makes this among the most powerful prefigures of Christ in the Jewish scriptures.

There is only one problem. These verses are not from the Hebrew Canon, but are from the book of *Wisdom* (Wisdom 2:12-20).

Therefore, those who wish to dismiss this Apocrypha book out of hand are confronted with a dilemma: since the above passage is a true prefigure of Christ, how can it be rejected as not being divinely inspired? And if one were to reject it as not divinely inspired, by what criteria would one then defend the divinity of those other prefigures found in the Hebrew Canon, since it is impossible to distinguish between the two?

And finally, in the simplest of suggestions, why not just read them for yourself? It amazes me how many Christians opposing these books simply recite denominational precept and doctrine without having themselves ever cracked their covers. Have no fear—God will not destroy you for reading them, nor will reading them destroy God. Both Wisdom and Sirach are of great religious significance (as apparently the New Testament authors agreed), and are useful in any effort to better understand the ancient Jewish principles regarding the Divine Order that shaped the creation. Their spiritual content must not be so easily disdained or dismissed, especially for the dubious sake of denominational bigotry.

The above positions outline the manner in which I believe the Bible must be approached if we are to have any chance at culling from these religious texts a dependable set of scientifically relevant principles. By diligently applying this method of interpretation to a reading of the Scriptures, we can peel back the veils of prejudice, preconception and partisanship that have for so long served to obscure the words of the Biblical authors so we can more easily discern the fundamental principles in which those ancient authors actually believed.

6

Science and the Scriptures

Truth Through Inspiration:
The Second Step Toward Unification

*Science without religion is lame; religion
without science is blind.*
                    —Albert Einstein

*The Religion that is afraid of science dis-
honors God and commits suicide.*
                    —Ralph Waldo Emerson

If we're to use the Bible in our search for the underpinnings
of a universe that occasionally acts supernaturally, it must first
be demonstrated that scientifically relevant information can be
gleaned from its pages. Of course, we're not talking about principles behind ancient technologies like building furnaces and
smelting metals. We're looking for evidence of knowledge for
which the technology needed to arrive at such physical wisdom
was not in their possession. Granted, perusing a book written
thousands of years ago for evidence of scientific knowledge is
an odd notion. But the possible rewards are well worth the effort. The evidence of such truth will help validate the Bible as a
viable source for cosmic theorizing, and will hopefully inspire

213

others to delve even deeper into its mysteries.

This data will no doubt draw protests from secular scoffers who resist any validating of Judeo-Christian mysticism. On one side are those who will dismiss the whole affair as lucky guesses or mere coincidence, while those at the other extreme will speak of extraterrestrial intervention. Either position is tenuous. The discovery of more than just a few scientifically significant concepts would propel the evidence beyond the statistical probability of random chance or lucky guesses. The other group has the burden of proving that such technologically advanced aliens existed, that they actually traveled to earth at that time and place, and then actually interacted with the ancient Jews repeatedly over a very long period of time. And even if that were so, they'd still have to explain why the messages these aliens delivered to the Jews were always spiritual in nature. Extraterrestrial evangelists? It's possible, but that's a hard sell.

There is a practical alternative to both these extremes. I believe it to be a valid, established fact that otherwise inaccessible truths can at times be revealed through inspiration. One of the conclusions drawn from the study of paranormal phenomena is that the information pertaining to the order and structure of all things is housed in the superphysical matrix of the universe's grand supergeometry. Recall too that transmental phenomena demonstrate the mind's ability to discern this superphysical information. Those who devote their lives to spiritual matters (like the many authors of the Bible) tend to focus their minds on the higher, invisible elements where this cosmic library of information dwells. We would then expect such inspirationally acquired knowledge to contain at least some information that is relevant to physics. There's no need to retreat behind random chance or extraterrestrials.

Of course, scientifically relevant materials are not just going to leap out at us from the pages of an ancient book of historical accounts and spiritual teachings. It often requires a between-the-lines examination for concepts that resonate with modern

214

scientific ideas. This presents us with the kind of interpretive challenges discussed in the previous chapter. If that weren't enough, the ancient languages themselves often pose obstacles. Today our languages are highly complex constructs containing a rich and robust vocabulary covering every category of modern thought. The ancient tongues were basic languages with far fewer words that served well during much simpler times. The Hebrew language of the period had perhaps several thousand words, a number dwarfed by our own voluminous vocabulary augmented by a seemingly limitless collection of highly sophisticated terms. Recall too that very few people had any formal education, which further narrowed their communicative skills. A good example of this can be found in the letters attributed to John, the wording of which is almost child-like in its simplicity (which is also part of its charm and beauty). At the other extreme is Paul, whose writings reveal a profoundly complex and intellectual man. His ability to communicate the intricacies of God that he perceived was hampered by a language lacking suitable words to express complex ideas. There are a number of passages in his letters that covey the sense of him struggling against the limits of the vocabulary in his effort to articulate his thoughts. Keeping these limitations in mind will help us better translate these ancient texts into concepts we can interpret in a modern way.

We must also accommodate the ancient worldview by being somewhat forgiving of the conceptual limitations under which the authors labored. Even in our own time, astronomers and physicists operated until almost the middle of the 20th Century under the mistaken belief that the Milky Way galaxy represented the entire universe. Structures that we now recognize as other galaxies were understood to be concentrated groups of stars within our own Milky Way. Because they were conceptually hampered by a single galaxy as the whole of creation, they would err in determining the actual locations of particular celestial objects, and sometimes drew flawed conclusions from their observations. This does not mean, however, that their observations were themselves inaccurate or that their reasoning abilities were less acute. In fact, these early observations laid the groundwork for what we know today, and their conclusions are quite understandable when viewed through our contemporary perspective.

The same can be said of the physical laws of Isaac Newton, which worked quite well within the confines of the reality visible to him, but failed when faced with the subatomic world he was unable to observe and so knew almost nothing about. Similarly, a person of two thousand years ago would not have been aware of the existence of things like microbes, or that there was anything beyond the heavenly firmament except the abode of God. Such an ancient person might disregard or grossly misidentify elements of a superphysical vision that did not fit into his known world. It wasn't that long ago when American Indians identified the first locomotive they encountered as an "iron horse," or when remote Asian tribes, upon seeing their first airplane, brought hay to feed it. That doesn't mean there was no underlying truth in it, for the airplane indeed consumed hydrocarbons originally derived from plant matter.

Hundreds of years from now, those who may read our own 21st century writings will have to make the same kinds of intellectual allowances if they sincerely wish to hear what we had to say. The Biblical text must likewise be studied with interpretive eyes, not with arrogant ones. We too will appear quite primitive and backward a thousand years from now.

Cosmology

Most everyone is familiar with the account of creation in the first chapter of Genesis. Secular scholars typically view this story as little more than Hebrew mythology. Perhaps it should not be so easily dismissed. If we re-examine this account while applying the interpretive considerations previously mentioned, we find many details remarkably similar to modern cosmology and biology.

> In the beginning, God created the heavens and the earth. (Genesis 1:1)

When you think about it, this simple statement says quite a lot. First, it indicates a true creation, that is, something arising from nothing. This is not unlike our own Big Bang theory where the universe emerged from a singularity described as infinitely small and infinitely dense. Although this sounds like it came from something, nothing we know of can be quantified as infinite. Therefore, "infinitely dense" and "infinitely small" is just another way of saying we have no idea what this nucleus comprised, or what produced the Big Bang. Being infinite, it was certainly not any "thing" in the conventional sense. Even our modern view of the universe is that of an expanding bubble beyond which is no "thing." So both the Bible and science agree that the universe was created from an infinite *no*-thing.

Another significant point is that the Genesis account differs significantly from many other ancient creation myths around the world. The universe did not come from the mouth of some primordial monster, nor was it the offspring of the mating between two deified beings, nor from the severed head of some prehistoric hero, and so on. It's instead depicted as a true creation in the modern sense of the word.

Also of interest is the use of the term "heavens" in the plural. The modern mindset reads this as meaning all that is skyward above the earth. But the ancient Biblical worldview beheld a multiple number of heavens when looking up. To them, the "universe" was a relatively small sphere with a hard outer shell or "firmament" having the earth at its center. The firmament itself was filled with tiny holes through which divine light shown through to form the stars. The firmament was suspended amid the heavens, which were divided into lower

217

and higher levels. The lower heavens contained the air, clouds, rain, snow, and all other meteorological elements. Above that were the higher heavens wherein dwelt the sun, moon, and planets. There were also a number of subdivisions within these main levels (the apocryphal books associated with the patriarch Enoch list either eight or ten levels of heavens depending on the translation). Beyond the firmament lay the highest heaven, which was the abode of God. We too divide the "heavens" into separate, spherical levels based on their composition like the atmosphere, stratosphere, ionosphere, solar system, and outer space. So this too is in a sense a very modern way of perceiving the layout of the heavens.

Finally, the phrase "In the beginning" is a temporal designation, indicating that time itself began with the creation of the universe. This again is a concept not common to other ancient creation stories, but is completely consistent with modern cosmology.

> The earth was without form and void, and darkness was upon the face of the deep.... (Genesis 1:2*a*)

If you were a person in ancient times, say 3000 years ago, with a very limited vocabulary, with little or no formal education, and having a conceptual repertoire completely devoid of anything remotely scientific or modern, how would you describe a vision of the primordial, nebulous, fluidic soup formed from the Big Bang? Give it a try for just a moment and you'll see what I mean. This passage can be viewed as a primitive but accurate metaphor for what the very early universe was like. The Big Bang had expanded into an immense broth of primordial matter and energy, but had yet to organize itself into stars and planets. The earth was indeed formless. The stars too had not yet formed to begin the process of stellar fusion that produces visible light, so that all was in darkness. And finally, "the deep" is a suitable ancient visualization for the cosmic background of

218

the vast, deep blackness of outer space against which the early formation of the galaxies took place.

> ...And the Spirit of God was moving over the face of the waters. (Genesis1:2*b*)

First, I think the traditional interpretation of "waters" as meaning the oceans is erroneous. Remember that the author just stated the earth was void and formless. He couldn't possibly be telling us now that oceans of water were "floating" on a bed of formless matter. For that reason, I believe he offered these mysterious, levitated waters as another metaphor for the primordial cosmic soup of the Big Bang. A great ocean would be a thing familiar to both he and his readers and that resembled his vision in both its appearance and in its fluidic movement. If you imagine how this expanding and fluxing dense cloud may have looked to an observer, and further imagine how the observer might interpret the movements within this cloud as being guided by the spiritual hand of his Creator, then the above quote is truly remarkable. Even we ourselves refer to it as a liquid "soup" rather than a nebulous cloud, so why would we assume others might not use a similar metaphor? Here we have the formless "waters" of the primordial cloud being moved by the Spirit of God against the backdrop of the "face of the deep," or in other words, the dark abyss of empty space.

> And God said, "Let there be light," and there was light. (Genesis 1:3)

Very early on, the primordial cosmic cloud began to segregate into areas of greater and lesser density (a mysterious event for which we still do not have a fully suitable explanation). The areas of greater density eventually began to coalesce into galaxies, and the areas of greater density within these began to condense into stars. When gravity compressed the cores of the stars sufficiently for nuclear fusion to commence, they began to

219

burn and emit light. This light would be the first prominent phenomenon visible to the unaided eye of an ancient observer. Therefore, from the author's perspective, light was indeed the first pronounced manifestation amid the "dark and formless void" of the early universe. He correctly places the formation of the stars—one of which is our own sun—before the formation of the earth.

> And God made the firmament and separated the waters which were under the firmament from the waters which were above the firmament.... And God said, "let the waters under the heavens be gathered together into one place and let the dry land appear. (Genesis 1:7-9)

A bit of interpretation is required here. First, God makes the firmament—the shell-like sphere surrounding the earth—that separates the "inner space" elements of the earth and its atmosphere from the "outer space" of the heavenly bodies. Again, I maintain that the author is not speaking of actual liquid water, since up until this point in the narrative, the earth is still formless, and so could not sustain a physical ocean. So what we have here are the "waters" (i.e., the primordial particle cloud) above the firmament that will gather to form the stars and planets, and the "waters" below the firmament that will coalesce into the earth. The particles below the firmament then gather together "in one place" and the dry land of the earth takes shape. If we concede that the old idea of a firmament was so ingrained in the ancient worldview that its inclusion would be almost compulsory to any description of the heavens, the picture drawn by Genesis is very much like that of modern science.

My assertion that the author is not referring to literal water in the Genesis account will no doubt meet with some skepticism. I ask the reader to once again consider all my premises— that the grand supergeometry of the cosmos contains within its matrix all the information about the origins of the physical universe; that the human mind on occasion has the ability to tap into this storehouse of information and retrieve comprehensible knowledge; that the author's interpretation of the vision he received from the supergeometric record would be limited by the cultural and conceptual confines of his day; that he could not have meant that a real ocean was resting on a formless void; that he was forced to express his vision using an archaic language; and that he wrote for a largely uneducated audience over three millennia ago. Given this scenario, would you or I describe the process of the Big Bang much differently? Think of the challenge in conveying the conceptual specifics of cosmology to an uneducated audience today, even though we are all surrounded by technology. What must it have been like in the primitive world of 3000 years ago?

Just one more critical point. The skeptic would charge that the Biblical creation account comprises merely a single possible scientifically relevant detail, and so would be in the statistical realm of chance, and therefore just a lucky guess. I went back and counted at least *seven* such "lucky guesses" in the Genesis account—that's way over the statistical odds.

Evolution

OK, so most people would think that the use of Biblical text to illustrate evolution is like using Marx's *Communist Manifesto* as a model for capitalism. However, you already know that I don't fully subscribe to either evolution or creationism in their current forms. The point here is to demonstrate that scientifically relevant information can sometimes be obtained though what is known as spiritual inspiration. Evolution is a reasonable theory based on observation, the fossil record, geological evidence and logical deduction. On the other hand, the Biblical creation account is based on spiritual inspiration. If both tell a similar tale, then that shows a correlation far beyond statistical

221

probability, and further evidence to support the argument that scientifically significant material derived from inspiration alone can be found within the Scriptures.

After describing the creation of the heavens, Genesis turns its attention to living things. The appearance of various forms of life follows the same basic sequence as that proposed by evolutionary theory.

> And God said, "Let the earth put forth vegetation...."
> (Genesis 1:11a)

Remember that the ancients had no direct knowledge of microscopic creatures. The only life forms with which they were familiar were those visible with the naked eye. According to evolutionary theory, the first macroscopic life forms to appear on earth were indeed plants.

> And God said, "Let the waters bring forth swarms of
> living creatures...." (Genesis 1:20a)

Evolution agrees that animals appeared after the plants, and in the sea before on land.

> And God said, "Let the earth bring forth living crea-
> tures according to their kinds...." (Genesis 1:24a)

This is also consistent with the sequence of events according to evolutionary theory, which maintains that land animals appeared later and actually evolved from the species in the oceans.

> Then God said, "Let us make man in our image, after
> our likeness...." (Genesis 1:26a)

The presence of human beings has changed the face of the earth more profoundly than any other evolutionary event save that of the formation of the first life itself. It is difficult to argue with the idea that humanity is the latest significant contribution to the process of the evolution of life.

The only discrepancy in the Biblical sequence when compared to evolutionary theory is in Genesis 1:20, which places the appearance of the birds before the advent of land animals. Yet that's still four out of five or 80%, a number beyond statistical chance. This one exception can't void the otherwise remarkable correlation of this very ancient document with both modern cosmology and evolutionary theory. We need to also take into consideration once again that such a scientifically accurate portrayal of the sequence in which various life forms appeared on earth is not typical of creation accounts from other religions and cultures.

Biology

The parallels between science and scripture continue into the field of biology:

> Then the Lord God formed man of dust from the ground.... (Genesis 2:7a)

Today it is common knowledge that our bodies are made of the same elements and minerals as those found in the earth.

> So the Lord God caused a deep sleep to fall upon the man, and while he slept took one of his ribs and closed up its place with flesh: and the rib which the Lord God had taken from the man he made into a woman, and brought her to him. (Genesis 2:21-22)

This fascinating account of the creation of the first woman Eve is one of the most unusual among the passages of Genesis. If such an account were found in a book written in modern times and with modern language, there would be little doubt that the text describes a surgical procedure complete with anesthesia, the apparent purpose for which was to extract genetic material suitable for cloning.

Organisms produced by cloning are exact duplicates of the original from which the genetic information was taken. When God presented the woman to the man, his first observation was that she was "bone of my bones, and flesh of my flesh" (Genesis 2:23). Similar words would likely come from the lips of any ancient man confronted with a woman identical to him in every aspect except for gender.

Some Christians will undoubtedly raise an eyebrow at such an unholy interpretation of these passages. There is also fuel here for the "extraterrestrial intervention" proponents with Von Däniken's ancient astronauts and other irreverent speculations. But before being myself accused of any radical heresy, I am *not* proposing that God actually cloned the first woman in a test tube. An omnipotent Creator would have no need to resort to such primitive manipulation. But if we assume as Einstein did that God created an orderly universe complete with a fixed set of physical principles, then it is natural to conclude that the account of Eve's creation would be consistent at least in principle with that order. Never mind that God had no need as we would for a physical laboratory complete with test tubes and incubator in order to perform such an act. The point is that the process of cloning is entirely consistent with the way in which the universe is put together, and therefore is described in the Bible in a scientifically understandable manner.

Physical law emerges from the matrix of supergeometry. Any inspirational picture derived from its pattern would therefore be a reflection of those physical laws, even though it might be expressed in primitive wording and imagery instead of equations, formula and processes.

There is an interesting footnote to this Biblical account of Eve's creation from Adam's rib. Most cell types like those from the blood, skin, hair, and muscle are inferior candidates for cloning because they are too specialized to provide the broad, non-specific genetic code necessary to replicate an entire animal. The ideal donor cells are the least specialized, like those from the stomach lining and from the *marrow of the bone*.

Medicine

The book of Leviticus prescribes the rituals for maintaining spiritual and bodily purity. Some of these display knowledge of sanitation thousands of years before the true nature of disease and its transmission were discovered. One could argue that these could simply be the result of wisdom acquired through hundreds of years of observation. But certain instructions seem to exhibit an awareness of the way in which diseases could be transmitted that is difficult to attribute to primitive observation alone. For instance, Leviticus describes the procedures to be followed after coming into contact with a dead animal carcass:

.... Whoever touches their carcass shall be unclean until evening, and he who carries their carcass shall wash his clothes and be unclean until evening; they are unclean to you. (Leviticus 11:27b-28)

And if any animal of which you may eat dies [of itself], he who touches its carcass shall be unclean until the evening, and he who eats of its carcass shall wash his clothes and be unclean.... he also who carries the carcass shall wash his clothes and be unclean until the evening. (Leviticus 11:39-40)

The concept of thoroughly washing to prevent the spread of microbial infection was unknown in the ancient world. Even our own modern medicine did not make the connection between unwashed hands and infections resulting from surgeries until the late 19th century. Also of note is the distinction made between animals that were slaughtered and those that died on their own, the latter being of a greater risk due to having possibly succumbed from a disease.

The serious health risks associated with the contamination of vessels of porous material used to store and prepare food seems also to have been recognized:

> And if any of them [i.e., a dead animal] fall into any earthen vessel, all that is in it shall be unclean, and you shall break it.... everything upon which any part of their carcass falls shall be unclean; whether oven or stove, it shall be broken in pieces; they are unclean, and shall be unclean to you. (Leviticus 11:33, 35)

Modern heath regulations describe the moisture content in foods as the *water activity level*. Dried foods may be stored almost indefinitely, but any food having a water activity level above a certain percentage point is considered to be a potentially dangerous substance and subject to contamination:

> And if any part of their carcass falls upon any seed for sowing that is to be sown, it is clean; but if water is put on the seed and any part of their carcass falls on it, it is unclean to you. (Leviticus 11:37)

Chapter Thirteen contains detailed instructions on the diagnosis of the disease of leprosy, including the modern practice of quarantine:

> When a man has on the skin of his body a swelling or an eruption or a spot, and it turns into a leprous disease on the skin of his body.... the priest shall examine the diseased spot on the skin of his body; and if the hair in the diseased spot has turned white and the disease appears to be deeper than the skin of his body, it is a leprous disease; when the priest has examined him he shall pronounce him unclean. But if the spot is white in the skin of his body, and appears

no deeper than the skin, and the hair in it has not turned white, the priest shall shut up the diseased person for seven days; and the priest shall examine him on the seventh day, and if in his eyes the disease is checked and the disease has not spread in the skin, then the priest shall shut him up seven days more; and the priest shall examine him again on the seventh day, and if the diseased spot is dim and the disease has not spread in the skin, then the priest shall pronounce him clean; it is only an eruption; and he shall wash his clothes, and be clean. But if the eruption spreads in the skin, after he has shown himself to the priest for his cleansing, he shall appear again before the priest; and the priest shall make an examination, and if the eruption has spread in the skin, then the priest shall pronounce him unclean; it is leprosy. (Leviticus 13:2-8)

Many more examples of similar health precautions can be found in Chapters Thirteen through Fifteen. Chapter Eighteen contains rules for sexual conduct among the people:

None of you shall approach any one near of kin to him to uncover nakedness. (Leviticus 18:6)

Today we know that the joining of close relatives increases the risk of birth defects, but this genetic knowledge was not available to the ancients, and was a very unusual taboo among the other religions and cultures of the time.

In the book of Numbers, rules are established for the purification of articles used in combat:

.... Whoever of you has killed any person, and whoever has touched any slain, purify yourselves and your captives.... You shall purify every garment, every article of skin, all work of goat's hair, and every article of wood.... only the gold, the silver, the iron, the bronze, the tin, and the lead, everything that can stand the

227

fire, you shall pass through the fire, and it shall become clean. Nevertheless, it shall also be purified
with the water of impurity; and whatever cannot
stand the fire, you shall pass through the water. You
shall wash your clothes on the seventh day, and you
shall be clean; and afterward you shall come into the
camp." (Numbers 31:19b-24)

The practice of sterilization has been adopted only in recent
times, and then only after the discovery that microbes (which
are destroyed by sterilization) were responsible for the spread
of many infections and diseases. Again, it is surprising to find
such modern concepts represented in so ancient a document
derived through spiritual inspiration, thousands of years before
the medical validity of these practices were confirmed by the
findings of modern science.

Astronomy

Barring any unforeseen cosmic catastrophe, astronomers
believe that the end of the earth will come as a result of our sun
burning out. The initial stage of this event will be the expansion
of the sun into a type of star known as a red giant. When this
occurs, the sun's expanding surface will come so close to the
earth that it will melt and burn the planet away. Although one
may think that this is strictly a modern idea, such a concept is
neither new nor confined to this century. The event is known in
the Bible as *The Day of the Lord*, the quintessential description
of which is found in 2 Peter:

.... And then the heavens will pass away with a loud
noise, and the elements will be dissolved with fire,
and the earth and the works that are upon it will be
burned up." (2 Peter 3:10b)

Physics

One of the concepts encountered throughout the Bible is the idea that the world of the physical is only temporary, and that all matter and energy is slowly but continually passing into nonexistence. The following passages illustrate this principle of Biblical physics:

> Of old thou didst lay the foundation of the earth, and the heavens are the work of thy hands. They will perish, but thou dost endure.... (Psalms 102:25-26*a*)

> Heaven and earth will pass away.... (Luke 22:33*a*)

> For the form of this world is passing away. (1 Corinthians 7:33)

> .... We look not to the things that are seen, but to the things that are unseen, for the things that are seen are transient, but the things that are unseen are eternal." (2 Corinthians 4:18)

This is the same conclusion mainstream science has arrived at based on a characteristic of the second law of thermodynamics known as *entropy*. The concept can be a bit tricky if you're unfamiliar with it, but it's necessary to understand in order to fully appreciate the significance of this Biblical idea of perishing or decaying matter. Entropy is the term used by physicists when referring to the unavailable energy in a thermodynamic system. For example, if you ever shopped for a refrigerator or an air conditioner, you'll see an efficiency specification like "97% efficient" or something similar. No thermodynamic system is 100% efficient—it always takes more energy input to run the system than what the system puts out. This is also why there can be no such thing as a perpetual motion machine, since more energy has to be continually fed into the mechanism to keep it moving.

In the case of the 97% efficient refrigerator, the process by which 3% of the energy input becomes unavailable in its output is a form of entropy.

We can construct a simple model to illustrate this principle. Figure 6.1 [next page] shows a basic thermodynamic system. Appliance *A* acts as a hotplate, outputting heat to warm the cup of coffee and maintain it at a specific temperature, say 150° F. Appliance *B* collects all the escaping heat energy radiating from the hot coffee cup and converts it to a form of energy (similar to how a solar battery collects light energy and converts it into electricity) for input into *A* so that it can continue to heat the coffee to the proper temperature. Now let's enclose this system in an imaginary container that is 100% insulated to prevent any energy from escaping and any foreign source of energy from getting in. This is known as a closed thermodynamic system.

Let's start the system running so that it heats the coffee to the desired temperature, and then close the container to allow the system to run isolated from any external energy source. Since the first law of thermodynamics states that matter and energy can neither be created nor destroyed, the total amount of energy enclosed in the system will always remain the same. Since no energy escapes, shouldn't our thermodynamic system be able to continue operating perpetually?

Well, not exactly. Remember that no thermodynamic system can run at 100% efficiency. Every time energy is recycled through the system, both appliances have to consume or "burn" a portion to keep running. When burning this energy, a small percentage of it is converted to a form that is unusable and unrecoverable. This unrecoverable portion is then *unavailable* to the appliances for the work of re-heating the coffee.

Let's say our elaborate warmer operates at 97% efficiency, or in other words, it converts only 3% of the available energy into an unusable form each time it runs through a complete cycle, which is actually quite efficient. Its second cycle consumes another 3% of the original volume of energy, leaving only 94%

available for the following cycle. The next run leaves only 91% available, and so on. This is what's known as *increasing* entropy. During this process, the temperature of the coffee begins to drop. Given enough time, a point will be reached where there is no longer sufficient energy of a usable, available state to heat the coffee any higher than the ambient background temperature. The system settles into a permanent state of equilibrium, and all thermodynamic processes effectively cease.

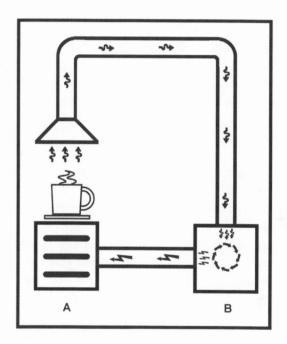

Figure 6.1 — A Closed Thermodynamic System. Appliance A heats a cup of coffee to a given temperature. Appliance B captures the excess energy and recycles it for use by A. The system is completely enclosed, preventing any energy from escaping or entering.

Herein lies the rub. Based on what hard evidence we have, the entire universe is very much like our hi-tech coffee machine in that it is one huge, closed thermodynamic system completely encapsulated within the boundaries of space and time. Although the total amount of available energy contained within it is so astronomical as to be incalculable by human standards, it is not infinite—there's only so much available energy in the universe. As far as science has been able to determine, the universe is a closed system, and so there is no source outside space-time pumping energy in to replenish its supply. And, if the conservation laws of energy hold true (i.e., it can neither be created nor destroyed), no new energy is being created within the boundaries of the universe itself. Nowhere in the universe has there ever been an example of *decreasing* entropy where more energy is produced by a system than it expends. This would be like having a refrigerator that ran at 103% efficiency, which, as far as we know, is a physical impossibility (physicists compare decreasing entropy to the arrow of time running in reverse, so that you would die and live your life before you were born!). Since the law of increasing entropy is universal, every process from the rotation of galaxies to the orbiting of electrons is subject to its degrading effect.

It gets even worse. Einstein demonstrated through his famous equation $E=mc^2$ that matter and energy are simply two different forms of the same thing. We might say that matter is actually a highly condensed and organized form of energy. This means that all the matter in the universe is also undergoing this same entropic decay. Although it may take untold billions of years, there will eventually be insufficient available energy to maintain all the processes in the universe, and the cosmos will slowly grind to a halt. Because molecular processes will also cease, matter itself will lose its cohesion and dissipate. This means that the entire matter/energy content of the universe is very slowly moving toward a state of relative non-existence (astronomers call this slow death the "Big Whimper").

There is yet another aspect to this law of increasing entropy that resonates with the Scriptures. Recall our coffee warmer's decay into a state of equilibrium. Scientists describe this by saying that the heated liquid moves from a *less probable* state (a technical way of saying "less likely") of being hotter than its surroundings to a *more probable* state of being the same temperature as its surroundings. This principle brings to light what scientists have puzzled over for decades, namely, that the very existence of the physical universe is highly improbable.

Since the whole universe is also in a state of increasing entropy, the implication is that all matter and energy is moving from a less probable state of existence to its more probable state of *non*-existence. This means that the transient nature of the physical realm known as the universe was built into it at the time of its creation.

The Judeo-Christian authors were absolutely correct—the world, and all that is in it, is indeed passing away.

Technology

A recent attempt to interpret a portion of the Scriptures in a technological way was made by Josef F. Blumrich, an engineer at NASA. Blumrich holds the NASA Exceptional Service Medal, and has developed several patents on rocket construction. In his book *The Spaceships of Ezekiel*, Blumrich puts forth the theory that the vision of the glory of the Lord in the book of Ezekiel (Ezk 1:1-28) is actually the recounting of a visitation from some sort of spacecraft. He goes as far as computing such things as the size and weight of the craft, fuel capacity, and generated thrust. He concludes that the craft described by Ezekiel employs a technology just slightly ahead of our time.

Of particular interest to Blumrich was Ezekiel's description of the wheels on this strange craft:

> Now as I looked at the living creatures, I saw a wheel upon the earth beside the living creatures, one for each of the four of them. As for the appearance of the

wheels and their construction: their appearance was like the gleaming of a chrysolite [a greenish gemstone]; and the four had the same likeness, their construction being as it were a wheel within a wheel. When they went, they went in any of their four directions without turning as they went. The four wheels had rims and they had spokes; and their rims were full of eyes about. (Ezekiel 1:15-19)

Having worked on landing gear designs for many different terrains, Blumrich was curious about the unusual features of these wheels. A landing gear sporting wheels that moved in any direction "without turning as they went" could be advantageous for maneuvering in certain alien environments. Working with Ezekiel's account, he devised a wheel that would both be true to the general description and practical for an extra-terrestrial vehicle. Instead of having a continuous solid rim, the perimeter of the wheel assembly consists of a series of rotatable cylinders. The mechanisms for driving the cylinders are contained within the wheel's spokes. The entire wheel assembly turns in a normal fashion when the vehicle is moving in forward or reverse. However, when the operator wishes to turn the vehicle, the rotatable cylinders are also engaged. By varying the combination of the forward/reverse movement produced by the rotating wheel assembly and the lateral movement produced by the rotating cylinders, the wheel is able to move the vehicle in any direction without turning left or right. Knobs or studs are added to the surfaces of the cylinders for better traction in a variety of terrains. [Figure 6.2, next page]

Blumrich's wheel satisfies the three major conditions set forth in Ezekiel's account—it can move in any direction without turning, its rim is filled with "eyes" (studs), and its functioning can be described as a "wheel within a wheel." Blumrich applied for and was granted a U.S. patent for his space-age invention—an invention based on a scriptural account written over 2500 years ago.

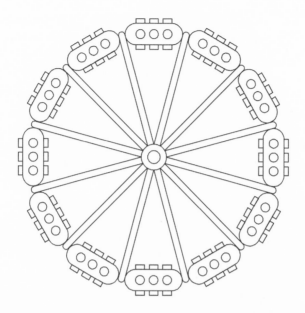

Figure 6.2 — Blumrich's Wheel. Blumrich's wheel design incorporates a series of rotatable studded cylinders around its perimeter. By combining conventional rotation with the movement of the cylinders, the wheel can be made to travel in any direction without having to be turned as in normal steering.

Blumrich's interpretation of Ezekiel is not being offered here as a proof for aircraft in Biblical times. If you set aside the mechanical elements in the text and focus instead on the substance of the messages Ezekiel received in his visions, all were clearly spiritual in nature. It is difficult to imagine some ancient aviator expending that kind of effort just to deliver religious instruction to a nomadic refugee. The purpose here, however, is not to debate the many means through which the prophets received their divine directives, whether in dreams, visions or physical manifestations. It is merely to demonstrate that the goal of finding inspirational messages in the Bible that are also scientifically relevant is indeed a viable one.

St. Augustine and His Relativistic Theory of Time

The first comprehensive thesis on the nature of the universe based upon Biblical principles was put forth by St. Augustine of Hippo. In his *Confessions* (397-401 AD), Augustine derives from the Scriptures a startlingly accurate description of the dimension of time, long before being re-discovered by 20th century science. Take a look at the following excerpt, in which Augustine compares the temporal nature of earthly time with God's eternity:

> So, since it is by your work that all times are made, how can it be said, if there was a time before you made heaven and earth, that you were abstaining from your work? That time itself was of your creation, and no times could pass by before you made those times. If, on the other hand, there was no time before the creation of heaven and earth, the question "What were you doing then?" is meaningless. For when there was no time, there was no "then." (Confessions 11:13)

Rejecting the notion that time existed before the beginning of the universe, Augustine places the commencement of time with the creation itself, an idea consistent with modern physics. Augustine continues:

> What then is time? I know what it is if no one asks me what it is; but if I want to explain it to someone who has asked me, I find that I do not know. Nevertheless, I can confidently assert that I know this: that if nothing passed away there would be no past time, and if nothing were coming there would be no future time, and if nothing were now there would be no present time. (Confessions 11:14)

In the classical physics of Newton prior to Einstein, time was always understood as being a separate, unvarying quantity.

236

However, with the advent of relativistic theory, time is now understood to be an integral and inseparable part of everything physical. The above passage reflects this ultra-modern view, linking the elements of the world with the dimension of time.

In the following passages, Augustine analyzes the first chapter of Genesis, where the formless void was transformed into physical reality (heaven and earth). Here we see an even stronger indication of his conclusion that time is linked to the spatial dimensions. He also puts forth the idea that time itself is a result of the spatial geometry of matter, and that the existence of both time and matter are co-dependent (a concept more advanced than those of Isaac Newton):

> For when there is no shape and no order, there is nothing to come into existence and pass away, and without that condition there are certainly no days nor any vicissitudes in the spaces of time. (Confessions 12:9)

> For where there is no variety of motion, there is no time, and there can be no variety of motion where there is no definition of form. (Confessions 12:11)

> .... Those who have the ability may understand that the matter of things was first made and called "heaven and earth," because heaven and earth were made out of it. But this matter was not made first in time, because the forms [i.e., spatial dimensions] of things give rise to time, but this matter was without form; only when time itself was in existence could it be observed in time. (Confessions 12:29)

Keeping in mind the fourth-century lingual and conceptual confines under which Augustine labored, this ancient but remarkably accurate portrayal of Einstein's relativistic space-time is nothing short of incredible. In light of this, I find it equally incredible that this has not received more publicity than it has. Not only that, but the above passages hint strongly at our own concepts of a pre-physical realm.

Augustine leaps ahead into the modern age of science again by introducing the concept of increasing entropy, and suggests that time itself, being inextricably linked to dimensional matter and space, also suffers from its decaying effect:

> But in what sense can we say that those two times, the past and the future, exist, when the past is no longer and the future is not yet? Yet if the present were always present and did not go by into the past, it would not be time at all, but eternity. If, therefore, the present (if it is to be time at all) only comes into existence because it is in transition toward the past, how can we say that even the present is? For the cause of its being is that it shall cease to be. So, that it appears that we cannot truly say that time exists except in the sense that it is tending toward nonexistence. (Confessions 11:14)

Since the matter/energy content of the universe is slowly passing toward non-existence through increasing entropy, then time itself, being intrinsically linked to the fabric of the physical universe, must also be passing away, and therefore "tending toward non-existence."

Our notion of the relative nature of time is based largely on the theory of relativity. We now know that time is not a fixed cosmic meter. The rate of its passing varies based on the location and velocity of both the observer and the observed, as well as their relative position to one another. The theory of quantum mechanics goes even further by stating that the observer actually becomes an integral part of the measurement of time, so that time passes at different rates depending on the presence or absence of the observer. We view with pride these concepts as the products of our modern science. But throughout Book Eleven of *Confessions*, Augustine makes many statements that indicate he deeply understood the principles of relativistic space-time, but struggled with the limited vocabulary and conceptualizations of his era to properly express it. The following examples are typical:

> How, then, do I measure time itself? Do we measure a
> longer time by means of a shorter time, as, for in-
> stance, we measure a rood [a unit of length varying
> locally from 5.5 to 8 yards] in terms of cubits? In this
> way, certainly, we seem to measure the quantity of
> syllables—the long by the short—and we say that a
> long syllable is double the length of a short. So we
> measure the length of poems by the length of the
> lines, and the length of the lines by the length of the
> feet, and the length of the feet by the length of the
> syllables, and the length of the long syllables by the
> length of the short ones. I do not mean measuring
> poems by pages; that is a spatial and not a temporal
> measurement. I mean the measurement of words as
> they are pronounced and pass away....

> Yet all this still does not give us a fixed measure of
> time. It may happen that a short line, if recited
> slowly, may take up more time than a longer line, if
> spoken hurriedly.... And so it seems to me that time
> can only be a kind of extension.... Could it not be, I
> wonder, an extension of the mind itself? What is it, I
> beseech you my God, that I measure when I say,
> either in an indefinite way: "This time is longer than
> that" or with precision: "This is double that?" That I
> am measuring time, I know. But I am not measuring
> the future, because it is not yet in existence; I am not
> measuring the present, because the present has no
> extension in space; I am not measuring the past,
> because it no longer exists. What then am I
> measuring? Is it time passing, but not past?

> Let us consider the case of a bodily voice. The voice
> begins to sound, it sounds, it continues to sound, and
> then it stops sounding.... Before it began to sound, it

239

was in the future and could not be measured because it did not yet exist, and now it cannot be measured because it no longer exists. Therefore, it could only be measured while it was actually sounding, because only then was there something in existence which could be measured. But even then it was not static; it was going, and going away into the past.... For while it was in the process of going away it was extended through a certain space of time which made measurement possible; for the present occupies no space.

Augustine's theory of time is truly remarkable in that it is based, not on any experimental measuring device or advanced mathematics, but solely on Scriptural principles and inspiration. I believe the reason why it has never been given the proper attention is that our modern prejudices preclude the pouring over of ancient religious texts in a search for physical principles. What other such precious gems lay waiting to be discovered in these old documents?

The examples in this chapter give evidence that there are indeed scientifically relevant concepts concealed within the pages of the Bible. There is every reason to believe that the inspirations of the human brain—a brain that is configured according to the pattern of physical universal laws—can reach beyond the limitations of current science to discover principles that will help us better understand the nature of the creation.

Having established a reasonable basis for exploring this premise, we can now move forward with the next step in our trifold TOE unification.

7

The Paranormal Bible

A Cornucopia of the Supernatural:
The Third Step Toward Unification

*There is more of man than the scalpel
ever dissected, or even the microscope
has ever beheld; and infinitely more of
the exterior universe than any physical
sense has yet discovered.*
                    —William Denton

We have accomplished much toward establishing the three-fold relationship between science, paranormal phenomena and Biblical principles essential to an all-embracing TOE. The final leg of this triangle is the correlation between the Bible and modern paranormal studies.

Fortunately, the Bible not only acknowledges the super-physical, but also celebrates it. Within its covers lives a world of miraculous events and fantastic imagery spanning virtually every class of supernatural phenomena. Biblical ideas about the nature of the spiritual realm are remarkably similar to modern superphysical concepts.

However, the Biblical way of describing these events is very different than that of a modern secular approach. The historical accounts of paranormal events in the Bible are presented as elements of a greater spiritual teaching. Descriptions of two very similar occurrences can be expressed quite differently depending on the religious lesson being conveyed in that particular passage. It's often necessary to drill down through the layers of the higher spiritual message in order to isolate the core event itself. Each of these events can then be identified and classified according to its distinct characteristics.

Take for example the Biblical teaching of a spirit's ability to influence or even control the behavior of an individual. The way in which the Biblical authors characterized this varies significantly based on whether the influencing spirit came from God or Satan. A person might be deemed as "having a spirit" if under demonic influence, but "moved" or "filled" if influenced by the Holy Spirit of God. But in spite of these diverse depictions, it's also apparent from the text that they understood the underlying physiological process to be the same in both instances. Both good and evil spirits were seen to travel from the invisible to the visible along the very same inner conduit within a human being. This conduit was a fundamental component of human anatomy like hands, heart or lungs. Moreover, this conduit was spiritually neutral, being of itself neither good nor evil. It was only the nature of the spirit traveling down the conduit that gave the resulting event its moral quality. *Do not believe every spirit, but test the spirits to see whether they are of God* (1 John, 4:1) illustrates that one cannot make a spiritual or moral judgment based solely on the human mechanism through which these spirits reached us. Yet religious tradition tends toward oversimplification, lumping all aspects of an event together as good or evil based on the nature of the spirit involved. Our task is to return to the ancient view and isolate the human mechanism from the traversing spirit.

The tendency to moralize supernatural phenomena as good or evil is indeed an interpretative challenge. Similar kinds of spiritual happenings attributed to God were also sometimes

242

manifested through what the Bible calls witchcraft, sorcery, soothsaying, or what we today often group together under the heading of the occult. All such practices were strictly forbidden as demonic. As a result, many Judeo-Christians hold a strong prejudice against anything labeled as paranormal, avoiding any in-depth discussion of the subject as taboo.

I too am very concerned with matters of good and evil. But I also understand—as did the ancient authors—that the question of morality pertains only to the nature and intent of the entity initiating a supernatural event. The paraphysical mechanics underlying these manifestations are themselves morally neutral. Take the account in the book of Exodus when Moses and Aaron confronted Pharaoh (Exodus 7:10-12). Aaron's staff transformed into a serpent, after which Pharaoh's magicians proceeded to turn their staffs into serpents. The moral distinction between the two actions was that the magicians used sorcery with the evil intentions of challenging God, whereas Aaron's staff was transformed by divine power for a righteous purpose. Yet the supernatural processes by which a piece of wood was transmuted into a living creature was identical in both cases, and both good and evil forces made use of it. It was only the nature and intent of the entity performing the act that gave each its moral distinction.

Another account tells of the time when Jesus cursed a fig tree and caused it to die. No one could consider this an evil act because Jesus himself performed it. But a person practicing witchcraft might also cause a fig tree to die, perhaps out of hate for the tree's owner or some other treacherous motive. Most would see that as an act of evil. But in each instance, whether with righteous or evil intentions, the tree is felled with the same supernatural axe.

A murderer may evilly dissolve a poisonous powder in a drink, while a mother might lovingly mix lemonade for her children. But the property of water to act as a solvent—the identical property that is being used by both the good mother and the evil murderer—is in itself neither good nor evil, regardless to whether or not the solution contains strychnine or sugar. And who would suggest that a chemist should be allowed only to investigate "good" chemistry while avoiding the "evil" ones?

I have covered this idea in some detail here to illustrate that the moralizing of paranormal mechanics, no matter how nobly motivated, is not really justified. Once the distinction between the superphysical mechanism versus moral intent is recognized, religious concerns about the morality of *scientific* paranormal research (and by this I certainly don't mean experimenting with occult practices!) can be duly satisfied.

The goal of this work is to identify the events and principles in the Bible that serve to illustrate the hidden processes behind paranormal phenomena, and to correlate them into our modern classification system and theoretical framework. We must therefore focus exclusively on the *actual phenomena themselves*, leaving the question of the initiators' morality to other, more appropriate pulpits.

Spirits of Emotion

A prime example of a Biblical phenomenon illustrating the morally neutral nature of paraphysical mechanics can be found in how the ancients described human emotions. Today we consider emotions to be a state of consciousness. If you are angry, for instance, you are considered to be in an "emotional state" of anger. Yet according to the Bible, emotions have nothing to do with a state of mind, but are instead the result of various spirits that might enter into a person. The person then assumes the mental and emotional characteristics associated with that particular spirit:

> .... For God did not give us a spirit of timidity but a spirit of power and love and self-control. (2 Timothy 1:7*b*)

And I will pour out on the house of David and the inhabitants of Jerusalem a spirit of compassion and sup-
plication.... (Zechariah 12:10a)
I dwell in the high and holy place, and also with him
who is of a contrite and humble spirit. (Isaiah 57:15)

.... The spirit of jealousy comes upon him, and he is
jealous of his wife.... (Numbers 5:14a)

This ancient definition for the nature of emotion is still represented in our language today when we speak of working together in a "spirit" of co-operation or when we say that someone has team spirit.

The reason why this principle is so often overlooked is that
we unconsciously apply our modern mindset to these ancient
texts. The natural inclination is to automatically assume the
modern concept of *emotional state* when we encounter the archaic term *spirit*. But our notion of emotional states is actually
a product of the contemporary discipline of psychology, a practice inconceivable to the Biblical authors, who might have seen
it as a profane human philosophy. Instead, they understood the
human psyche as a sort of living conduit through which the
essences of various spirits projected. According to the Scriptures, these emotional spirits are genuine ethereal forces, each
having its own characteristic essence or personality. Entering a
state of anger, for example, is not merely the result of a change
in mood, but is the consequence of a spirit of anger literally
entering into a person. In a process similar to possession, the
invading spirit influences and even dominates the individual,
who then begins to display that spirit's personality. The passage
*the spirit of jealousy comes upon him, and he is jealous of his
wife* clearly describes the husband's attitude as being caused by
an occupying, jealous entity. This fundamental Biblical principle—one that almost every fellow Christian I've encountered is
largely unaware of—is a perfect example of how easily we can
completely overlook concepts of great significance by trying to

245

interpret the Scriptures through a modern mindset.

It's important to realize this supernatural mechanism was not just limited to emotions. All kinds of human qualities and behavior were influenced and induced spiritually through this same inner channel:

> And Joshua the son of Nun was full of the spirit of wisdom, for Moses had laid his hands upon him.... (Deuteronomy 34:9*a*)

> Now therefore behold, the Lord has put a lying spirit in the mouth of all these your prophets.... (1 Kings 22:23*a*)

> The Lord has mingled within her a spirit of confusion; and they have made Egypt stagger in all her doings.... (Isaiah 19:14*a*)

> For the Lord has poured out upon you a spirit of deep sleep.... (Isaiah 29:10*a*)

> For the spirit of harlotry is within them, and they know not the Lord. (Hosea 5:4)

> .... God gave them a spirit of stupor, eyes that should not see and ears that should not hear.... (Romans 11:8*b*)

The following passages illustrate that the influencing spirit entering through a person's inner pathway can have either a good or evil source. The following first four examples are Godly, while the last four are demonic:

> But the Spirit of the LORD took possession of Gideon; and he sounded the trumpet, and the Abiezrites were called out to follow him. (Judges 6:34)

> .... God did not give us a spirit of timidity but a spirit

246

of power and love and self-control. (2 Timothy 1:6)

The Spirit of the LORD will come mightily upon you, and you shall prophesy with them and be turned into another man. [!] (1 Samuel 10:6)

For you did not receive the spirit of slavery.... but you have received the spirit of sonship. (Romans 8:15)

As we were going to the place of prayer, we were met by a slave girl who had a spirit of divination and brought her owners much gain by soothsaying. (Acts 16:16)

Teacher, I brought my son to you, for he has a dumb spirit; and wherever it seizes him, it dashes him down; and he foams and grinds his teeth and becomes rigid.... (Mark 9:17-18a)

And in the synagogue there was a man who had the spirit of an unclean demon; and he cried out with a loud voice, "Ah! What have you to do with us, Jesus of Nazareth? Have you come to destroy us?" (Luke 4:33-34)

And there was a woman who had had a spirit of infirmity for eighteen years; she was bent over and could not fully straighten herself. (Luke 13:11)

The Bible clearly makes a distinction between the process of receiving a spirit and the nature of that spirit. Demonic entities, emotional and behavioral traits both desirable and undesirable, and even the Holy Spirit of God are all described as entering into a person in a similar manner. The process is in itself neither divine nor occult, since spirits both good and evil enter via the same pathway. It is therefore unreasonable to prejudicially avoid discussing such phenomena as "unholy" simply because the force that is responsible for the event can at times be evil.

Whether that force is divine or diabolical, the mechanics of the phenomenon itself operate according to the same superphysical principles, and according to the way in which the Creation was assembled. The ancient Biblical writers clearly held a similar view.

CORRELATING BIBLICAL PHENOMENA WITH MODERN PARANORMAL CLASSIFICATIONS

As we've been discussing, Biblical labeling of paranormal occurrences can vary based on their moral and spiritual context. Modern paranormal terms tend to be secular and thus far less complex. Telepathy, for example, is a suitable term to describe any event in which a human mind receives information from a remote source by means other than the five physical senses. The Bible, on the other hand, also takes into consideration its religious implications, so that one is denoted a "word of knowledge" when received from the Spirit of God while others can be labeled with such diverse terms as "soothsaying" or "divination" when the source is demonic. Both, however, work through the same human faculty.

Isolating these Biblical phenomena and classifying them under our modern system is the first step toward better understanding them. Having a uniform set of reference terminology is vital to the kind of three-fold relationship being forged in this book. This cannot be accomplished sensibly if we're forced to switch to a completely disparate set of terms each time we shift discussion from one discipline to another.

The first effort at assembling such a system of classification comes from the Bible itself. In 1 Corinthians, the apostle Paul offers a list of phenomena conveyed to the believer through the Holy Spirit, establishing an "official" name for each:

> Now concerning spiritual gifts, brethren, I do not

> want you to be uninformed.... To one is given through
> the Spirit the utterance of wisdom.... to another the
> utterance of knowledge.... to another gifts of heal-
> ing.... to another the working of miracles, to another
> prophesy, to another the ability to distinguish bet-
> ween spirits, to another various kinds of tongues, to
> another the interpretation of tongues. (1 Corinthians
> 12:1-10)

Paul proceeds from here to analyze this list in greater detail,
even assigning to each gift a relative order of magnitude and
spiritual authority.

It's important to remember that these spiritual definitions
are of a profound religious significance, extending far beyond
the limited scope of secular paranormal research. This contrast
between sacred and secular can complicate efforts to establish a
good correlation between the two. But if we stay focused on the
root phenomena, a workable translation into our modern revised classification system is possible:

- *Utterance of wisdom.* The possession of higher learning
  and insight beyond the usual capabilities, experience,
  and educational background of the speaker. This inspiration comes to the individual through the same inner
  pathways that play a role in transmentation. In modern
  terms, we might say that the recipient is in transmental
  communion with the Divine Word through the Holy
  Spirit of God.
- *Utterance of knowledge.* Similar to the above, except
  that the information received contains factual details
  about specific people, places, and things that would be
  otherwise unknowable to the speaker. The information
  comes through the same human faculty as other transmental phenomena.
- *Gifts of healing.* The elimination of sickness, injury or
  deformity by supernatural means. All these fall under

the category of transmutation.

- *Working of miracles.* This is a very broad category that could include almost anything supernatural having a positive effect. Depending on the event, a miracle can be a translocation, transmigration, or transmutation.
- *Prophesy.* Virtually identical to precognition, except that the prophet receives the foreknowledge of future events directly from God for a divine purpose.
- *Distinguishing of spirits.* The ability to see and categorize the nature of various spirits (for instance, whether they might be good or evil), and to discern whether an individual is under the influence of such spirits. The term has no exact secular equivalent. While it might be tempting to equate this talent with that of a modern psychic or spirit medium, a "distinguisher of spirits" as mentioned by Paul does not become one with an occult entity, nor does he or she allow such a malevolent spirit to enter into them so that it might speak. Instead, the distinguisher possesses an acute, God-given perceptiveness to the Holy Spirit of God, who then reveals these things from outside the physical realm. This spiritual gift can then be classified as a distinct and very high form of transmentation.
- *Speaking in tongues.* First mentioned in the Bible in *The Acts of the Apostles,* it is the ability to communicate via a language normally unfamiliar to the individual. The language spoken can either be an established human tongue or one of "heavenly" origin (i.e., a spiritual *uttering*). Again, this term has no secular equivalent. One might say that other languages can also be spoken through a person acting as a spirit medium, but this is too broad a stroke, and implies something other than the specific phenomenon referred to in the text. Since the sudden ability to speak in a strange language cannot possibly be acquired through the normal senses, it must

operate via the same internal mechanism as trans-mentation.

The scriptural references that follow show how these and other supernatural Biblical phenomena can be placed within the framework of modern paranormal classification.

Transmentation

The terms *ESP, psi, telepathy,* and the like are recent additions to our language. The closest ancient equivalents are *vision, revelation,* and *prophesy* on the Godly side, and *divination, witchcraft* and *soothsaying* as being demonic. Once again, keep in mind that our modern terms do not carry with them the broader religious connotation of these Biblical terms.

Telepathy. The communal spirit of the new Christians inspired many to sell their possessions and offer the proceeds to the church for distribution among the needy. At one such offerings ceremony officiated by the Apostle Peter, a certain husband and wife sold their possessions, but held back some of the money for themselves. Peter immediately recognizes the couple's deception with an *utterance of knowledge*:

> But a man named Ananias with his wife Sapphira sold a piece of property, and with his wife's knowledge he kept back some of the proceeds, and brought only a part and laid it at the apostle's feet. But Peter said, "Ananias, why has Satan filled your heart to lie to the Holy Spirit and to keep back part of the proceeds of the land? ....You have not lied to men but to God." When Ananias heard these words, he fell down and died. And great fear came upon all who heard it....
> After an interval of about three hours, his wife came in, not knowing what had happened. And Peter said to her, "Tell me whether you sold the land for so

much." And she said. "Yes, for so much." But Peter said to her, "How is it that you have agreed together to tempt the Spirit of the Lord?".... Immediately she fell down at his feet and died. (Acts 5:1-5:11)

Clairvoyance. Clairvoyance is seen by some today as a natural (though largely undeveloped) mental faculty. The ancients held that ethereal agents both good or evil delivered information to the recipient through this faculty from the spiritual domain. Spiritualists today still adhere to this traditional view, using the title of *medium* to describe a person who acts as an intermediary or conduit between a spiritual messenger and the physical realm.

Those who acted as professional clairvoyants were described as practitioners of divination or soothsaying. The Bible has very few detailed accounts of such professional mediums primarily because Judaic law forbade the practice. Far more common are the accounts of holy visions and revelations, where information is received spiritually through either angelic messengers or divinely induced dream states. However, according to our generic classifications, these are all examples of transmentations. What distinguishes Godly visions and revelations from divination and soothsaying is the spiritual source of that information, the motivation behind seeking the information, how the information is used, and whether or not this talent was practiced as a profession for monetary gain.

The book of 1 Samuel (1 Kings in the Latin Vulgate) contains an account of a professional medium that holds a séance at the request of King Saul. The king had fallen out of God's favor and no longer received answers to his prayers. Saul was about to go into battle and had previously depended on God's oracles to insure victory. He decided to seek advice from the spirit of the deceased prophet Samuel. During the séance a ghost is seen, and a disembodied voice is heard:

Then Saul said to his servants, "Seek out for me a

woman who is a medium, that I may go to her and inquire of her." And his servants said to him, "Behold, there is a medium at Endor." So Saul disguised himself and....came to the woman by night. And he said, "Divine for me by a spirit [a very important detail!], and bring up for me whomever I shall name to you." The woman said to him, "Surely you know what Saul has done, how he has cut off the mediums and the wizards from the land...." Then the woman said, "Whom shall I bring up for you?" He said, 'Bring up Samuel for me.' When the woman saw Samuel, she cried out with a loud voice; and the woman said to Saul, "Why have you deceived me? You are Saul." The king said to her, "Have no fear; what do you see?" And the woman said to Saul, "I see a god coming up out of the earth.... An old man is coming up, and he is wrapped in a robe." Then [the ghost of] Samuel said to Saul, "Why have you disturbed me by bringing me up?" Saul answered, "I am in great distress; for the Philistines are warring against me, and God has turned away from me and answers me no more.... therefore I have summoned you to tell me what I shall do." (1 Samuel 28:7-15)

The book of Acts tells of another professional clairvoyant:

As we were going to the place of prayer, we were met by a slave girl who had a spirit of divination and brought her owners much gain by soothsaying. (Acts 16:16)

Occasionally, hidden knowledge was received in dreams. Genesis recounts an instance when Abraham and Sarah were journeying through a foreign land known for its violence and immorality. Abraham feared he would be murdered by men who might wish to seize his wife, so he presented themselves as brother and sister. A local ruler, desiring Sarah and believing her to be unwed, ordered her to be brought to him:

> But God came to Abimelech [king of Gerar] in a
> dream by night, and said to him, "Behold, you are a
> dead man, because of the woman whom you have
> taken; for she is a man's wife." Now Abimelech had
> not approached her; so he said, "Lord, wilt thou slay
> an innocent people? Did he not himself say to me,
> 'She is my sister'? And she herself said, 'He is my bro-
> ther'. In the integrity of my heart and the innocence
> of my hands I have done this." (Genesis 20:3-5)

The wife of Pilate also had such a dream, and tried to warn
her husband that Jesus was no typical prisoner:

> .... While he [Pilate] was sitting on the judgment seat,
> his wife sent word to him, "Have nothing to do with
> that righteous man, for I have suffered much over
> him today in a dream." (Matthew 27:19b)

An event involving the prophet Elisha and one of his servants is recorded in 2 Kings (4 Kings in the Vulgate). Elisha re-
fuses a monetary reward from a man whom he has just healed
from leprosy. The servant, seeking to take advantage of the
man's gratitude, slips out to ask the cured man for money in
Elisha's name. Upon returning, the servant lies about where he
has been, but Elisha "sees" his actions:

> He went in, and stood before his master, and Elisha
> said to him, "Where have you been, Gehazi?" And he
> said, "Your servant went nowhere." But he said to
> him, "Did I not go with you in spirit when the man
> turned from his chariot to meet you? Was it a time to
> accept money and garments..." (2 Kings 5:25-26a)

Precognition. It is difficult to determine where to begin citing
examples of precognitive phenomena from the Scriptures, as we
encounter them on almost every page. From the warnings pro-

nounced by the prophets concerning the future of the Jewish nation to the strange and powerful prophetic images of the Revelation, prophecy resides at the very heart of Judeo-Christian mysticism.

The most dramatic Biblical prophecies are presented in the form of Divine Edict. However, two examples of "simple" precognition can be found in the Second Book of Kings. In the first, a woman in the town of Shuneum showed unusual kindness to the Prophet Elisha, who repaid her by predicting the birth of a son:

> And he said, "What then is to be done for her?" Gehazi answered, "Well, she has no son and her husband is old." He said, "Call her." And when he had called her, she stood in the doorway. And he said, "At this season, when the time comes round, you shall embrace a son." And she said, "No, my lord, O man of God; do not lie to your maidservant." But the woman conceived, and she bore a son at about that time the following spring, as Elisha had said to her. (2 Kings 4:14-17)

The second tells of a great famine in the land. Benhadad, king of Syria, was angry with God for the famine and sought to behead God's servant Elisha. The king sent a messenger ahead of him to find out if Elisha was at his house. But a message came to Elisha from God alerting him to the king's intentions:

> Elisha was sitting in his house, and the elders were sitting with him. Now the king had dispatched a man.... but before the messenger arrived Elisha said to the elders, "Do you see how he has sent to take off my head? Look, when the messenger comes, shut the door, and hold the door fast against him. Is it not the sound of his master's feet behind him?" (2 Kings 6:32)

Translocation

The most spectacular translocation in history has to be the parting of the Red Sea in Exodus. Yet there are sufficient reports of translocations on a smaller scale to establish a correlation with our modern classifications.

Telekinesis. In the following passage, the prophet Elisha causes a submerged iron axe head to rise and float on the water:

> .... as one was felling a log, his axe head fell into the water; and he cried out, "Alas, my master! It was borrowed." Then the man of God said, "Where did it fall?" When he showed him the place, he cut off a stick, and threw it in there, and made the iron float. And he said, "Take it up." (2 Kings 6:4-7)

Levitation. One of the most famous Biblical accounts is when Jesus was levitated on the surface of the water:

> Immediately he made his disciples get into the boat and go before him to the other side.... when evening came, the boat was out on the sea, and he was alone on the land. And he saw that they were making headway painfully, for the wind was against them. And about the fourth watch of the night he came to them, walking on the sea. He meant to pass by them, but when they saw him walking on the sea they thought it was a ghost, and cried out; for they all saw him, and were terrified. (Mark 6:45-51)

Poltergeists. Examples of poltergeist activity also make appearances in the Bible. The most common ones recorded are apparitions or ghosts. The idea of a ghost as a disembodied, visible spirit able to move unhindered by physical forces and barriers has changed little since ancient times. The ghost of Samuel in the séance mentioned earlier is a prime example.

When the disciples saw Jesus walking on water, they were terrified, believing they had seen a ghost. Matthew's account of this occurrence is the most dramatic of all the gospels:

> But when the disciples saw him walking on the sea, they were terrified, saying, "It's a ghost!" (Matthew 14:26)

Jesus was again greeted with a similar reaction when he suddenly appeared in the midst of his disciples after his death:

> And as they were saying this, Jesus himself stood [i.e., suddenly appeared] among them. But they were startled and frightened, and supposed that they saw a spirit. (Luke 24:36-37)

Audible translocational phenomena are also reported, such as the 'ghost battle' heard by the Syrian army in the Second Book of Kings (the battlefield at Gettysburg is a modern hotspot for such reports):

> So they arose at twilight to go to the camp of the Syrians; but when they came to the edge of the camp of the Syrians, behold, there was no one there. For the Lord had made the army of the Syrians hear the sound of chariots, and of horses, the sound of a great army, so that they said to one another, "Behold, the king of Israel has hired against us the kings of the Hittites and the kings of Egypt to come upon us." So they fled away in the twilight and forsook their tents, their horses, and their asses, leaving the camp as it was, and fled for their lives. (2 Kings 7:5-7)

Transmutation

Physical healings are the most common form of transmutational phenomena mentioned in the Scriptures. A classic example is the cure of the man with a withered hand:

> Again he entered the synagogue, and a man was there
> who had a withered hand.... and he said to the man,
> "Stretch out your hand." He stretched it out, and his
> hand was restored. (Mark 3:1-5)

Here is another healing involving a visible transmutation:

> Now Peter and John were going up to the temple....
> And a man lame from birth was being carried, whom
> they laid daily at the gate of the temple.... to ask for
> alms of those who entered the temple.... But Peter
> said, "I have no silver and gold, but I give you what I
> have; in the name of Jesus Christ of Nazareth, walk."
> And he took him by the right hand and raised him up;
> and immediately his feet and ankles were made
> strong.... And all the people saw him walking and
> praising God, and recognized him as the one who sat
> for alms.... (Acts 3:1-10a)

Water seems to have been a popular candidate for transmutation. At a party, Jesus changes water into wine:

> On the third day there was a marriage at Cana in
> Galilee, and the mother of Jesus was there; Jesus was
> also invited to the marriage, with his disciples. When
> the wine gave out, the mother of Jesus said to him,
> "They have no wine.".... Now six stone jars were
> standing there.... each holding twenty or thirty
> gallons. Jesus said to them, "Fill the jars with water."
> And they filled them up to the brim. He said to them,
> "Now draw some out, and take it to the steward of the
> feast.".... the steward of the feast tasted the water now
> become wine, and did not know where it came
> from.... (John 2:1-9a)

Moses turns the waters of the Nile to blood:

Moses and Aaron did as the Lord commanded; in the sight of Pharaoh and in sight of his servants, he lifted up the rod and struck the water that was in the Nile, and all the water that was in the Nile turned to blood. (Exodus 7:20)

Elisha cleanses a polluted spring:

> Now the men of the city said to Elisha, "Behold, the situation of this city is pleasant.... but the water is bad, and the land unfruitful." He said. "Bring me a new bowl, and put salt in it." So they brought it to him. Then he went to the spring of water and threw salt in it, and said, "Thus says the Lord, I have made this water wholesome; henceforth neither death nor miscarriage shall come to it." So the water has been wholesome to this day, according to the word which Elisha spoke. (2 Kings 2:19-22)

Transmigration

Transmigration is yet another class of miracle that frequents the pages of Scripture. Lamps that never run out of oil, apostles who pop in and out of the physical plane, and food that replicates itself are all examples of Biblical transmigrations.

Dematerialization. After his death and resurrection, Jesus appeared to his disciples on several occasions. In one instance, he joined two of them as they were walking. His outward appearance differed from what they were accustomed to, for they did not recognize him at first. As soon as they realized who he was, Jesus instantly dematerialized:

> So they drew near to the village to which they were going. He appeared to be going further, but they restrained him, saying, "Stay with us".... When he was at table with them, he took the bread and blessed, and

259

broke it, and gave it to them. And their eyes were
opened and they recognized him; and he vanished
out of their sight. (Luke 24:28-31)

Materialization. Shortly after his resurrection, Jesus materialized within the midst of his disciples, who initially thought he
was a ghost. Jesus had to demonstrate that he was not an ethereal spirit, but was in fact fully materialized:

> .... They were startled and frightened, and supposed
> that they saw a spirit. And he said to them.... "See my
> hands and my feet, that it is I myself; handle me and
> see; for a spirit has not flesh and bones as you see
> that I have." (Luke 24:37-41)

Another form of materialization found in the Scriptures is
known as *multiplication*. The Second Book of Kings records a
typical account of this phenomenon:

> Now the wife of one of the sons of the prophets cried
> to Elisha, "Your servant my husband is dead.... the
> creditor has come to take my two children to be his
> slaves." And Elisha said to her, ".... what have you in
> the house?" And she said, "Your maidservant has no-
> thing in the house, except a jar of oil." Then he said,
> "Go outside, borrow vessels of all your neighbors,
> empty vessels and not too few. Then go in, and shut
> the door upon yourself and your sons, and pour into
> all these vessels; and when one is full, set it aside." So
> she went from him.... and as she poured they brought
> the vessels to her. When the vessels were full, she said
> to her son, "Bring me another vessel." And he said to
> her, "There is not another." Then the oil stopped flow-
> ing. She came and told the man of God, and he said,
> "Go, sell the oil and pay your debts.... (2 Kings 4:1-7)

Teleportation. A classic example of teleportation is recorded
in Acts, when the Apostles miraculously escaped from prison:

But the high priest rose up and all who were with him.... and filled with jealousy, they arrested the apostles and put them in a common prison. But at night an angel of the Lord opened the prison doors and brought them out and said, "Go and stand in the temple and speak to the people...." Now the high priest.... called together the council and all the senate of Israel, and sent to the prison to have them brought out. But when the officers came, they did not find them in the prison, and they returned and reported, "We found the prison securely locked and the sentries standing at the doors, but when we opened it we found no one inside...." And someone came and told them, "The men whom you put in prison are standing in the temple and teaching the people." Then the captain with the officers went and brought them, but without violence, for they were afraid of being stoned by the people. (Acts 5:17-26)

Peter himself was later freed from imprisonment in the same manner:

About that time Herod the king laid violent hands upon some who belonged to the church.... he proceeded to arrest Peter also.... when he had seized him, he put him in prison, and delivered him to four squads of soldiers to guard him.... The very night when Herod was about to bring him out, Peter was sleeping between two soldiers, bound with two chains, and sentries before the door were guarding the prison.... an angel of the Lord appeared, and a light shone in the cell; and he struck Peter on the side and woke him, saying, "Get up quickly." And the chains fell off his hands. And the angel said to him, "Dress yourself and put on your sandals.... Wrap your mantle around you and follow me." And he went out and followed him; he did not know that what was done by the angel was real, but thought he was seeing a vision. When they had passed the first and second guard, they came to the iron gate leading into the city. It opened to them of its own accord, and they went out and passed on through one street; and immediately the angel left him. And Peter came to himself, and said, "Now I am sure that the Lord has sent his angel and rescued me...."Now when the day came, there was no small stir among the soldiers over what had become of Peter. And when Herod had sought for him and could not find him, he examined the sentries and ordered that they should be put to death. (Acts 12:1-19)

Bilocation. The most famous bilocation is that of Jesus feeding over five thousand people with a handful of fish and bread:

When it was evening, the disciples came to him and said, "This is a lonely place, and the day is now over; send the crowds away to go into the villages and buy food for themselves." Jesus said, "They need not go away; you give them something to eat." They said to him, "We have only five loaves here and two fish." And he said, "Bring them here to me." Then he ordered the crowds to sit down on the grass; and taking the five loaves and two fish he looked up to heaven, and blessed, and broke and gave the loaves to the disciples, and the disciples gave them to the crowds. And they took up twelve baskets full of the broken pieces left over. And those who ate were about five thousand men, besides women and children. (Matthew 14:15-21)

This was not an act of producing a multitude of different loaves and fishes—all those people feasted on the *same* loaves and fish. The five loaves and two fish were manifested in thousands of different locations at the same time.

Synchronicity

There are a number of simultaneous events in the Bible that convey a genuine impression of synchronicity. One that readily comes to mind is that of Peter's denial of Jesus. Each time Peter denied knowing him, a cock crowed, the two events being synchronized:

> And as Peter was below in the courtyard, one of the maids of the high priest came; and seeing Peter warming himself, she looked at him, and said, "You also were with the Nazarene, Jesus." But he denied it, saying, "I neither know him nor understand what you mean." And he went out into the gateway, and the cock crowed. And the maid saw him, and began again to say to the bystanders, "This man is one of them." But Peter denied it. And after a little while again the bystanders said to Peter, "Certainly you are one of them, for you are a Galilean." But he began to invoke a curse on himself and to swear, "I do not know this man of whom you speak." And immediately the cock crowed a second time. And Peter remembered how Jesus had said to him, "Before the cock crows twice, you will deny me three times." And he broke down and wept. (Mark 14:66-72)

Several uncommon events occurred synchronously with the death of Jesus. The sky darkened, the curtain in the temple tore, the earth shook, and the dead rose from their graves:

> Now from the sixth hour there was a darkness over all the land until the ninth hour. And about the ninth hour Jesus cried with a loud voice, "Eli, Eli, lama sabachthani?", that is, "My God, my God, why hast though forsaken me?".... And Jesus cried with a loud voice and yielded up his spirit. .... And behold, the curtain of the temple was torn in two, from top to bottom; and the earth shook, and the rocks were split;

the tombs were also opened, and many bodies of the
saints who had fallen asleep were raised, and coming
out of the tombs.... they went into the holy city and
appeared to many. (Matthew 27:45-53)

As we have seen, phenomena in the Scriptures correspond
very closely to paranormal events we encounter today. Because
of this correlation, both the ancient and modern events can be
incorporated together as a single body of data under the modern revised system of classification.

PARAPHYSICAL PRINCIPLES AND THE BIBLE

In addition to accounts of paranormal events, the Bible also
presents spiritual principles associated with the supernatural.
These are very difficult to correlate with modern superphysical
principles because they are religious in nature. They refer to
things like faith, divinity, prayer and morality, but without addressing the underlying physical processes. You might say that
the supernatural principles put forth in the Bible are more
along the lines of "how-to" as opposed to "what-is."

A study of these Biblical accounts, however, reveals an implicit belief in the same kinds of principles expressed by the
four paraphysical principles established in this book. Here they
are again:

- There exists a means by which information can be
  gathered, stored, and transmitted outside of normal
  space-time.
- Matter and energy can be influenced and manipulated
  by some unknown mechanism, the source of which is
  non-physical and which originates outside normal
  space-time.
- Matter and energy can pass in and out of normal space-
  time. During this passage, the original pattern of matter

and energy is maintained.

- There exists a non-physical pattern or matrix on a grand scale. Seemingly unrelated physical things and/or events are in fact related though their alignment and resonance with this non-physical matrix. The existence of this matrix can be recognized by the occurrence of meaningful coincidences.

The key to bridging these principles and those of the Bible is in translating our modern semantics into the ancient. Most significant are the terms *outside space-time*, *non-physical* and *matrix* (or *supergeometry*, as we are now calling it). The ancient equivalents are *Kingdom of Heaven* or *Kingdom of God* (an eternal place residing outside normal space and time), *the invisible* (or the *spiritual*), and *Divine Wisdom* (Judaic) or *Word of God* (Christian). Were we to re-write these four principles in the ancient vernacular, they'd look something like this:

- The order and form of all things is established in and emanates from the eternal, invisible Kingdom of God.
- From His eternal, invisible Kingdom, God directs the workings of the world and all the things in it.
- People and things can pass from the visible world into the invisible and back again. They can even appear spontaneously from the invisible, and can be multiplied so that each additional "copy" is identical to the first.
- All things were made through Divine Wisdom, which is the Word of God. The Word determines the order of all things, and in the Word the shape of all created things are sustained.

I think you'd find that most Christians would uphold the spiritual truth of these four principles. They are virtually identical in substance to our modern terms. The only difference is that our generic, secular concepts have been elevated to their

Behind The Cosmic Veil

Biblical equivalents.

Of all these elements, the Biblical concept of Divine Wisdom stands out as a direct parallel to supergeometry. The basic precepts of supergeometry are:

- Every physical thing in the universe has a corresponding pre-physical pattern or supergeometry, which exists independently of its physical counterpart;
- The form, character, and behavior of all things in the universe is determined by the information contained in these supergeometric patterns;
- A variation in the supergeometric pattern (and thus in the contained information) results in a corresponding change in the state of physical reality.

These supergeometric characteristics are virtually identical to Divine Wisdom or the Word of God, which establishes and maintains the order of everything in the universe. Since supergeometry also bears solid parallels to modern scientific thought, it is the strongest bridge joining the three disciplines.

Divine Wisdom

Professor David Bohm was one of the more influential physical theorists of our time. During a lecture he gave at Berkeley in 1977, Bohm proposed an intriguing idea:

> There is a similarity between thought and matter. All matter, including ourselves, is determined by 'information.' 'Information' is what determines space and time.

It may be surprising to hear such a philosophical statement offered up by a leading physicist. However, the idea that the structure of the universe is dictated by "thought" is not new.

266

Theologians and philosophers have long asserted that some sort of cosmic consciousness is behind all we see. The Bible expresses this in several ways. In the Old Testament, the concept is known as *Divine Wisdom*. Wisdom represents the intellect or "mind" of God. The structure of all things is determined by this divine order [italics added]:

> I learned both what is secret and what is manifest, for wisdom, *the fashioner of all things,* taught me. (Wisdom 7:21-22)

> .... She [Wisdom] pervades and penetrates all things. (Wisdom 7:24*b*)

> .... He poured her out upon all his works. (Sirach 1:9*b*)

> When he [God] established the heavens, I [Wisdom] was there, when he drew a circle on the face of the deep, when he made firm the skies above, when he established the fountains of the deep, when he assigned to the sea its limit, so that the waters might not transgress his command, when he marked out the foundations of the earth, then *I was beside him, like a master workman....* (Proverbs 8:27-30*a*)

The ancients saw in the workings of creation a reflection of the "thought processes" of God that continually shaped and sustained all things:

> For she [Wisdom] is.... a spotless mirror of the working of God. (Wisdom 7:26)

> Though she is but one she can do all things, and....she renews all things.... (Wisdom 7:27a)

> She reaches mightily from one end of the earth to the other, and she orders all things well. (Wisdom 8:1)

> .... What is richer than wisdom who effects all things?
> (Wisdom 8:5b)

Wisdom came into being before the creation. Although the physical universe was fashioned after its pattern, Wisdom existed prior to and independently of the physical:

> The Lord created me [Wisdom] at the beginning of his work; the first of his acts of old. Ages ago I was set up, at the first, before the beginning of the earth. (Proverbs 8:22-23)

> Wisdom was created before all things.... (Sirach 1:4a)

In the New Testament, the Judaic concept of Wisdom evolves into the Christian *Word of God*. When God "spoke" his Word, things came into being according to its pattern:

> By faith we understand that the world was created by the word of God, so that what is seen was made out of things which do not appear. (Hebrews 11:3)

> In the beginning was the Word, and the Word was with God, and the Word was God. All things were made through him.... (John 1:1-3a)

From its very first pages, the Bible expresses the notion that the Word of God gave shape to all things. The book of Genesis states that when the world was first created, it was "without form and void." What ultimately gave it shape and form was God's speaking through the Word, *Let there be light*, *Let there be a firmament*, etc.

According to the Christian faith, Christ is considered to be the human personification of this Word. He is a form of intellectual emanation from God, extending into the physical world and existing in the flesh [italics added]:

And the Word became flesh and dwelt among us....
(John 1:14*a*)

He [Christ/The Word] is the image of the invisible
God, *the first-born of all creation*; for in him all things
were created.... He is before all things, and in him all
things hold together. (Colossians 1:15-17)

The principle of Wisdom/Word/Christ is a remarkable parallel to the concept of supergeometry. God's Wisdom provides
the superphysical patterns or blueprints for everything in the
physical universe while existing independently of it. The patterns of information contained within its matrix determine the
forms, characteristics, and behavior of all things. Variations
within this matrix (brought about by the "thought processes" of
God) produce an equivalent change in physical reality. Our
equivalent term for the all-encompassing nature of Divine Wisdom is *grand* supergeometry.

Even though this work occasionally blurs the traditional
line between spiritual and secular, there is one spiritual aspect
of Divine Wisdom that should not be forgotten. We must recognize that Divine Wisdom represents something alive and
conscious. Even physical theorists (who generally subscribe to
the notion that the universe is the result of random occurrences) find it difficult to escape the fact that there appears to
be an implicit order or grand design behind the physical laws
that govern the universe. Whatever determined these laws
existed before the world of matter and energy came into being.
This pre-existing order implies a *purpose* behind the way in
which the universe was designed, and purpose implies *intent*.
Intent implies *consciousness*, and consciousness implies something *alive*. These qualities should be assigned to the notion of
grand supergeometry—it is not merely a static pattern, but a
dynamic, conscious, and animated implicitness.

David Finkelstein's theory of quantum topology states that
the fundamental building block of the universe is some type of

pre-physical event or process. If supergeometry is indeed conscious, then these events must be the "thought processes" that
occurr within it. This thought produces the "information" spoken of by David Bohm, which determines both the structure of
matter and the geometry of space-time. As he described it, the
explicate order of space, time, matter and energy unfolded from
a deeper, pre-physical *implicate order*.

Bohm presented another fascinating proposition:

> The ultimate perception does not originate in the
> brain or any material structure, although a material
> structure is necessary to manifest it. The subtle mech-
> anism of knowing the truth does not originate in the
> brain.

This is a remarkable statement. It harmonizes with the concepts of both a superphysical realm and a *conscious, thoughtful*
supergeometry. It also echoes both the Biblical principle of
non-physical spirits influencing the human mind and the paranormal phenomenon of transmentation.

By combining in this way the elements of scientific thought,
supergeometry and Biblical Wisdom, we are able for the first
time to finally get a detailed model of how it all works. The
non-physical Divine Wisdom/Word of God contains the master
blueprint or grand supergeometry of every particle and process
in the physical universe. The pattern of this blueprint reflects in
some way what we might call the Mind of God (I believe this is
the concept envisioned by Einstein when he referred to "The
Old One"). Divine Thought produces variations in the grand
supergeometry that result in corresponding changes in physical
reality. Think about the graphic images of brain activity generated by medical scanning devices. The patterns in these images
change and fluctuate according to the type of thought and
mental activity taking place in that Mind. Just as our changing
thoughts produce a variety of images, the diverse processes
within the grand supergeometry produce variations in the pre-

geometric patterns. This is the crucial theoretical element.

The first physical manifestations of supergeometry take the form of the tiniest subatomic particles like quarks. Quarks then combine to form elementary particles, which in turn progress to atoms, compounds, etc., eventually resulting in the whole of the universe. The way in which these particles combine and interact is in part determined by their relative position and hierarchy within the matrix of grand supergeometry with all its subsidiary or secondary supergeometric systems.

There are times when simple supergeometric patterns combine to form broader, more complex patterns. Because of their size and complexity, these begin to reflect certain aspects of the grand supergeometry itself, and therefore take on some of its characteristics—animation, metabolism, purpose and intent, or in other words, *life*. Such highly developed patterns stand as independent entities, and are the complex supergeometries that give rise to more complex life forms.

The concept of grand supergeometry as reflected in the Biblical principle of Divine Wisdom correlates perfectly with our paraphysical principles. It is the common thread that binds together the essential elements of both systems:

- It ties the theories derived from the study of paranormal phenomena to the physical theories derived from anomalous scientific observations;
- It gives greater definition and clarity to the idea of pre-physical patterns and how they might be formed;
- It explains how these patterns can be altered, resulting in a corresponding change to physical reality;
- It suggests a mechanism for the origins of life from inanimate matter.

Finally, it demonstrates that there is indeed strong common ground between science, the paranormal, and the Scriptures. All three have at their very core certain principles that are closely related if not at times identical.

Time to recap: We've established that the human brain is constructed according to the same physical laws that apply to all other structures in the universe. Therefore, the products of the brain/mind must function within those same laws. This forms a sturdy bridge between science and thought. Biblical principles effect the functions of the mind in a positive, powerful way, showing they are in accord with the physical laws governing the brain's construction. This bridges physics and spirituality. We've shown how these Biblical principles at work in the brain relate to paranormal activity and can even amplify the effect—another bridge. We've assigned to the paranormal a sound scientific definition, and then demonstrated how aspects of physics are indeed paranormal—still another. We've shown how the patterns of Scriptural principles at work in the brain produces scientifically valid information. And we've shown how certain modern scientific theories resonate with both Biblical principles and the principles governing the behavior of paranormal events.

No matter how narrow one might argue that this triangle of bridges is, they are sufficiently solid and logically defensible for a reasonable person to travel across them from one discipline to the other while maintaining intellectual integrity and without grossly violating any of them. Moreover, aspects of each can now be approached with a single common set of terminology and principles. We've not had this before. With the establishment of this narrow but firm common ground, it is no longer necessary to see these three great disciplines as fundamentally opposed to one another.

There is yet one more important task to close the circle on our new TOE. A grand cosmological framework must be found in which to place all the ideas and principles that have so far been presented in their proper perspective and order. To accomplish this, we turn once again to the Scriptures.

8

The Cosmology of the Scriptures

The Universe According to the Prophets and Apostles

> *If we believe in only one universe, then the remarkably uniform arrangement of cosmic matter, and the consequent coolness of space, are almost miraculous, a conclusion which strongly resembles the traditional religious concept of a world which was purpose-built by God for subsequent habitation by mankind.*
>
> —Dr. Paul Davies

For nearly two millennia, the story of creation in the book of Genesis served as western civilization's model for how the universe began. Even today, when science has abandoned such traditions in favor of reason and pragmatism, this ancient tale remains a source of spiritual inspiration to millions of people.

However, there is another cosmology described in the Scriptures of greater complexity and depth. It is not in plain sight like the creation account, but is woven within the philosophies and teachings of the Bible. The Biblical authors embraced a mystical view of the universal order that is reflected in their writings. A careful examination of their words reveals this hidden cosmological picture.

Extracting this mystical cosmology from the vast body of Scripture is no small feat. In a previous chapter, I explored the many challenges facing anyone undertaking a novel approach to Biblical interpretation. The challenges here are much more formidable. We are about to examine this ancient work for material having cosmological rather than religious significance. Any method so extraordinary is bound to provoke controversy. Even conventional interpretations of the Bible are hotly contentious—just consider the countless Christian denominations that have adopted opposing theological positions based on the very same documents.

Fortunately, most of what I'll present does not involve any reinterpretations of the Bible, but will just apply its principles in ways perhaps not considered before. It really is not a radical departure from Biblical thought, but rather a rediscovery of the archaic all-in-all principle concealed within. What makes this approach even conceivable is that we now have the advantage of knowledge acquired through our 21st century sciences, which is a far cry from the primitive Aristotelian system that distorted the viewpoint of our predecessors. Armed with this knowledge, a fascinating picture of Biblical cosmology emerges.

Some of the new ideas presented in this chapter have never been described before, at least not in this context. Certain concepts will be so unusual that no terminology for them yet exists. Engineering new words can be a tricky process, but today it's done in the computer industry almost daily, so at least we are more accustomed to it than in years past. I rendered each first use of a new term in bold along with a detailed explanation.

The introduction of so many new terms in such a short span can be a bit unsettling for both reader and writer alike. It surely isn't light reading. But consider the alternatives. Yes, we can choose to return to those ambiguous and outworn clichés traditionally used to describe ideas like what realms might lie beyond space and time. But most of these contribute almost nothing toward understanding the subject. This is certainly not the case here—specific realms are identified, and their respective qualities and functions well defined. Our only other choice is to continue using descriptive phrases to represent these new concepts. But how many times can the phrase "the non-physical realm containing the opposing forces of God and Satan" be repeated before reader and writer together sink into the all-too-familiar earthly realm of deep slumber? To facilitate reasonable discussion, new terminology is essential.

The following is a list of principles that outline the spiritual cosmology of the Scriptures, along with detailed explanations. Virtually all of them will be readily familiar to any Bible-reading Christian. What's new is the understanding that these are not just religious precepts, but are also elements of the ancient, mystical 'physics' of the Bible.

The Principle of Three Fundamental Realms

The first cosmological principle of the Bible is the ancient overview of what represented the whole of creation. To them, "everything created" comprised both the visible *physical* realm and the invisible *spiritual* realm. The physical includes literally "the heavens and the earth" mentioned in the beginning of Genesis. Today, we understand this as meaning the total matter and energy content of the entire universe.

We tend today to interpret *the heavens* as all that is skyward. But the ancient perception of this is far more complex. The *heavens* were subdivided into various layers, hence the use of the plural form of the word. Looking up from the surface of the earth, the first heaven was the layer containing the visible atmosphere and the weather. Each subsequent higher layer underwent a gradual transition from the visible/physical to the invisible/spiritual, culminating in the layer where God resided on His Throne, or in other words, the *highest heaven* (which is the original meaning behind this phrase). This commonly held view is reflected in the writings of Paul when he refers to being taken up to paradise, which he called the *third heaven*.

Looking down through the surface of the earth (according to the ancient perspective), there are additional layers that also graduate from the physical to the spiritual. Although these layers are not specifically defined in the text, the ancient belief in them is expressed through various accounts like the journey of a dead person passing from the visible, physical world to the invisible, spiritual realm of the underworld, or Hell.

Various spirits, angels and demons dwell within these two respective invisible domains and make regular excursions into the physical. The result is a three-tiered creation having the non-physical realms of Heaven above and Hell below, with the physical realm of the universe sandwiched between, all three being physically and spiritually connected. This three-tiered picture of creation is sketched out rather well in the Scriptures, and so there's nothing new here.

The Principle of Spiritual Predominance over the Physical

Next is the idea that the spiritual realm holds a position of prominence over the physical, so that much of what occurs in the physical is dictated by events taking place in the spiritual. The concept of predestination—God predetermining the fate of humanity on earth from the spiritual realm above—arose from this belief. Another derivative is the image of God sitting on His throne in Heaven above while the physical creation rests below Him as His footstool.

The belief that events in the superior spiritual realms determine those in the inferior physical realm is well expressed in Colossians 1:15-17. Paul explains the role of Christ over creation, which He wields from His seat at the right hand of the Father in Heaven above (italics added):

> He is the image of the invisible God, *the first-born of all creation*; for in him all things were created, in heaven and on earth, visible and invisible.... *He is before all things, and in him all things hold together.... that in everything he might be pre-eminent.*

There is another aspect to this principle, however, that we must always keep in mind. To the ancients, the arrangement of spiritual over the physical was more than just a religious metaphor—it was also *literally* true. Remember that the spiritual abode of God was situated *above* the physical firmament of the planets and stars in the lower heavens. The spiritual realm was a real location, so that its superior placement over the lower heavens and earth was as much physical as it was religious and authoritative.

We thus have three fundamental principles concerning the dominance of the non-physical over the physical:

- The invisible spiritual realm is relatively timeless and stable when compared with the temporal and corruptible nature of the visible physical realm;
- The spiritual realm holds an authoritative position over the physical realm, and so actually determines much of what takes place in the physical;
- The superior placement of the spiritual realm over the physical realm is not just symbolic or figurative but is also literal, being bodily situated higher in the order of creation than the physical.

Good and Evil: The Principle of Non-Physical Absolutes

The Bible asserts that there are two cosmic forces at work in the universe, namely good and evil. The source of each is represented in the persons of God and Satan. The pinnacle of each force is concentrated in its source, so that at the core of God is absolute good, while the core of Satan is absolute evil. Both are centered or 'enthroned' in their respective domains of Heaven and Hell. Heaven is situated above us while Hell is below, with the physical earth straddled between. Both forces exert their influence over the entire creation from the invisible spiritual realm into the visible physical realm.

From a faith-based perspective, the conventional personifications of God and Satan are functional concepts for the practice of the faith. But these humanized images don't lend themselves easily to cosmological theorizing. The titles *God* and *Satan* bring with them a rich diversity of spiritual meaning. It is unwieldy, imprecise and perhaps even irreverent to continue using these titles to describe what amounts to just a singular dimension of their respective natures. We need to isolate only that aspect of God and Satan to which the Bible directly attributes the form and function of the universe. I believe writer Charles Fort best expressed this idea when he coined the term *positive absolute*. I see no reason not to benefit from his earlier work, especially since I've not found a better way to articulate it. Therefore, we shall label that aspect of God relating to the creation as the **positive absolute**, and that of Satan as the **negative absolute**. It is applied in the same way physicists use the term *absolute zero* for the lowest possible temperature—the terms *positive absolute* and *negative absolute* both represent the most extreme and pure manifestation of each.

We must keep in mind that for the limited purposes of this book, these terms will be handled as completely secular with no religious or moral connotation, and will be confined to describing the *physics* of creation.

The Principle of Eternal Absolutes

An important aspect of the positive and negative absolutes is that both are understood to be eternal. Everyone knows this is the case with God, but few see Satan this way because of his eventual defeat. That doesn't mean he won't still be around:

> .... And the devil who had deceived them was thrown into the lake of fire and sulphur where the beast and the false prophet were, and they will be tormented day and night for ever and ever. (Revelation 20:10)

Not only is Satan eternal even in defeat, but also the realm to which he is banished. This means that both the positive and negative absolutes exist outside normal time. Were we to express this in scientific terms, we might say that they are both *non*-temporal. Being non-temporal, they are also non-physical, and so exist in a realm outside space-time.

Frequent reference has been made throughout this work to a non-physical realm. Though conveying the proper idea, it says little about what might be there. Now that we have identified specific elements of this realm, it's time to give it a proper title. Because it's non-physical, there is nothing in it, or to be more precise, no-*thing*. It is completely void of anything physically tangible, and contains only pure unalterable absolutes (positive and negative). It is therefore the only realm that is truly *non*-physical. Because of this, words like "area" or "region" convey too strong a sense of physical location. The word *domain* comes nearest to the desired meaning, indicating a range of influence or presence of authority. We should then call this area the **domain of absolutes**.

The Principle of Corruptible, Perishable Matter

The Biblical characterization of the physical world is quite different than that for the non-physical domain of absolutes. According to the ancient authorities, God is perfect, unchanging and incorruptible (James1:17); He is eternal, having no beginning or end (Deuteronomy 33:17); the realm in which He dwells is also eternal (Isaiah 57:15). On the other hand, the physical world is bound to space and time, having both a beginning (Genesis 1:1, Isaiah 42:5) and—according to both scientific theory *and* the Bible—an end (2 Peter 3:7, Revelation 21:1). Everything in the universe is subject to decay and change (1 Corinthians 7:31), or in other words, is corruptible and perishable. All physical substances continually break down and are recombined into other material forms.

279

The Principle of Necessary Evil

The contrast between eternal and temporal raises an intriguing and vitally important question. If such an unchangeable, eternal God were to create a corruptible, changeable and temporal physical universe, where could he actually place it? He certainly could not position it within Himself, because physical matter (being dependent on the presence of dimensional time and space for its existence) could not be formed or sustained in the dimensionless realm that is the abode of God. This view is reflected in 1 Corinthians 15:50, which states that "flesh and blood [i.e., matter] cannot inherit the kingdom of God, nor does the perishable inherit the imperishable."

To create a physical universe subject to space and time, God had to first create a different realm *outside* Himself. That Satan plays an essential role in this other realm is asserted numerous times throughout the Bible. The following passages clearly describe the very close relationship between the adversarial Satan and the world of the physical [italics added]:

> The Lord said to Satan, "Whence have you come?" Satan answered the Lord, "From *going to and fro the earth, and from walking up and down on it*." (Job 1:7)

> And the devil took him up, and showed him all the kingdoms of the world in a moment of time, and said to him, "To you I will give all this authority and their glory; *for it has been delivered to me*, and I give it to whom I will." (Luke 4:5-6)

> *The world* cannot hate you, but it hates me, because I testify that *its works are evil*. (John 7:7)

> .... Now shall *the ruler of this world* be cast out. (John 12:31*b*)

> Now we have received not *the spirit of this world*, but

the spirit which is from God.... (1 Corinthians 2:12a)

.... *The god of this world* has blinded the minds of the unbelievers.... (2 Corinthians 4:4a)

....When we were children [i.e., spiritually immature], we were slaves to the *elemental spirits of the universe.* (Galatians 4:3b)

.... You were dead through the trespasses and the sins in which you once walked, following the course of *this world,* following *the prince of the power of the air....* (Ephesians 2:1b-2a)

And the great dragon was thrown down, that ancient serpent, who is called the Devil and Satan.... was *thrown down to the earth....* (Revelation 12:9a)

The book of Revelation contains a most remarkable passage that not only links Satan with the physical, but also indicates his presence is actually required for the very existence of physical matter. Revelation 20:7-10 tells of the final defeat of Satan by being thrown into an eternal pool of fire. The very next passage tells the fate of the physical world immediately following Satan's permanent removal [italics added]:

Then I saw a great white throne and him who sat upon it; from his presence earth and sky fled away, *and no place was found for them.* (Revelation 20:11)

Without the presence of the adversarial Satan, there is "no place" where corruptible, physical matter can be sustained.

The Principle of Primal Conflict

Why would the presence of a spiritual being like Satan be a

"necessary evil" for the existence of the physical creation? To understand this, we need to consider the perishable quality of matter in greater depth. Recall that both the creational, positive absolute and the opposing, negative absolute are non-physical, and so are completely without spatial or temporal dimension. In contrast, the physical universe is completely bound by the dimensions of geometric space and time. How can something without dimension give rise to a dimensional universe?

To answer this question, we must first take a closer look at what is meant by *dimensions*. Dimensions are essentially expressions of *differences*. For example, the measurement of space between my eyes and the computer monitor I am now looking at is approximately twenty-four inches. Another way of saying this is that the distance in space between the location of my eyes and the monitor screen is a *difference* of two feet. Time too can be expressed in terms of differences. The time between the moment I typed the first word in this paragraph and what I am typing right now is a difference of approximately two minutes. The dimensions of time and space are expressions of these differences—differences between 'here' and 'there' or between 'then' and 'now'.

A fundamental quality of spatial and temporal dimensions is that they can be measured. One might even say that measurability is *proof* of dimensionalism. If there were no differences between locations and events—if all things were in exactly the same place at exactly the same moment—there would be no possibility of measurements. Without measurements, there can be no dimensions. Without dimensions, there can be no space and time.

Here is where our 21st century understanding of physics—specifically, our knowledge of the dimensions of space and time—can be effectively applied to Biblical principles. Both the non-physical absolutes are pure, uniform essences lacking any internal variation. Without any differences or variations, there is nothing to measure. There are no geometric points between which to take measurements, and there is no passage of time by which to measure a sequence between any two events. Being immeasurable, they are by definition non-dimensional.

Yet within this immeasurable, non-dimensional realm of absolutes, there is actually *one* significant difference from which measurable dimensions might arise—it is the very difference between the positive and negative absolutes themselves! As exact and total opposites, the two absolutes are as different from one another as anything could possibly be (the name *Satan* literally means *adversary*).

The Scriptures are filled with accounts of the struggle between these opposing absolutes. One might even say that the Bible is a history of humanity's plight amid the theater of this cosmic conflict. It depicts the physical world as being squarely in the middle of the collision between these two great forces. God is above and Satan is below, while the world lies between, "groaning and travailing" (Romans 8:22) in perpetual flux and turmoil from the effects of the ongoing conflict.

According to this Biblical model, the two opposing absolutes collide against each other in the non-physical, spiritual realm. This clash generates an area of turbulence that I call the **zone of conflict**. The turbulence within this zone would certainly generate the differences necessary for the formation of dimensions (and consequently the physical universe).

Picture the surface of a perfectly calm lake. The flat, smooth surface is like a non-dimensional realm in that there are no geometric structures above or below the featureless surface that can be measured in terms of height, width or depth (i.e., spatial measurements), nor is there any movement that can be timed. Now imagine that two separate streams converge as they flow into the lake. The collision of the two flows disturbs the calm surface of the lake and produces conflicting patterns of waves, the peaks and valleys of which project above and below the plane of the lake's surface. There are now features that can be measured in their height, depth and width. In addition to the measurable peaks and valleys of the swells, there is now also a movement of waves along the surface, the sequence and progression of which can be timed. In short, the waves have *dimensions* that emerge from the colliding flows of the two streams. They have measurable spatial and temporal variations that are lacking in the dimensionless plane of the previously pristine surface of the lake.

This **primal conflict** (as we shall call it) between the positive and negative absolutes produces waves of turbulence in the otherwise dimensionless domain of absolutes. The fluctuations and movements of these waves provide the dimensional differences necessary for the formation of the physical universe.

The notion that conflict and motion are both essential for the existence of the universe is in perfect harmony with current scientific thought. Einstein's relativistic theories proved that there is no such thing in the universe as absolute motionlessness. Everything in the universe is in motion, and this motion is the result of opposing or conflicting forces. Without conflict, there can be no motion. Without motion, there can be no time, no space, no universe.

A TOE that has gained much attention within the scientific community is that of *superstrings*. According to this modern theory, subatomic particles are not really particles at all in a physical sense, but are infinitesimal vibrating strings. All strings are identical, but each is capable of vibrating at many different frequencies. The unique qualities of each kind of particle catalogued by physicists is determined by a different frequency of string vibration. What physicists are actually seeing when they observe a particle is a cross-sectional view of its corresponding vibrating superstring. This cross-section is the only part of the superstring that exists in our dimensional realm of space-time, while the ends of the superstring extends beyond space-time and therefore cannot be directly observed.

Physicists who support this theory assume that *something* must cause these strings to vibrate, but offer no explanation as to what that something might be. In light of our ongoing discussion, it's enticing to think these superstrings could be set in motion by the wave frequencies produced in the primal conflict between the positive and negative absolutes within the pre-physical zone of conflict. It may even be that the vibrating waves of primal conflict are *themselves* the actual superstrings.

The re-discovery of this ancient principle of primal conflict and its relevance to the physical world also provides us with a tremendous spiritual benefit by finally answering the age-old question, "If God is so good, why is there evil, sickness, disease and death in the world?" It finally puts to rest the need for Christians to rely on Hebrew mythology or the dual-deity solution of Gnosticism, neither of which are truly satisfying or are completely consistent with the Scriptures. The simple truth is that in order for God to create a universe that is physical, temporal and dimensional, He *had* to create an adversarial force having an opposite nature to His own so that the differences necessary for the formation of space and time could be established. This ancient principle is the only one that is logical, scripturally consistent in its entirely, and scientifically sensible. Consequently, we must accept all the "necessary evils" of this world as simply the cost of being alive. The spiritual teachings of the Bible are to help save us from having our minds and souls enslaved by *the spirit of this world* that is required for our very existence. God's working these things made it possible to have life. To my mind, this means that even though this world has its tribulations, we should embrace it with gratitude, for the alternative is nonexistence.

The solution to this puzzle frees us from futile debates over the world's evils and elevates our attention to what is truly the fundamental question at hand: *Why* did God choose to create a physical universe? Although I have my own ideas, I think that we humans can never fully know the mind of God. At least the ancient principle of primal conflict enables us to raise the bar of our understanding in these things to a higher level than before.

The Principle of Formless Matter

Genesis 1:2 recounts that when the physical world was first created, its initial state was *without form*. This formlessness was later shaped into the physical forms and structures that make up the universe. This does not mean, however, that this formlessness was a mere nothingness. The ancients understood this to be a real, tangible, pre-material substance from which the creation was fashioned, just as a shapeless lump of clay is molded into figures. Wisdom 11:17 echoes this same notion, reiterating that God *created the world out of formless matter*.

The turbulence resulting from the vibrating waves of primal conflict perfectly fulfills the role of the formless pre-matter of Genesis. Both absolutes have no material form or dimension on their own, yet in collision produce the "substance" from which physical matter is created. We can liken this process to rubbing together the palms of the hands vigorously. The resulting friction produces heat, just as the conflict between positive and negative absolutes produces waves of pre-matter.

It's time once again for new terminology. We speak of "vibrating waves" as the product of primal conflict. Yet this is only a metaphor to help convey the proper idea, since *wave* represents something dimensional. The domain of absolutes has no dimensional environment in which a physical wave might be propagated. The word *substance* is another term having strong physical characteristics. We need instead a word that will define this pre-physical substance while avoiding too many physical connotations.

We can begin by replacing *substance* with *influence*. An influence is something invisible yet still has a significant presence and exerts a tangible effect on its surroundings. Taking this a step further, we can say that the positive and negative absolutes project **positive influence** and **negative influence** respectively. Within the zone of conflict, the positive and negative influences encounter one another in opposition, creating an area of incredible turbulence where these two opposite polarities collide.

Taking this a step further, we can see that this pre-material substance must also be *bi-polar* in that it contains a mixture of both positive and negative influences. We'll call this mixture **diffluence** (dif′ floo • ens), the prefix *di-* representing the twofold, bi-polar nature of this turbulent fluid.

Diffluence is the formless matter mentioned in the Scriptures. Forged in the furnace of primal conflict, diffluence meets the requirements set by both science and religion for a true creation—it is some-*thing* (*pre*-physical) produced out of the void of no-*thing*-ness (*non*-physical).

Now that we have further defined the composition of the superphysical realm outside space-time, we are again in need of additional terms. The realm where the non-physical influences confront one another in primal conflict is responsible for the creation of the physical universe and for establishing and sustaining of all its functions, structures and order. It quite literally gives birth to the universe, and so is in a manner of speaking, is its parent. Combining the Latin prefix *patri* meaning "father" (sorry ladies, but I needed to pick just one gender, and went with tradition) with the suffix "verse" gives us patriverse for this realm above the physical universe.

The next step in defining this superphysical realm is to give a name to the sum total of "all *things* visible and invisible"—the combined realms of both the superphysical patriverse and the physical universe. Welcome to the **omniverse**. The omniverse comprises the entire creation: *pre*-things (patriverse), and *all*-things (universe).

The Principle of Primary Imbalance

The principle of **primary imbalance** is derived from the Scriptural teaching of the relative strengths of God versus Satan. God is depicted as superior to Satan in power, thereby inferring that the positive influence is greater than the negative influence. This would create an initial state of primary imbalance in the superphysical patriverse, resulting in the bi-polar diffluence being more positive than negative.

The evidence for the primary imbalance of diffluence can be seen everywhere in our physical universe. We often think of forces in the universe as being in a state of balance. But like so many other mental conventions, a careful examination reveals that this is not the case. Take for example the orbit of the earth around the sun. The momentum of the earth's orbit would send it hurtling into space were it not for the sun's gravity holding it in place. It is therefore natural to assume that the forces of the earth's momentum and the sun's gravity are in a state of balance so that they cancel each other out. We could express this perfect balance with the equation $[+1] + [-1] = 0$, the positive and negative values completely negating one another. But a sum of zero would result in a static system with no variations in movement or force. In contrast, the solar system is dynamic, full of movement and struggle between opposing forces. It is not truly balanced at all, but is actually in a state of perpetual *imbalance*. If perfect balance were ever achieved, all movement would stop, and the planets would hang motionless in space. In order for physical reality to exist and function, all interactions of forces in the universe must be in a continual state of orderly imbalance.

The principle of primary imbalance offers a possible explanation why the Big Bang produced an orderly universe. Recall that, given the initial conditions immediately following the Big Bang, the formation of a universe with order and structure was an extremely unlikely event. The chaotic movement of the primitive particles and forces should have immediately scrambled and dispersed any newly forming structures. However, primary imbalance implies that from the very beginning, the game was 'rigged' in favor of order. According to Biblical theology, God is not a God of confusion (1 Corinthians 14:33) but a God of order, while Satan is the source of all confusion, disorder and chaos. Since the positive orderly influence is a greater force than the negative chaotic influence, order was able to overcome chaos to some degree, causing the featureless primitive soup of the early universe to spontaneously differentiate into orderly structures throughout the cosmic cloud. These emerging orderly structures ultimately gave birth to the universe's atoms, molecules, stars, and galaxies.

Another aspect of primary imbalance is that it causes the diffluential waves to flow in a certain direction as they travel from the pre-physical toward the physical. This directional flow could not occur if the positive and negative influences were in perfect equilibrium. The primary imbalance principle states that the positive influence dominates the negative influence, forcing the flow of diffluence in a given direction from the pre-physical to the physical, or from patriverse to universe. This directional flow also provides for the existence of time itself and its movement in one direction from past to future.

The Principle of Duality

If all things in the universe are a result of the dual interactions of positive and negative influences, then all things in the universe should in some way exhibit this dual nature. Most philosophies and religions teach the duality of all things—light and darkness, matter and energy, male and female, etc. The Oriental philosophy of *yin-yang* is a prime example, classifying all things as being either yin (sky, fire, sun, male, etc.) or yang (earth, water, moon, female, etc.). Supergeometric theory expresses this a bit more precisely in terms of opposite polarities of conflicting absolutes. The duality of the resulting diffluence is reflected in all physical things.

Physicists can also see another kind of duality in all things based on the research into the dual nature of light. When first discovered, this luminary duality was a baffling paradox, since it

289

was difficult to imagine how a material particle could also manifest itself as a wave, or how a wave could manifest itself as a concrete, physical particle. Yet it was soon discovered that other particles like electrons also behaved like waves. Subsequent experiments revealed this duality was not limited to just subatomic particles—larger atoms and molecules were also shown to have these corresponding *matter waves* as they are called. Physicists have since demonstrated that *all* things in the universe possess this dual nature, having both material-like and wave-like qualities.

This kind of physical duality is perhaps best described by the Chinese name for physics, *Wu Li*. *Wu* represents matter and energy, while *Li* roughly translated means "universal order" or "organic patterns." We can simplify this by saying that Wu Li stands for both *substance* and *form*. For example, a snowflake consists of ice, which is its "Wu" or substance, while its beautiful crystalline shape is its "Li" or form. Applying this concept to an electron or photon, its particle-like state is its form, while its wave-like state is its substance. Relating this to our own emerging model, diffluence is the substance and supergeometry the form. All things in the universe have duality, both in form and substance (supergeometry and diffluence), and in opposing polarity (positive and negative influences). It is a philosophical way to describe physical nature, yet it is an accurate reflection of observable reality.

The Principle of Grand Supergeometry

We covered in a previous chapter the Biblical idea of Wisdom or the Word of God as a divine order which shaped the universe and all that is in it. This Judeo-Christian principle is fundamental to the cosmology of the Bible. It happens to be virtually identical to the paraphysical principle of grand supergeometry, the giant "cookie cutter" of the cosmos, which contains in itself all subsidiary supergeometric systems, as well as all the simple and complex patterns within those systems. By combining this with the idea of a pre-physical substance (diffluence) having a given direction of flow (from the pre-physical toward the physical), and the principle of duality (all things have both form and substance), we can now begin to draw a picture of how these elements might work together to produce a universal creation that was truly something out of nothing. The raw pre-physical diffluence (which is made of the duality of positive and negative influences) provides the substance from which physical things are formed. Supergeometry serves as the pre-physical model or pattern that shapes the "clay" of raw diffluence into recognizable structures having both physical form and sub-stance. [Figure 7.1]

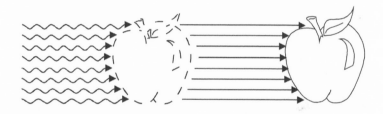

Figure 7.1 — Physical Materialization. The pre-physical waves of diffluence flowing toward the physical plane are shaped during their transit by the pre-physical patterns of supergeometry to produce a physical, dimensional object having both form and substance.

The Principle of Light

Light occupies a unique position within the hierarchy of science. The velocity of light (186,300 miles per second) is the only universal constant. Its speed is always the same relative to all other things in the universe. Nothing can travel faster than it, and therefore light is a sort of barrier residing at the uppermost limit of the physical universe.

Behind The Cosmic Veil

Light holds an identical position of prominence in the Bible. According to Biblical teachings, there are two kinds of light in the world—visible light, and spiritual or inner light. The Scriptures often refer to both types of light as metaphors for the authority and wisdom of God. These metaphors provide clues to the mystical role that light plays in Scriptural cosmology.

The First-Born Light. When God created light, he placed it in the uppermost region of the heavens above all other things. But there is more to light's position of prominence in the Scriptures than just its physical location. Light was also understood to be the first visible, tangible manifestation of the creation. When light was made, all other things were still in a state of invisible, pre-material formlessness. Because of this, light was seen as the "first-born" of creation, a position of prominence and authority in ancient Jewish tradition. The first-born son was first in line to inherit the father's properties and titles. He was also second-in-command of the Jewish family, given broad administrative powers by the father over his family's affairs. In the absence of the father, the first-born *was* the father, and was treated as such by other members of Jewish society. The first-born sat down to table at his father's right hand, and was set above all other family members.

Two examples of light being equated with a first-born son can be found in 1 Kings and in Psalms, where God insures the ascension of David's son Abijam to his father's throne [italics added]:

> Nevertheless, for David's sake the Lord his God gave him a *lamp* in Jerusalem, setting his son up after him.... (1 Kings 15:4a)

> There [in Zion] I will make a horn [i.e., a son] to sprout for David; I have prepared a *lamp* for my anointed. (Psalms 132:17)

The above metaphor of a lamp as the first-born (here, and in many other Scriptural passages) further illustrates that the physical location of light in the heavens is not the reason for its first-born status in the creational order. Even the relatively insignificant light from an oil lamp was also understood to be of the same special substance as that which emanated from the sun, moon, and stars. This means that *all* light, no matter what the source, possessed the same quality and mystical significance as the light from celestial bodies. Light "earned" this position at the top of the creational order by being the first-born of the creation. The conceptual placement of light by the Biblical authors at the uppermost level of the creation regardless to its physical source is identical to the cosmological position assigned to it by science.

Light as a Metaphor for God. Just as visible light illuminates all things in the world, the "light" of Divine Wisdom also illuminates all things to reveal their true nature. Both visible light and inner, spiritual light are very closely related in the Bible. Both are equal signs of the influential presence of God in this world.

The following are a few of the many examples where God and his Wisdom are compared with spiritual or inner light:

> The Lord is my light and my salvation.... (Psalms 27:1a)

> Thy word is a lamp to my feet and a light to my path. (Psalms 119:105)

> For the commandment is a lamp and the teaching a light.... (Proverbs 6:23a)

> For it is God who said "Let light shine out of darkness," who has shone in our hearts to give the light of the knowledge of the glory of God.... (2 Corinthians 4:6a)

The following are several passages where God Himself is equated with physical or visible light:

.... God is light, and in him is no darkness (1 John 1:5*b*)

O Lord my God.... who coverest thyself with light as with a garment.... (Psalms 104:1-2*a*)

.... He [God] knows what is in the darkness, and the light dwells with him. (Daniel 2:22*b*)

Of all the elements in the physical world, nothing resembles the qualities of God more closely than light. Visible light was therefore seen as the tangible, physical equivalent to the invisible Creator.

Light's Proximity to God. Genesis states that God created the heavens and the earth, the word *heavens* indicating a plurality. The Old Testament describes this multiplicity of the heavens as being loosely divided into three levels. The lower or first level is the atmosphere, wherein resides the wind, rain, snow, and all other meteorological phenomena. The second or middle level is the firmament, wherein the sun, moon, and stars are placed. The third and highest level is the *heaven of heavens*, where God resides. The two lower levels are physical, while the highest level is a spiritual realm. In this ancient cosmology, light (in the form of the heavenly bodies) is the highest *physical* element of the creation, and therefore the one substance that is closest in proximity to God. In other words, light is virtually the closest physical element in this world to *being* God—no *physical* creation exists above light.

This ancient Hebrew concept of multiple heavenly layers is presented in much greater detail in the apocryphal book *The Secrets of Enoch* (also known as 2 Enoch). The three main levels of the heavenly realm above the earth is subdivided into numerous strata spanning from the first or lowest stratum of heaven comprising the atmosphere to the throne of God in the highest heaven. Of particular interest is a set of passages in Chapter 25 that not only mirrors the cosmology of the canonical Scriptures, but also contains a fascinating reference to light [italics and brackets added]:

> I [God] commanded in the very lowest parts, that vis-
> ible things should come down from invisible, and
> Adoil came down very great, and I beheld him, and
> lo! he had a belly of great light.... And I said to him:
> "Become undone, Adoil, and let the visible come out
> of thee." .... And he came undone [i.e., like the Big
> Bang], and a great light came out. And I was in the
> midst of the great light, and as there is born light
> from light, there came forth a great age [i.e., the be-
> ginning of time], and showed all creation, which I had
> thought to create.... And [God] said to the light: "Go
> thou up higher and fix thyself high above the throne,
> and be a foundation to the highest things." And *above
> the light there is nothing else....*

Stripped of its religious allusions, this account bears a remarkable parallel to role of light in modern cosmology.

In conclusion, both the Scriptural and scientific definitions of light have positive correlations. The most significant of these is that light exists at the highest level of the universe. All other things in the worldly order are positioned below light. Light defines the border between what is physical and what is super-physical.

PUTTING IT ALL TOGETHER

It is now time to assemble all these principles into a coherent image of Biblical cosmology according to the progression of creation from the non-physical to the pre-physical to the physical. First, let's review:

1. The aspects of God and Satan that contribute to the formation of the physical are called the **positive absolute** and
   the **negative absolute**. Both are non-physical without spatial or temporal dimension. The two are in complete anti-
   thesis to one another. These reside in a **domain of absolutes** that is also completely non-dimensional.

2. Each of the absolutes exert their own unique influence on
   the creation. The positive absolute exerts **positive influence** and the negative absolute **negative influence**. Both
   influences are of opposite "polarity" to one another.

3. Both the positive and negative influences collide and grind
   against one another in a process called **primal conflict**.
   The area in which these two clash and grind is the **zone of
   conflict.** The zone of conflict is more than non-physical,
   but less than physical—it is *pre*-physical or *super*physical.

4. Primal conflict between the two influences produces vibra-
   tions or waves in the otherwise featureless background. The
   frequency and amplitude of these waves are a kind of pre-
   physical "substance" containing the temporal and spatial
   variations from which the physical universe unfolds. Since
   this substance is a mixture of the two oppositely polarized
   influences, it is called **bi-polar diffluence** (or simply **diffluence** for short). It is the "formless matter" referred to in
   the Bible. It is also the invisible, spiritual "force" referred to
   in many other philosophies and religions.

5. Because the positive influence is greater than the negative,
   the diffluence resulting from primal conflict is said to be in
   a state of **primary imbalance**. Primary imbalance serves
   two purposes—it tends to progressively intensify the frequency and amplitude of the **diffluential waves,** and it
   gives those waves a direction of flow from the non-physical

through the superphysical and into the physical. This uni-directional flow also gives rise to the progression of time which science typically represents with an arrow.

6. As the diffluential waves increase in intensity, they begin to slow down, eventually decelerating to the speed of light. Once at the speed of light, the diffluence begins to densify or solidify into physical matter and energy. Light itself is the first physical manifestation of this deceleration, and so it exists at the uppermost edge of the physical creation. As the diffluence further decelerates below the speed of light, the pre-dimensions that are tightly wrapped inside the waves begin to unfold, expanding into the hard temporal and spatial dimensions of our physical universe.

7. The various physical forms that diffluence will eventually assume are determined by the superphysical patterns of **grand supergeometry**, which is the cosmic order known in the Bible as *Wisdom* or the *Word of God*. Supergeometry interacts with diffluence and shapes it according to the laws contained within it into the recognizable structures, characteristics and interactions of all matter and energy, as well as the geometry of space and time.

8. The highest realm in Biblical cosmology is the non-physical **domain of absolutes**. The middle realm is the **patriverse** in which the positive and negative influences clash to yield the diffluence that is shaped by grand supergeometry into the lowest realm of the physical **universe**. The patriverse and the universe are collectively known as the **omniverse**.

Every theory needs a name, and this one is no exception. Since the geometry of universal order lies at the very heart of the creation, I decided to call it the **Theory of Supergeometry**.

COSMOLOGICAL MODELS

We can now begin to construct visual models based on the above principles and interactions. But first, we have to concede that there are certain limitations to what any such model can depict. Supergeometric theory contains many elements that are either pre-dimensional or non-dimensional. It is impossible to construct a truly accurate model of these superphysical elements within the confines of a two-dimensional sheet of paper. No flat or even three-dimensional representation can ever hope to correctly portray something that extends beyond space and time.

The following example illustrates this difficulty. Begin by drawing a single straight line, which according to Euclidean geometry has no width or depth, and so represents a true one-dimensional object. Of course, this model is already undone because any visible line, no matter how finely drawn, will have a width that violates the definition of a Euclidean line. But without width, the line would be invisible, so we'll have to mentally allow for it. Next we'll square this line to itself to produce a square, a two-dimensional object having length and width, but still lacking depth. Next, square the square to itself and you will have drawn a three-dimensional cube having length, width, and depth. If we're drawing this on paper, we've already abandoned any hope for accuracy because we can only render it in a flat perspective view, and have to depend on our imaginative minds to interpret the implied depth.

Now what if we were to leap to the next step by squaring the cube to itself? Mathematicians call this object a *tesseract*, a hypothetical figure projected into four spatial dimensions. Although a tesseract can be expressed in mathematical terms, it is impossible to draw it on paper or to construct a physical model of it. Even with the aid of our imagination, we cannot form an image of such an object in our minds (take a moment to try this for yourself, and you will quickly see how perplexing it is). No matter how we conjure, draw, or sculpt, the resulting image will always be cast as a three-dimensional figure. The fourth spatial dimension of the tesseract cannot be represented or even conceptualized within the confines of our three-dimensional space.

Similarly, supergeometric cosmology is like a multi-faceted, superdimensional jewel of which we can observe only one facet at a time from our limited perspective. The best we can do is to represent each of those facets by its own individual model, each model illustrating in turn a different perspective of this cosmological map. By combining all these various models, a coherent mental image of the structures and processes represented in the different drawings emerges.

We should also keep in mind that these two-dimensional models will only be mere abstractions. None will be adequate to completely represent the actual cosmological processes that take place beyond space-time. It's very similar to the miniature solar system presented to high school students as a model for the atom—it's not truly an accurate representation, but in the most rudimentary way conveys a sufficiently reasonable approximation.

The model of the omniverse begins by drawing the positive and negative absolutes opposite one another and causing them to overlap in the middle, creating the zone of conflict between the two. The overlapping area is known as the patriverse. [Figure 7.2, next page]

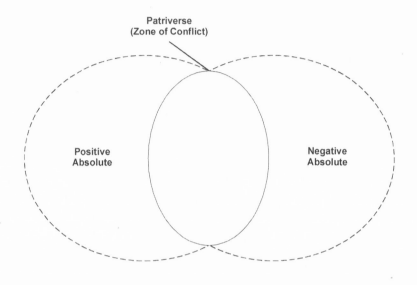

Figure 7.2 — Supergeometric Model #1. The positive and negative absolutes collide, creating a turbulent zone of conflict.

Primal conflict within the patriverse produces turbulent patterns of waves. These pre-material waves are the bi-polar diffluence from which the physical universe will eventually arise. The conflict intensifies as we move closer to the center, and so the diffluential waves become increasingly dense. [Figure 7.3, next page]

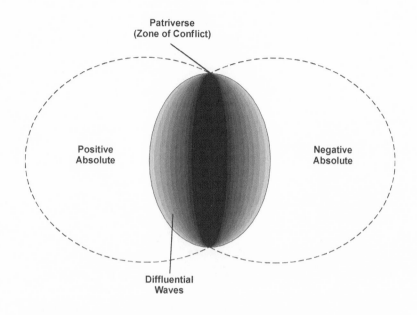

Patriverse
(Zone of Conflict)

Positive
Absolute

Negative
Absolute

Diffluential
Waves

Figure 7.3 — Supergeometric Model #2. The conflict between the two absolutes produces pre-dimensional waves of diffluence, which grow increasingly dense as the conflict intensifies. The conflict is most intense in the center where the clashing is most severe.

The increasing intensity of primal conflict decelerates the superlight diffluential waves down toward the speed of light. As the diffluence crosses the light barrier, it solidifies or "particulates" (becomes particles) into physical matter and energy. The pre-dimensions within the diffluential waves also begin to unfold into the dimensional space-time that will suspend and sustain matter and energy within its matrix. Particulation becomes increasingly intensified and the dimensions of space-time more defined as the velocity falls further and further below the speed of light. [Figure 7.4, next page]

301

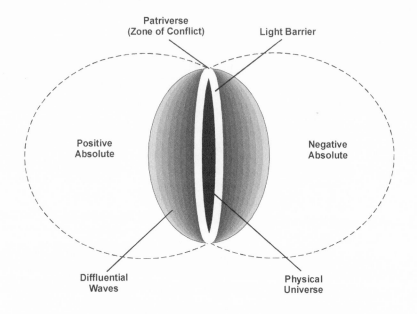

Figure 7.4 — Supergeometric Model #3. The superlight waves of diffluence begin to slow from the progressively stronger effects of primal conflict, solidifying into physical matter, energy, space and time as they drop below the speed of light.

A horizontal cross-sectional view (overhead) of the above model provides a different perspective. Note the bands of increasing density from the non-physical to the physical. [Figure 7.5, next page]

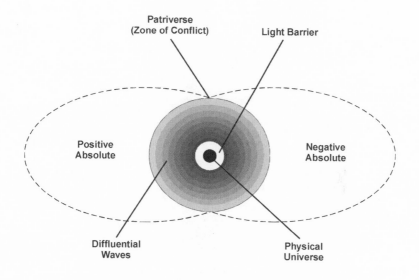

Figure 7.5 — Supergeometric Model #4. An overhead view of the omniverse, showing the graduation from non-physical to superphysical to physical.

Although this model provides a basic overview of the new cosmology, its bilateral symmetry prevents it from illustrating the principle of primary imbalance. To do this we must draw another model from a different perspective. Notice in this model that the stronger positive influence produces a flow from left to right. A time arrow has been added to show that primary imbalance also determines the flow of time. [Figure 7.6, next page]

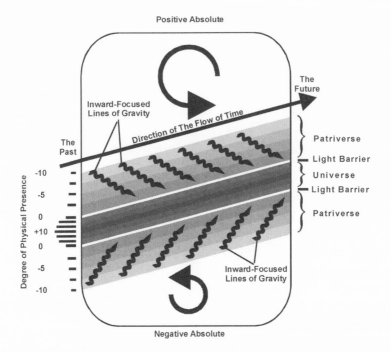

Figure 7.6 — Supergeometric Model #5. A view of the omniverse from a different perspective, showing how primary imbalance determines both the direction of gravity and the flow of time. The scale on the left shows the degree of physical density or "presence" in negative numbers above the speed of light and in positive numbers below. The one-to-ten scale is arbitrary and is for illustrative purposes only, although such a practical scale might possibly be ascertained with more research.

Notice that the force of gravity as well as time has been added to Figure 7.6 with directional arrows illustrating how these flow into physical reality. The fascinating and unexpected consequence of this supergeometric model in its revealing previously unidentified characteristics of gravity and time will be covered more thoroughly in the next chapter. The goal for now is to focus on illustrating the fundamental principles of supergeometric theory.

Diffluence is shaped into physical forms by the patterns contained within the grand supergeometry. Because grand supergeometry and its myriad of subsidiary supergeometric forms is dispersed throughout the zone of conflict, it is difficult to illustrate in the previous overview models. It can best be shown through a linear model. [Figure 7.7]

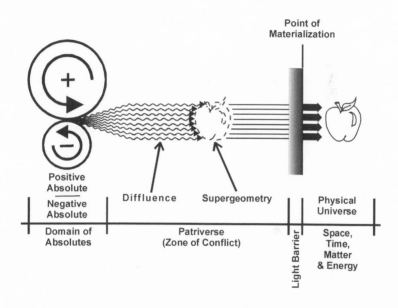

Figure 7.7 — Supergeometric Model #6. A linear model of the omniverse showing the process by which the waves of diffluence are formed, shaped, and materialized into physical matter and dimension.

Together, the above models represent a reasonable depiction of reality as defined by the theory of supergeometry.

SUMMARY

Much ground has been covered toward a new TOE since the foundation for our theorizing was established in the first chapter. Evidence has been collected from diverse fields, organized into a coherent system of classification, and sound principles have been established through analysis and argument. These principles were then used to derive a new coherent cosmology comprising physical, superphysical and non-physical elements. Finally, well defined models were produced to illustrate its workings.

But is this supergeometric functional? Can the processes described really provide any valuable insights into the anomalies of science and the paranormal? In the following chapter, we'll put this new theory to the test.

9

Correlations

Fitting the Pieces into the Cosmological Puzzle

> For the scientist who has lived by his
> faith in the power of reason, the story
> ends like a bad dream. He has scaled
> the mountains of ignorance; he is
> about to conquer the highest peak; as
> he pulls himself over the final rock, he
> is greeted by a band of theologians
> who have been sitting there for centur-
> ies.
>
> —Robert Jastrow

That a collection of religious principles can give rise to a superphysical theory of reality is remarkable to say the least. But regardless to how cleverly devised such a theory might be, it must satisfy the hard questions posed to it. If this so-called theory of supergeometry is to merit consideration as a viable portrayal of reality, it must provide reasonable explanations for the many anomalies thus far discussed.

Chapter Two presented a collection of recognized scientific anomalies, while Chapter Three covered the mysteries of the paranormal. It is time to return to these scientific and paranormal puzzles, touching on each in the approximate order that they were first introduced, and see how they might fit within the framework of a supergeometric cosmos.

EVOLUTION

Supergeometry leads us to the heart of the debate between evolution and creationism or intelligent design. Proponents of each sometimes muddy the waters by bringing with their arguments an underlying agenda. Supporters of intelligent design seek through rhetoric to re-introduce the teaching of God into the public classroom, while proponents of evolution adhere to a preconceived notion that almost any idea, no matter how awkward, can be entertained *except* the existence of an influence outside the physical environment. These kinds of blind agendas hijack the quest for Truth and replace it with the counterfeits of politics, propaganda and protectionism.

Supergeometric theory unquestionably implies intelligent design, but with two big differences. First, it does not deny the anthropological evidence on which the theory of evolution is based. The process of superphysical elements progressively working toward the creation and expansion of physical reality suggests that life would likewise develop in a progressive manner, just as the theory of evolution describes. Secondly—and most significantly—the supergeometric model implies that at some level, evolution *is* intelligent, and so intelligent design *is* evolution. Evolution is not the refutation of intelligent design as its proponents argue, but is actually the hard evidence to support it. Supergeometric mechanics validate evolution as a viable system, and bolsters it with "intelligent" solutions for the handful of nagging but substantial questions that observable evidence alone cannot fully explain. Supergeometric evolution would indeed leave the exact kind of physical evidence that is displayed in the fossil record while offering insightful explanations for its anomalies.

Co-Evolution

One of these anomalies is the co-evolution of various inter-related features within a single organism. The previously cited examples—the highly specialized organs of the whale, the inter-dependency of the giraffe's long neck and its unusual circulatory system, and the many unique co-dependent features of the woodpecker—are all instances of the synchronous co-evolution of biological subsystems within a single organism. The simultaneous co-evolution of these various interrelated parts cannot be fully explained through random genetic drift (which is just a fancy name for genes that appear to change all by themselves for no predetermined reason).

What if the physical form of a creature is brought about in some way by its supergeometric pattern? It would certainly provide a more workable explanation for co-evolution than the idea of random change. Recall that with supergeometry, every functioning organism has a distinct, stable, coherent supergeometric pattern. Each localized area within the pattern's matrix is harmoniously synchronized with the greater overall pattern. Any localized change in the pattern would send out ripples of discord throughout the rest of the matrix. If the change were sufficiently distinct, the entire pattern would quake and flux until it re-established its internal harmony. Every area of the pattern would undergo slight adjustments to accommodate or absorb the original discord, resulting in an overall, synchronous change. Each one of these overall "adjustments" would yield a corresponding, interrelated change in the physical form of the creature. This would perfectly explain why the evolution of the giraffe's neck was matched by a corresponding increase in the strength of its circulatory system.

But how can we assume that such localized supergeometric changes would result in a corresponding change to the greater pattern in a highly organized and functional way? Why, for example, does a seemingly random change in the pattern of the giraffe's neck not result in an equally random or chaotic change elsewhere in the pattern so that the front left hoof begins to grow three times larger? Why instead do multiple traits change simultaneously in an orderly and synchronous way as if there were some sort of intelligence guiding them?

The answer to this lies in the nature of supergeometry itself. Remember that according to the conclusions reached from the analysis of both paranormal phenomena and Biblical principles, there is an implicit order in the grand supergeometry of the omniverse. Our four-dimensional physical reality that emerges from supergeometry is therefore not chaotic, but orderly and *meaningful*. This is because grand supergeometry is a reflection —or perhaps more accurately, an image—of a Supreme Order. Were we to express this religiously, we might say that supergeometry is an aspect of the Mind of God, and so is both infinitely intelligent and purposeful. The physical laws that govern all matter, energy, space and time in the universe arise from this superphysical order. Even that which appears chaotic has an inherent order. A molecule comprising two hydrogen atoms and one oxygen atom at standard temperature and pressure will always yield a clear liquid at all times and places in the universe. Order was built into the physical elements at the very beginning of creation, and that order remains to this day. This is essentially the same belief held by Isaac Newton that led him to his vision of a clockwork universe, the order of which was engineered by God and then set into motion. Einstein also subscribed to such an intrinsic order for similar reasons.

As a result, "evolving thoughts" within the grand supergeometry produce changing patterns that are intrinsically orderly. The strengthening of the giraffe's circulatory system in response to the lengthening of its neck is not a result of some arbitrary stroke of luck, but is instead *reasonable* and *sensible*. It is in fact evolution as we know it, but it is also intelligent and purposeful. In the case of our woodpecker, specialized feet, hardened bill, thick skull, and unique tongue evolved together in response to

the overall supergeometric scheme being *meaningfully* recon-
figured. As a result, the new creature is no oddity of random
mutation that will disappear within a generation—it is a harmoniously designed stable organism with a sustainable genetic
code.

The Origin of Species

Let's consider the origin of species itself. Again, we're not
speaking here of minor sub-special adaptations in response to
localized environmental influences (what is called *speciation*),
but the emergence of new and distinct genera. Sometimes the
ability of microbes to mutate within a few generation is cited as
a possible cause for speciation, as when bacteria quickly develop immunity to antibiotics. But this doesn't work for higher,
infinitely more complex creatures. The lack of evidence in the
fossil record of a contiguous, unbroken line of one genera and
species morphing into another over vast expanses of time is a
major bone of contention with the opponents of evolution.
However, the sudden appearance of a new organism from the
spontaneous altering of its overall pattern would help explain
the wholesale lack of gradually changing intermediate forms in
the fossil record *without* invalidating the basic concept of what
is commonly known as evolution.

Bear in mind, however, that explaining the rise of a distinctly new creature covers only half of the evolutionary puzzle. We
also need to consider how this singular novelty of nature grows
to become established as a new and separate species without
having another of its own kind to mate with. Let's look at the
giraffe again. Say that somehow some early predecessor with a
short neck suddenly gives birth to one with a slightly longer
neck and stronger heart. Now what? How does this lone variant
individual survive and propagate to the extent that it replaces
the race of its parents? Isn't it limited to mating with members
of its parents' species having only the previous characteristics?

And remember, it is the parents' species that is the stable, established, and fully adapted standard model of the creature, the genes of which evolved into the dominant, not the recessive set. Without a similarly formed partner, the recessive genetic code of this newcomer will be diluted or lost by mating with one of its evolutionary predecessors—that is, if such a mating between new and old would even be genetically possible. So where does a similar mate come from? Or are we to believe that, if a mating between the new giraffe and the old giraffe were even possible, this singular individual would be capable of passing on its genes to the entire species on such a scale that it alone could "convert" the entire population of giraffe to a new species? Even if the newcomer's own genetic code is fully stable and functional, it would still be a one-of-a-kind mutant among its more typical contemporaries. Traditional evolution simply assumes—quite unscientifically—that somehow this conversion takes place without finding the evidence for it in the fossil record, or even to explain in a convincing way how this process might take place. Nor is it explained how this lone mutation manages to become the dominant gene, while the dominant gene of the established species suddenly turns recessive. They just *assume* that it must all happen by some means in an inexplicable way. It's a trade secret.

This is where the influence of supergeometry once again comes into play. An entire species has its own greater supergeometric pattern that also encompasses the pattern of every individual of that species. If one of these patterns were to undergo even the slightest localized change, it would send ripples throughout the species' entire supergeometric system, which would then adjust itself by re-synchronizing its overall pattern to restore inner symmetry. At times this re-synchronization results in the eradication of the new individual by the dissipation of its pattern into the greater supergeometric whole. At other times, however, this re-synchronization may have the opposite effect in that the greater whole will resonate with the

312

change that produced the new individual, replicating its pattern throughout the entire matrix. In a process not unlike that of quantum entanglement, other individuals similar or identical to the first newcomer will begin to appear everywhere throughout that species. The new variety can then reproduce with others of its own newly evolved kind, and in time come to dominate and replace its predecessors, just as traditional evolution describes, and as is reflected in the fossil record.

In this way, supergeometry allows for the sudden leaps that seem to contradict the standard evolutionary model of gradual change. For example, let's assume we have an imaginary species of red canaries. Let's further assume an occasion where an odd, yellow canary hatches from a single clutch. It appears to be the kind of random genetic drift suggested by evolution. But the fossil record actually leans more toward a scenario where yellow canaries suddenly begin popping up in every nest around the same time. The newborn species spontaneously and universally appears in its completed form, even co-habitating with its predecessors for a time. This type of supergeometric replication does not refute the gap-filled fossil record, but confirms its accuracy. As the change in the overall pattern becomes coherent, yellow canaries begin to appear in every nest. If the new pattern proves stable, the yellow variety completely supplants its red parents.

Okay, I hear the catcalls now. One might reasonably argue that all research to date indicates that genes alone are responsible for such changes, and so no unseen influence is needed to explain genetic mutations. Let's set aside for a moment (just as evolutionists habitually do) the anomalies of evolution that cannot be explained by genetics alone. There's no question that changes to genes indeed have physical consequences. But it does not rule out the kinds of non-local influences demonstrated in the physics experiments discussed earlier. Or is the matter and energy from which are made the genes and bodies of living creatures of a different kind than all other matter and energy, or do their molecules obey a different set of subatomic laws?

Supergeometry implies that physical things can be manipulated from any level in the omniverse, whether in the physical or the superphysical. If a physical pair of hands works a physical lump of clay, the corresponding superphysical supergeometric hands are also working the supergeometric clay at the same time. This is admittedly a difficult thing to envision because a portion of it is superdimensional. Everything that occurs in the superphysical has physical consequence, and everything that occurs in the physical has its superphysical counterpart. Our inability to reduce superdimensional elements into a linear, three-dimensional mental image does not preclude its reality—the functioning of creation is not bound by the confines of human understanding.

I hear more jeers. These voices chime there is sufficient evidence to show that the surrounding local environment is the sole determiner of evolutionary adaptation. Forgive me, but this is still conventional thinking. After all, isn't the environment also part of the physical? If so, it too has its own supergeometry that will interact with the supergeometry of the living creatures within it. Furthermore, if physicists have already established that certain physical processes have non-local causes, how can anyone declare with certitude that absolutely no evolutionary process might possibly have a similar, non-local cause? So yes, I agree that evolutionary adaptation is tied to the environment. But there is also an interconnection beyond the physical between subject and environment that has already been scientifically demonstrated. Although it is highly unusual for those in the natural sciences to think of their disciplines in terms of physics, just the briefest of contemplation leads quickly to the conclusion that it must be so.

What induces supergeometric patterns of creatures and their environment to undergo change in the first place? Perhaps they are like the chemical elements on earth, which are rarely found in pure form but instead exist in compounds that constantly break down and re-combine into new combinations of chemical substances. In much the same way, supergeometric patterns are dynamic, forming new combinations of matrices in a never-ending progression of "evolutionary" transformation. The dynamism observed in the physical universe is a reflection of the dynamism inherent in the grand cosmic supergeometry.

Of course, even if we accept the supergeometric model of evolution, a debate could still be waged as to whether super-physical changes are guided by randomness rather than some governing intelligence. I believe that the universe is too orderly to be the product of randomness. To me, changes within the grand supergeometric scheme are evidence of the "thought" processes of God. The actual cause for the origin of new genera then lies somewhere between the two extremes of miraculous spontaneous creationism and mundane impersonal evolution. Change occurs over time, but is brought about in incremental spurts by a conscious order. These spurts would by nature be orderly, purposeful and meaningful, just as the evidence shows.

As we explore further into space, exobiologists are confident that we will find life wherever conditions are right for it. Why? Because they believe—that is, they *have faith*—that there is an intrinsic and implicit order in the universe. But this belief flies in the face of the very same godless evolution to which their discipline also adheres, namely, that the appearance and development of life on earth is simply the result of a dumb-luck, one-in-a-billion throw of the cosmic dice without purpose, meaning or design. Do you see the hypocrisy in this?

Yes, I agree that evolution can be studied as a viable and fruitful discipline just like electrical engineering or chemistry without a belief in intelligent design. But unlike the firm foundations of our physical sciences, we still have no idea how life emerged from inanimate material, or why it appears to be more than just the sum total of its chemistry. Without the possibility of intelligent design, the very lump of synapses and cells subscribing to this nature-bound evolutionary view is by its own admission nothing more than an accidental collage of random minerals and elements sloshing inside a bony cranium without inherent purpose or meaning, and so is compelled to entertain such ostentatious concepts as evolution to attain some self-ascribed illusion of significance.

Symbiosis

Supergeometric theory also provides for the co-evolution of interdependent species. Recall that in such instances, two or more species in unusually close symbiotic relationship (like the Corianthes orchid/orchid bee or the bot-fly/mosquito/human interconnections discussed earlier) act collectively as a distinct biological unit or system, behaving at times more like a single organism than as separate individuals. These complex, interdependent systems have their own greater governing supergeometry through which all the symbiotic individuals within the system are interconnected. A change in the supergeometry of such a system affects all its synchronized members at the same time. Any change, for example, in the supergeometry of the Corianthes orchid is matched by a corresponding change in the orchid bee, thereby maintaining both members of the system in a state of synchronous, co-evolutionary harmony.

Many communal insect societies also act collectively as a single organism. The various members of an ant colony each go about performing its own specialized task that when combined produce a remarkably intricate and coherent society. Yet no individual or group of individuals possesses the master plan for the collective whole. It is the supergeometry of this giant, single organism that contains the plan, expressing itself through the biomass of the colony as synchronous behavior. The primitive nature of their brains help facilitate this supergeometric influence, since they lack a strong independent thought that might interfere with the collective commands as it does in the higher animals. To the ant, it's all spontaneous intuitiveness.

Other Related Structures

Supergeometry can also account for the development of nearly identical structures in otherwise dissimilar species. For example, wings are a characteristic structure in birds that allow them to fill an ecological niche in the sky. Yet the same structure appears in species normally associated with earth-bound environments. Mammals and reptiles both produce varieties with wing-like structures that enable them to take to the air. Some, like the flying dragon of Borneo and the flying squirrel, possess little more than extra flaps of skin that allow them to glide short distances. Yet others like the bat and the extinct Pteranodon are true fliers having wings virtually identical to those of birds (except for feathers). Such flying non-birds are genuine anomalies among the animal kingdom.

Strong arguments are made by traditional evolution for why these winged oddities evolved. For example, the bat's ability to fly (along with its other co-evolutionary anomaly of sonar and specialized ears) allows it to take advantage of the abundant food supply of nocturnal flying insects not exploited by day-feeding birds. However, these arguments seem less convincing when you consider creatures like the flying squirrel. All other squirrels have always been flightless and yet are very successful species, competing and surviving quite nicely in environments *identical* to those occupied by their flying cousins. Only a tiny fraction of the world's squirrels can fly, which is the proof that this ability is not required to significantly enhance the survival of the species. Yes, perhaps it's due to that mysterious evolutionary aberration called genetic drift—but why would their genes randomly drift in *that* particular direction?

The flying fish is another species whose wings are difficult to justify. Thousands of fish species adapt and survive quite well without the ability to fly. To say that this skill helps the flying fish to better escape predators is inadequate, since if this tactic was so much more effective than those typically employed by

317

other prey species, many more fishes would have developed it. Besides, because of this behavior, flying fish fall prey to certain birds that specialize in dining on this weird winged creature while it's airborne. So why did it acquire wings? So that frigate birds would have something to eat during their forays over long expanses of water far from land? Now that *would* be intelligent.

Grand Supergeometric Systems

Flight itself appears to have its own supergeometry. Remember that the air through which creatures fly also has its own superphysical pattern. The supergeometry of the atmosphere itself may work in sympathy with those of various creatures to form one grand supergeometric system of flight. The medium (in this case, the atmosphere) exerts influence over the evolving creature's pattern, inducing the formation of wings, feathers, etc., which can then operate in, or *synchronize* with the air. The creature and the medium are thus only individual components of a greater, harmonious system formed by the larger overlaying supergeometric pattern of flight.

An even stronger argument for this idea can be found in the relationship between light and the formation of eyes. Evolution would cite the loss of eyes in many cave-dwelling species as the evidence that the formation of eyes occurs as a reaction to the presence of light. However, this apparently natural conclusion seems less convincing when one considers the bizarre creatures that occupy the deepest parts of the oceans. Just as in the deepest caves, there is no visible light in the ocean depths. Yet unlike the cave dwellers, many deep-sea inhabitants do in fact have fully formed eyes and are not blind. Instead, they produce their own light from their very bodies by means of bioluminescence. Think about this—*light* evolving in response to darkness? Evolution does not provide for a physical substance (in this case light) to "evolve" to fit its environment— light *is* the environment! Only living things evolve, and only in response to the existing physical elements in the surroundings. Yet in these luminescent creatures, both eyes and light "co-evolved" simultaneously in the same environment. It appears as if the very same invisible hand responsible for shaping these deep-sea eyes as receivers for light also shaped the light source for those eyes to see by. In other words, the same supergeometry responsible for fashioning eyes is also responsible for fashioning the light source itself. Eyes and light are merely different physical manifestations of the same supergeometry that governed the simultaneous formation of both. Very intelligent indeed.

The Enigma of Humanity

Modern evolutionists have long wrestled with the question originally posed by Alfred Russell Wallace—how did the human brain evolve far beyond what is required for simple survival by adaptation to its environment? A number of theories have been proposed, some of which are quite clever. Yet no single theory is so attractive as to cause the majority to rally around its banner. What environmental influences prompted the brain of some primordial primate to make the leap from using a twig for prying insects from a nest to assembling from the physical elements a spaceship with which to travel to the moon?

The simple truth is that there is no known environmental influence (much to the chagrin of Darwinian fundamentalists) that might produce such an "astronomical" leap, just as Wallace asserted. He was convinced that in the case of humans, some other outside, non-local influence must be responsible for this leap. Supergeometric theory provides Wallace with his answer. According to the theory, grand supergeometry is the master blueprint for the entire cosmos, from which all things were fashioned. Surely, there would come a moment in the history of life where the influence of this creative mind would begin to shape a creature that in some way resembled its own image and likeness. Perhaps humankind is precisely what the Bible says—a being shaped both *from the dust of the ground* (the physical elements and environmental influences) and the "breath" of God (grand supergeometry). One would expect the combination of these two ingredients to produce just the kind of animals we are, part carnal creature and part spiritual creator. Our unique capacity to create—to transform invisible thought into visible reality—coupled with the ability of our unique hands to carry out what our creative minds imagine, is a direct result of the influence of grand supergeometry upon the whole of our "evolutionary" development.

This process of supergeometry working progressively upon the face of reality has surprising and far-reaching implications beyond evolution. Recall that the Biblical concept of the Word or the Divine Wisdom of God was understood to be a creative force, containing within it the blueprint for the entire cosmos. We can imagine this creative supergeometry ascending through the primordial cloud, imposing its high degree of order on a chaotic infant universe and initiating the formation of galaxies, stars, and planets. Ascending further through the coalescing elements of early earth, grand supergeometry began to fashion the first rudimentary forms of life (being a living thing itself). Ascending still further throughout the environment, it gave rise to a multitude of organisms of both increasing diversity and complexity. Darwin caught a glimpse of the trail left by this ascension and gave it a name—*evolution*.

Inevitably, grand supergeometry would shape the raw materials of physical matter into a form that more closely reflected its own nature—*homo sapiens*. Ascending even further through humankind, grand supergeometry would ultimately shape a human most closely emulating its own nature—in other words, a very 'godly' person, or a *Christ* if you will (*And the Word was made flesh and dwelt among us*). Cast in this light, the existence of a God-like man possessing the miraculous power to spontaneously transmute matter (healings, the multiplying of bread and fishes, etc.) can now at least be brought into the realm of reasonable discussion instead of being confined exclusively to the domain of devotional faith. Such a man would truly be *an image of the invisible God*, the *Son of God, born of the Father*, and *of one substance with the Father*. He would indeed be—as close as is possible in this corruptible, physical world—the incarnation of God on earth.

The idea of grand supergeometry working ever increasingly upon the face of matter not only reflects the process known as evolution, but the advent of humanity as well. In addition, supergeometric evolution leads us to the remarkable conclusion that the appearance of a Christ is not only reasonable, but also *inevitable*, being built into the system at the very foundations of creation. It's hard to imagine any stronger correlation between Christian faith and scientific thought.

There's little doubt from the evidence that creatures change to meet the challenges posed by a changing environment, just as evolutionary theory maintains. Yet supergeometric theory is able to fill certain gaps in the traditional evolutionary picture. The combining of these two theories yields a picture of the development of life on earth that is neither quite evolution nor intelligent design, but something in between—*supergeometric evolution*. Simply put, supergeometric evolution states that life on earth originated through self-assembly according to a superphysical order, and continued evolving in collective response to both local (physical) *and* non-local (superphysical) influences.

PHYSICS & COSMOLOGY

Scientific anomalies are vital to unlocking the mysteries of the universe. Many past attempts to explain enigmas like the paranormal founder because they fail to address the underlying physics, without which no one can come to true understanding. Supergeometry provides solutions to these scientific puzzles, which then reveal the answers to the other deep mysteries.

Behind The Cosmic Veil

Universal Order

Just as naturalists explain how life developed in terms of evolution, cosmologists seek to similarly explain the formation of the universe as a process of evolutionary steps from the Big Bang through the present. However, as is the case with the evolution of life, there are serious gaps in the evolutionary map of the cosmos. Supergeometry provides a key to unlocking some of the missing pieces to this cosmological puzzle.

Recall that the giant primordial cloud resulting from the Big Bang was a homogenous mixture having within it no recognizable forms or structures. In direct violation of the laws of chaos (which would disrupt any forming structures), this cloud began to segregate into organized regions of nebulae, galaxies, stars, and planets. Supergeometric theory provides for this seeming violation of chaotic law. As the organized patterns within the grand supergeometry began to unfold, the particles throughout the primordial cloud aligned themselves to its superphysical matrix. As the grand supergeometric blueprint evolved into even more complex patterns, the particle cloud followed suit, eventually resulting in the highly organized and very structured universe we can now observe.

It's extremely unlikely that matter determined its own physical laws during its formation. Instead, the substances of the early universe formed into atoms and molecules according to a set of laws that existed *before* matter began to take shape. Contained within the grand supergeometric scheme were these predetermined laws to which primordial matter conformed.

Non-Local Causality

Recall the two scientific experiments that demonstrate non-local causality, namely the two-slit and the entangled photons experiments. To recap the former, individual photons are fired at a board having two slits, after which the final destination of each is recorded on a screen beyond. Although the photons are fired one at a time, the resulting hits do not collect as the uniform randomness expected, but instead form a pattern of waves as if many photons were fired at the same time and interfered with one another. Without other "local" photons to affect each single photon as it travels along its path, conventional science can offer no explanation for how they collectively form a pattern of interfering waves. Physicists accept this strange quality of light as a proven but inexplicable phenomenon.

To understand how supergeometric theory explains this, it is first necessary to take a closer look at the dual nature of light. Light manifests itself both as a particle and a wave. This dual personality—being both matter and energy simultaneously—is very strange at first sight, since experience and reason tell us that a thing must be either one or the other at any given time. Yet photons are not the only particles that sport this duality. The electron that orbits the nucleus of an atom exists as a wave function until it is measured. The act of measuring then collapses the wave pattern into a solid particle.

The most significant characteristic of photons in relation to the supergeometric model is that they travel at the speed of light. We know that this velocity is unique in that it is the only constant in the physical universe. No matter what speed and direction an observer is traveling relative to a beam of light, the speed of that beam is always observed to be 186,300 miles per second. This unique, immutable velocity holds the key to light's dual nature. It is not a question of duality being an intrinsic quality of light, but that its velocity at the fringes of physical creation causes it to behave as both a particle and a wave.

A deeper look into the bizarre nature of physical reality at the speed of light reveals exactly why this is so. Recall that matter cannot be sustained in its usual form at the speed of light. The proof for this is strictly mathematical, since we do not yet possess the means to propel a physical mass at velocities anywhere near the speed of light. It has been mathematically

323

demonstrated that as a mass approaches the speed of light, the energy required to propel it grows exponentially. As the mass creeps ever closer to lightspeed, vast quantities of energy are expended for each tiny increment of increased acceleration. At the moment an object reaches the light barrier, the value in the equation representing the amount of energy required to propel it goes off the scale to infinity, indeed a physical impossibility. What is it that prevents mass from traveling at such speeds, while permitting a photon (which is a particle and thus itself a piece of matter in theory) to do so?

Physical matter requires four dimensions in which to exist, which are the three spatial dimensions of length, width, and depth, and the temporal dimension of time. Yet at the speed of light, the distinction between these four dimensions begins to break down. We have all heard the hypothetical story of a person who sets out in a spaceship traveling just under the speed of light for a journey of one year, only to find upon returning to earth that many years have passed, and that all the people he or she knew are either very old or deceased. This phenomenon, known as *time dilation*, was first described in Einstein's theory of relativity. It is whimsically illustrated in the following well-known limerick:

There once was a lady in flight
Who could travel much faster than light.
She set out one day
In a relative way
And returned home the previous night.

The point is that at the speed of light, the dimension of time essentially collapses in on itself. A person in a spaceship traveling at the speed of light can look out the front portal and see at its outer edges the stars that the ship has already passed! Although a sub-light observer some distance away sees the ship pass each star in the usual way, the person in the lightspeed ship observes these same stars as if they were just being encountered —past, present, and future appear condensed into a single, almost flat field, with the past around its perimeter and the future at its center. The phenomenon is eerily similar to what was said about the way God views time from His perspective: *His gaze spans the ages*, so that He sees past, present and future in its entirety at once. [Figure 8.1]

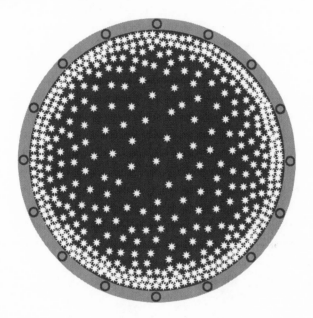

Figure 8.1 — View Through the Front Portal of a Spaceship at Lightspeed.
Time folds in on itself at the speed of light, merging the past and the future into the present. Looking through the front portal of a spaceship moving at the speed of light, an observer sees time compressed into a single, almost flat field. The approaching stars of the future are at the center of the portal, while those already passed are seen condensed around its perimeter.

If the existence of matter is dependent on *all* four dimensions, what happens then if you remove the dimension of time? For a material object to maintain a coherent form (i.e., to retain its characteristic structure and mass in all frames of reference and from all angles of observation), it needs to have the time to do so, or in other words, it needs a certain amount of temporal dimensioning. Yet how can one measure the temporal co-ordinates of "then" and "now" that are necessary for the dimension of time when at the speed of light, past, present, and future are so tightly condensed together that it is difficult to distinguish any difference between them? Since time practically stands still, there is not enough temporal dimension for a physical object to maintain a coherent structure.

It is therefore easy to see why light cannot materialize into either a particle or a wave—plainly speaking, it simply doesn't have the *time* to do so. Instead, it exists in an incoherent state somewhere between the two. The photons do not have the time to solidify and sustain themselves as either distinct particles or waves. Of course, once a photon encounters interference like a measuring device, the resulting deflection introduces a sufficient amount of localized time to "materialize" or collapse it into a particle.

In a supergeometric cosmos, only diffluential waves (superphysical substance) and supergeometry (superphysical form) can be sustained at superlight speeds. Physical reality begins to emerge when primal conflict sufficiently slows the flow of diffluence. As its velocity descends to the speed of light, diffluence begins to coagulate and densify, solidifying into hard, physical reality once it drops below lightspeed. But in that narrow band of lightspeed between the not-yet-physical superlight realm and the fully physical sub-light realm, all reality exists in a transient state. Anything within this narrow lightspeed band would naturally be chameleon-like, behaving sometimes as a particle or sometimes as a wave (depending on how, when or from where we observe it), but never fully committing to being one or the other. Once velocities drop below the speed of light, the dimensions of space-time unfold sufficiently to manifest stable and coherent material forms.

This supergeometric principle provides a reasonable mechanism for both the anomalies of the dual nature of light and the non-local causality demonstrated in the two-slit experiment. In the lightspeed realm of the photon, temporal and spatial dimensions are still so tightly wrapped together that there is not enough differentiation to allow any material structures to take a coherent form. It is for this reason that light expresses itself as both a wave and as a particle simultaneously. In the two-slit experiment, the individual photons are actually "wave-particles" that align themselves to the pre-existing wave-particle patterns inherent in the supergeometry of light. Since light is the only constant in the universe, its supergeometric pattern must likewise be constant and unchanging. Therefore, in whichever way light is introduced into the experiment (either as individually fired photons or a full beam), its photons will collectively draw the identical wave pattern on the screen because the pattern is already established in the superphysical. Since the supergeometry of light is unchanging, the pattern traced by the emitted photons will always be the same whether or not they are fired individually or en masse, just as the experiment demonstrates. Supergeometry is thus the "local" causality that produces this otherwise mysterious phenomenon. These are the non-physical guide waves Louis de Broglie proposed in the last century.

What this all means is that at sub-light speeds, the four dimensions of space and time are sufficiently unfolded and solid to give the appearance that physical masses and actions all have physical, local causes. Only at lightspeed do these hard dimensions become sufficiently indistinguishable to reveal the non-locality (i.e., causality by *non*-physical means) underlying the whole of physical reality.

As a side note, the ideal that hard dimensions only begin to unfold just below the speed of light (where particles acquire mass) should also hold true for gravity in a supergeometric universe. We know that gravity is associated with mass. Therefore, if mass is acquired at just below the speed of light where the dimensions of space-time unfold, then gravity too would only begin to unfold at this sub-light band. This would explain why physicists have been frustrated in their attempts to devise a model of quantum gravity, or in formulating a mathematical expression of gravity projected through the four dimensions of space-time. A few pioneering theorists have speculated that gravity does not even operate on the subatomic quantum level. According to supergeometry, there's a chance they may be right —gravity emerges with sub-light space.

The second light experiment demonstrating non-local causality is the one involving entangled photons. Recall the example where a pair of photons, one having an up spin and the other a down spin, are joined together or *entangled* in a balanced or correlated pair. The pair is then split apart so that each travels away from the other in opposite directions while retaining its original directions of spin. When one of the photons is passed through a polarizing filter that reverses its spin, its partner instantly reverses its spin as if by magic, thus re-establishing the pair's original balance. Physics can offer no explanation as to how the second photon might "know" what is happening to the first photon, which is now far removed and thus non-local to its partner.

Supergeometry provides the missing link for this quantum entanglement as it is called. The entangled photon pair has its own collective supergeometry through which the individual photons are connected, even after they have been *physically* separated. The supergeometric pattern of the photon pair has an inner harmony that is disturbed when the spin of the first photon is altered. The interconnected pattern then forces the second photon to likewise reverse itself, re-establishing the original balance and inner harmony of the pair.

Remember too that at lightspeed, the spatial dimension of distance (as in the distance between the two separated photons) has not yet fully materialized. The sub-light observer can clearly perceive and measure the physical distance between the two lightspeed photons because the geometric space being observed is also sub-light, and so its dimensions are completely unfolded to the observer's eyes. But the photons themselves occupy a band of velocity at the very outer fringe of the physical universe where there is only quasi-dimensionalism. The sub-light observer cannot see that inside the area defined by the perimeter of the photons is a realm of reality where the normal spatial dimensions are so compressed that no such geometric measurement of distance is possible. In this higher temporal realm, the two lightspeed photons cannot be geometrically separated because the geometry of space that would define such a separation is not yet unfurled.

Imagine poking both ends of a U-shaped wire through a sheet of paper so that only the tips protrude. You would see two separate objects from the top side of the paper. From a certain perspective, they would even appear as two distinct round balls or particles. But if you peeked around to the realm on the other side, you'd see what was really happening. You'd also see that the perception of two distinct round objects is an illusion.

If we were able to extend our observations to a perspective above the speed of light, we would see the spatial and temporal dimensions that define distance in our physical space to be completely collapsed. Even if we allowed the separated photons to travel so far from one another as to be separated by galaxies, this *physical* distance would be of little consequence in the realm of superlight velocity. Within this realm, wherein dwells the supergeometry of quantum entanglement, the two photons are still intrinsically linked as a single unit.

Relativity Vs Quantum Theory

The discussion of the speed of light and how the normal quality of space-time changes at that velocity leads us back to the conflict between relativistic and quantum theories. Recall that according to relativity, all events are ultimately predictable if given enough information. Quantum theory instead proposes that no event can be exactly predicted regardless to how much information is gathered—only the percentage of probability of a particular event can be determined. Relativity has proved ideal for describing the universe at large, while quantum theory better explains the mysterious world of the subatomic realm. The obvious problem is that we should not need two very different systems to adequately describe a single universe. Even though some physicists maintain this division is an illusion, claiming that the quantum effect can be observed in the world at large, they are still unable to describe that world using quantum mechanics. Science has not yet been able to successfully reconcile the macroscopic with the subatomic.

Within the supergeometric model itself, however, there is no paradox. As the wheels of primal conflict grind out the face of creation, the resulting friction works on the pre-dimensional, superlight waves of diffluence and slows them. As these waves slow to the speed of light, dimensional space and time begin to unfold, although the spatial and temporal dimensions are so tightly bundled at this velocity as to be nearly indistinguishable from one another. As the velocity falls below the speed of light, dimensional space and time gradually become the distinct reference points with which we are accustomed. The growing state of dimensionalism at these lower velocities allows matter to begin to take shape and hold firm, a thing not possible at lightspeed or faster. Form and substance—the two elements necessary for the existence of hard reality—increasingly become the separate and sovereign qualities with which we are familiar as velocities progressively drop below the speed of light. The result is a single, continuous model of a graduated reality rather than a divided reality requiring two separate theoretical systems to define it.

There is strong evidence to support this graduated cosmological picture of increasing dimensionalism with decreasing velocity. One example is the concept of *matter waves*. Physicists have known for some time now that all matter has wave-like qualities. The discovery that photons manifest as both particles and waves led physicists to experiment with other particles to see if these also displayed the same dual nature. Those experiments revealed that not only single particles, but also atoms and molecules have their own associated wavelengths. These matter waves are an integral part of all physical things from atoms to airplanes. It was further proven that the wavelengths of these matter waves grow longer as the momentum of the associated particle diminishes, almost as if these matter waves expand as velocity decreases. By the time subatomic matter finally descends below the speed of light into the macroscopic sub-light world, the matter waves are so dissipated as to be virtually undetectable. These matter waves are proof that reality undergoes progressive changes relative to velocity.

Another piece of correlating evidence can be found in the phenomenon of time dilation. Recall that the occupants of a spacecraft traveling at near-light velocity for one year will return to earth to find that many years had passed. It's clear that time dilation is intimately linked to velocity. As the spacecraft increases its velocity toward lightspeed, the dimension of time decreases proportionately. Just as matter waves become increasingly shorter in wavelength as a particle accelerates, so too does time become more tightly wrapped or "shorter" as the spaceship gains speed. If it were possible for the ship's mass to reach the actual speed of light, the dimension of time would appear to virtually stand still when compared to that on earth, where the temporal dimension is much more thoroughly unfolded due to its slower velocity.

This gradual unfolding of dimensional time and space based on velocity leads to the startling conclusion that space-time is not divided into quantum units or "quantized" as is currently defined (hence the "quantum" in quantum physics), but is instead *stratified* according to velocity. Light occupies the highest stratum of space-time, since the speed of light is the uppermost universal velocity as well as being the only universal constant. Below lightspeed, space-time unfolds into layer upon layer of progressive strata, each representing an increment of decreasing velocity. A particle jumping from one stratum to the next only gives the illusion of a quantized cosmos.

In each of these lower strata, spatial and temporal dimensionalism increases incrementally. To put it another way, time passes more quickly in the lower strata because there is literally *more time* there to pass. As we ascend to the higher strata, time passes more slowly because it is more tightly bundled, and so there is less of it available to pass. At the speed of light, the dimension of time is so compacted that almost none of it is available for passing, and so time seems to stand still. Time passes much more slowly inside a spaceship traveling near lightspeed when compared with time's rate of passing on earth because a ship at this velocity occupies a much higher stratum of space-time than the lower stratum occupied by the earth's surface. In short, not just time, but all dimensionalism, is relative to velocity according to the supergeometric model.

Returning now to the conflict between quantum mechanics and relativity, we know that in the macroscopic world of relativity, no physical matter can travel as fast as light. But in the subatomic world of the quantum, lots of things whirl around at or near lightspeed. This means that the subatomic world occupies a much higher stratum of space-time than does the macroscopic world, and therefore exists in a place where space-time is not yet fully unwrapped and so is much less defined. It is for this reason that events in the quantum world seem unpredictable. One cannot make precise predictions for any event without fixed reference points from which to take firm measurements. For example, we are able to predict solar eclipses because we know the exact location of the earth, moon, and sun, and know precisely how fast and in what direction they are moving. But in the strata where subatomic processes occur, there are insufficient spatial and temporal dimensions to fix such concrete points of reference. It is only as velocity slows to a sub-light speed that the geometry of space-time begins to unwrap into a stable gridwork on which the fixed reference points that make reliable event prediction possible can be established.

The duality of wave/particles in the subatomic world is not then simply a question of the properties of particles, but of their *velocity*. Light manifests as both a wave and a particle because at the speed of light, there is not enough temporal dimension-alism for either a photon or a wave to manifest as a distinct, separate entity. Therefore, light particles and light waves (i.e., the *form* derived from light's supergeometric pattern and the *substance* derived from its diffluence) co-exist within a tightly wrapped package of wave/particles, awaiting the dimension of time to separate them into independently recognizable forms. As velocity decreases and reality moves toward the lower strata of the macroscopic world, time unfolds, making things become more spatial and temporal so that particles and waves can then be recognized as distinct independent qualities.

This *stratum theory* seems to compliment existing quantum theory quite well. Quantum theory describes the behavior of a particle and at what velocity it travels based on the amount of energy it contains. The notion of a stratified universe tells us something about *why* a particle behaves in such a way at a given velocity. Combining these two provides a better understanding of both the nature of the subatomic world and of space-time itself.

Most physicists today embrace the idea that unpredictabil-ity is a fundamental quality of the quantum universe. Yet Ein-stein was firmly convinced that all of reality, whether at the subatomic or macroscopic level, was ultimately predictable if given enough information. Supergeometrically speaking, he was most likely correct. As suggested by the physicist de Broglie, reality on the quantum level may appear to be unpredictable simply because we try to measure it from the lower strata of space-time to which we and our instruments are confined. The missing information that Einstein and de Broglie envisioned resides outside the physical where we cannot directly observe or collect it, and so we get the false impression of unpredictability. An observer unaware that automobiles have human drivers would find their behavior on the highways quite perplexing!

Were the relationship between dimensionalism and velocity better understood, we might see quantum theory and relativity, not as two contrasting ways to describe the universe, but as a single system, becoming gradually more or less quantized or relativistic based upon the particular stratum of space-time an observed particle occupies.

Science Creeps Ever Closer to the Solution

The apparent conflicts between the theories of relativity and quantum mechanics is so compelling that many physicists have for decades devoted themselves to unraveling the mystery. Fundamental to their thinking is the need to explain the non-local causality demonstrated by both the two-slit experiment and the behavior of entangled photons. An excellent article entitled *A Quantum Threat to Special Relativity* by David Z. Albert and Rivka Galchen published in the March 2009 issue of *Scientific American* describes the latest ideas in this field of inquiry (it's a must-read for anyone interested in the subject of this book). To summarize the concepts presented in the article:

- The non-local nature of certain aspects of quantum mechanics demonstrates that, contrary to conventional reasoning (and conventional physics), the universe is more than can be accounted for by the sum total of all the physical particles and forces comprising it;
- That quantum non-locality is not something that just appears to be real because of our limited ability to observe, nor is it an artifact from some other unknown physical process, but that non-locality is quite literally

and unquestionably a part of physical reality;

- Subsequently, the underlying "cause" for all of physical reality is non-local, so that any theory accurately portraying the nature of the universe would also have to describe a non-local, non-physical cause for all things in the universe (!);
- That at some deep level of reality, events take place with "absolute spontaneity" or in other words, a given event happens everywhere in the universe simultaneously without the need for its cause to travel to the location of that event across any span of space, or at any given velocity, or without any passage of time, meaning that every fundamental eventful cause occurs at a level of reality where the normal confines of space and time do not apply except for a state of absolute "here" (everywhere in the universe at once) and absolute "now" (again, everywhere in the universe at once);
- That the non-local, absolute spontaneity of geometric space and the matter occupying it also indicates that time itself has a non-local origin—that events of the past must occur simultaneously on some level with the present in order to determine the future (!!);
- That quantum non-local causality is the result of some unknown wave function;
- That according to the math, these wave functions cannot occur in the physical realm of four-dimensional space-time, but only in a superdimensional realm called *configuration space* from which the *illusion* of four-dimensional space-time and its relativistic local causality emerge.

Paranormal? You bet.

You can imagine my excitement when first reading these cutting edge concepts in theoretical physics that validate the very same conclusions reached in this book, the fundamentals of which were first conceived almost three decades ago. The timeless and spaceless superphysical patriverse, the super-dimensional wave functions of diffluence, the curved geometry of space-time unfolding from it, the underlying interconnection of all things, the non-local origin of local reality—it's all there. If you fill in the missing parts by inserting the physical concepts derived from the study of paranormal phenomena and the principles of Biblical cosmology, both of which are completely consistent with and complimentary to these ultra-modern ideas from the scientific community, a comprehensive vision of reality within this "configuration space" finally emerges. It is quite literally the very same supergeometric model set forth in this work.

All this gives us cause to reflect once more on the previous discussion regarding evolution. One of the principle precepts in evolutionary theory is that the consideration of any element outside the physical environment as being in any way responsible for the evolution of species is absolutely forbidden. But the growing consensus among physicists that reality emerges from an extra-physical, non-local source is gradually eroding that dogmatic view. By persisting in this no-possible-external-cause framework, evolutionists will increasingly distance themselves from the field of modern physics until they eventually find themselves in a conceptual vacuum completely isolated from the rest of the scientific community.

The Mystery of Gravity

Science traditionally categorizes gravity as being one of the four basic forces of nature. It certainly appears to behave like a force, displaying qualities very similar to electromagnetism. Yet unlike electromagnetism, no graviton or gravity wave has ever been discovered. Without such waves or particles, it is impossible to say for certain exactly what gravity is, or how gravity is generated or conveyed. We're unable to even determine at what velocity gravity is propelled, or if indeed it has a velocity at all. Without a wave or a particle to study and measure, none of these qualities can be established with any certainty.

The lack of any evidence for these has led some to simply accept that gravity is not a conventional force as dictated by the Standard Model, even though its true nature is not fully understood. It may be, as Einstein proposed, simply the result of the curvatures in space-time that surround every object large and small. This would make gravity merely another characteristic of the geometric dimensions of space. If so, then gravity is more likely to be some sort of driving force, acting in reverse of what conventional thought would indicate.

Supergeometric cosmology lends support to the idea that gravity is a type of repulsive or pushing force. According to this model, the supergeometric substance of diffluence has a direction of flow from the superphysical to the physical, solidifying into matter as it crosses the light barrier and slows to sub-light speed. This means that every physical object is surrounded by an inward-focused field of diffluential waves. The greater the mass of the object, the greater the volume of diffluential current focused in on it. This directional field creates the effect we know as gravity in dimensional space-time.

A massive object like a planet has a proportionately more massive diffluential field of inward-directed current surrounding it than that of a much smaller object like a meteor. If the meteor happens to cross into the larger diffluential field of a planet, its smaller field is caught up in the stronger diffluential "wind" that then carries it down toward the surface of the planet [Figure 8.2, next page].

Supergeometric gravity acts quite differently than classical gravity. In the latter, smaller objects like meteors are caught up in the gravitational field of a larger object like a planet, which then pulls the meteor into itself like a magnet. In supergeometric gravity, the inward-focused flow of the planet's surrounding diffluential field overcomes the smaller field of the meteor and carries it down toward and onto the planet's surface. Supergeometric gravity then is not like a magnet, but more like a strong wind, driving smaller objects down and holding them onto the surface of larger ones. This also means that the cause of gravity is both non-physical and non-local, just as Theodore Kalusa had ultimately concluded.

This is indeed a challenge to conventional reasoning—is the meteor pushed, or pulled along?

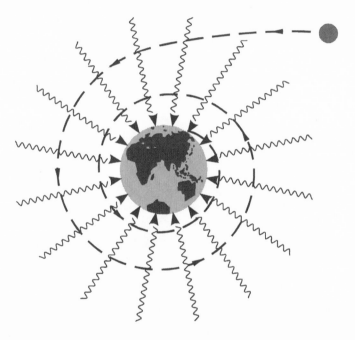

Figure 8.2 — Supergeometric Gravity. Gravity is produced by the inward-focused diffluential field surrounding an object, which is the force that bends space-time. A smaller object passing nearby gets caught in the larger field, carrying in downward.

This model of gravity would certainly explain the failure of science to isolate a graviton or a gravity wave. The diffluential fields surrounding objects are superphysical and therefore invisible to current measuring devices that are capable of detecting only *physical* waves or particles. Once diffluence solidifies, the resulting matter and energy are easily detected by our technology. But the underlying diffluential fields remain hidden outside the scope of these instruments, just as de Broglie and Kalusa postulated.

Einstein demonstrated that space-time is curved in the presence of matter. It is believed that the field of gravity emitted by a mass presses these divots into the space-time landscape. However, without a graviton or gravity wave with which to experiment, science can only assume that gravity is the cause. All that is known for certain is that space-time indeed warps in the presence of matter, resulting in a sort of bubble in space that surrounds each object, and that these bubbles are associated with gravity.

The supergeometric model of space-time curvature, which works in reverse of the conventional model, is highly intriguing with fantastic implications. According to this model, it is the increased flow of diffluence across the light barrier in specific areas that causes space-time to warp. These localized flows of additional diffluence into sub-light space result in a space-time fabric littered with bends, twists and depressions. Within these sub-light "potholes" or bubbles of dimensional space, diffluence and supergeometry converge to produce physical matter. These depressions serve as crucibles or "wombs" in which matter is born, shaped, and held together. In other words, it is not matter that is the cause of gravity as assumed, but it is instead the forces that warp space-time into gravity-filled bubbles that are the cause of matter!

It's time to introduce a new term for these potholes in the fabric of space. A **diffluential field bubble** is a sub-light depression in the geometry of space-time produced by a localized flow of diffluence across the light barrier and into dimensional space. Diffluence combines with supergeometry within these spatial depressions to coalesce into physical matter. Diffluence wraps around a supergeometric pattern, creating a bubble in which the resulting object materializes. A diffluential field bubble takes the form of an inward-focused diffluential field surrounding that object. These inward-focused bubbles produce the phenomenon of gravity as well as the curvatures in space-time.

A diffluential field bubble is highly stable when the matter within it is moving at sub-light speed. However, when accelerated to the speed of light, these bubbles lose their cohesion and "burst." When a diffluential field bubble bursts, the material within it breaks down and looses its mass, after which it is then dispersed as pure energy—a form of matter that *is* capable of traveling at lightspeed.

This supergeometric model is opposite that of conventional physics. According to the current scientific viewpoint based on the standard model, all matter generates a gravitational field, which in turn bends or curves the surrounding space-time. But when you stand back and look at Einstein's fundamental vision, there really isn't anything that contradicts our supergeometric model. Einstein envisioned the universe as a continuous plane of space-time geometry, interrupted by protrusions or pimples —what he called *matter points*—that marked the presence of matter. It is only the strict materialistic view of physics that assumes these pimples in the otherwise featureless fabric of space must have a material cause. But if you look beyond this materialistic prejudice and consider a non-local cause, there is nothing to say these matter points aren't instead the *source* of the matter they represent. An image of space-time based on the supergeometric mechanics of diffluential field bubbles would be *identical* in appearance to Einstein's pimpled plane. Space-time curvature, gravity, and even matter itself are then simply three different manifestations of the same singular process of diffluence wrapping around a supergeometric pattern to produce a bubble of space-time in which matter is materialized and sustained. [Figures 8.3 and 8.4, next two pages]

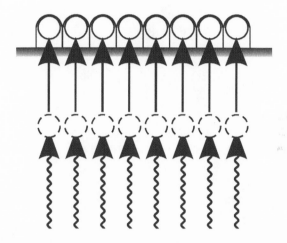

Figure 8.3 — Diffluential Field Bubbles. Localized areas of increased diffluential waves push across the light barrier, creating depressions or bubbles in the fabric of space-time. Diffluence then combines with supergeometric patterns within these bubbles to produce physical reality, in this case a field of atoms.

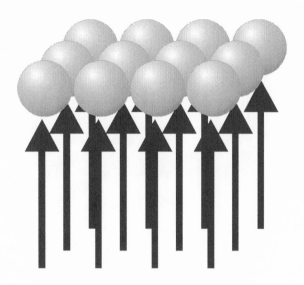

Figure 8.4 — A Field of Atoms. This representation of an electron-microscopic picture of a field of atoms portrays exactly what supergeometric theory predicts, which is a series of bubbles filled with matter and energy. The arrows show the superphysical flow of diffluence into these atomic bubbles. From our perspective in the physical, the field of bubbles comprising the atoms would look like a box of ping pong balls, which is exactly what electron microscope images depict.

Dark Matter and Dark Energy

Supergeometric gravity eliminates the need for astrophysicists to evoke imaginary substances like dark matter to provide a source for all the gravity required to hold the cosmic web of galactic material in place. The supergeometric model with its diffluential fields furnishes a much more reasonable (although admittedly, a non-materialistic) solution to this phenomenon. Diffluential fields are indeed invisible and immeasurable, just like dark matter is said to be. But unlike this dark matter, they are *super*physical, and therefore are *supposed* to be invisible. There is no need to fabricate explanations for how solid matter

342

can somehow magically become transparent so that it cannot even be detected with photons *and* yet have sufficient density to generate most of the universe's required gravity. According to supergeometric mechanics, diffluential fields generate gravity by warping space and provide the source for the missing gravity in astronomers' equations. In a very real sense, supergeometric diffluence *is* dark matter.

Moreover, supergeometry implies that gravitational fields exist everywhere in the universe, even in empty space. Since diffluential waves are the result of primal conflict, and since primal conflict extends throughout the entire physical realm, then diffluence too must be present throughout the universe. In those places where localized coherent supergeometry is also present (these are Einstein's matter points), diffluence wraps around it, creating a bubble having an inward-directional focus and with it a locally concentrated field of gravity. But wherever the pattern is too diffuse for a distinct object, such as in the great vastness of open space between the stars and galaxies, the diffluential effect is dispersed as a *non*-directional field along the featureless fabric of space-time throughout the cosmos (just like the alleged distribution of dark matter). The strength of this diffused field might be too small to measure locally, but is observable through gravitational lensing (gravity bending space to produce a lens-like effect) across vast expanses of space. The result would be—as Einstein imagined—that the entire face of the physical universe is curved, or in supergeometric terms, is one gigantic diffluential field bubble containing a myriad of lesser bubbles (its perimeter looking more like broccoli than a sphere). A vast cosmic field of diffluence could easily supply the missing gravity astronomers seek. What this all means is that the very curvature of space-time itself generates its own gravity.

This would also provide an explanation for the accelerated expansion of the universe that is normally attributed to the imaginary force known as dark energy. The supergeometric model indicates that the process by which a focused diffluential flow forms an expanding space-time bubble is progressive. This means that the expansion rate of the grand diffluential field bubble we call the universe progressively increased over time. One of the predictions that we can then make based on this accelerating expansion is that the total volume of gravity in the universe likewise increased over time in proportion to its expansion. Since gravity is a product of the curvature of space, the expanding curves of the growing bubble generates progressively more "ambient" or background gravity over time.

This presents a problem for dark matter. According to the laws of conservation, the matter/energy content of the universe is constant—no more can be created. Presently, the visible matter/energy content in the universe accounts for only about 10% of the total volume of universal gravity—dark matter supposedly generates the rest. But if the supergeometric model of cosmic expansion is correct, then the total amount of cosmic gravity would have been *less* in the past. If dark matter was truly the primary source of the universe's gravity, then the total sum of gravity-generating dark matter would have likewise been less. Once the accelerated expansion began about five billion years ago, the universe would have had to somehow break its own conservation laws by progressively creating more dark matter to generate the ever increasing volume of gravity as the universe got bigger. If we were able to confirm that the cosmic volume of gravity has indeed increased over time, then this would be a serious blow to the concepts of dark matter and dark energy.

While we're on the subject of cosmic expansion, there's another prediction about the early universe that emerges from the supergeometric model of creation. According to the theory, the universe arises from a superphysical, superlight realm, which then coagulates into physical matter and energy only when the diffluential flow decelerates down to lightspeed and below. This indicates that at the very first moment of the Big Bang, the bubble that was to become the physical universe was expanding at superlight speed. When matter, energy, and even time began to materialize in the forms we now recognize, the universe had already expanded significantly. I imagine it to have been like an exploding fireworks shell, that blasts out a ring of burning stars that suddenly slow and hang almost motionless in the air once their momentum has been expended, except that in the Big Bang, the stars don't start visibly burning (i.e., reach full physical presence) until the moment the force of their initial momentum is exhausted. As far as we can tell, the universe indeed experienced this same kind of deceleration before its expansion once again picked up speed.

Astrophysicists conclude from mapping the cosmos that the supposed concentrations of dark matter appear to be located in the same regions as the concentrations of normal matter. They thus see dark matter as a sort of pre-established cosmic scaffold around which the stars and galaxies ultimately formed. But the superstructure of grand supergeometry would also provide this skeleton around which to form and arrange cosmic material without the need to invent a new type of invisible matter.

I would ask all astrophysicists to humor me with a single mental experiment. We know the curvatures of space caused by this proposed dark matter can actually be seen by viewing how light from distant objects is bent by them as if through a lens. Here's the experiment: For just five short minutes, examine the available physical evidence with the same mindset from which Einstein viewed the Michelson-Morley experiment. He accepted the experiment's results at their face value without prejudice, and so concluded that the experiment demonstrated exactly what it appeared to demonstrate—namely, that there was in fact no ether. Now look upon the gravitational lensing along the cosmic web, envision the associated gravitational fields that bend the space, but also embrace with this vision what the failure of every known detection instrument and procedure appears to indicate—that there is really no local causal matter within these gravitational space-time curvatures. Yes, I know it's highly non-materialistic, but humor me—contemplate it sincerely, earnestly, for just five minutes out of your entire life. Do you see it now? There they are. The diffluential fields and the bubbles they form that cause gravitational lensing on a grand scale. There's your missing gravity. And now you can see the galactic matter formed within them. It's all exactly as it appears. It's a glimpse behind the cosmic veil of physical reality.

Senior scientist Chris Quigg of the Fermi National Accelerator Laboratory wrote "Physicists have an obligation to test any theory by considering its implications as if all its elements were real." I ask nothing more or less.

THE PARANORMAL

Perhaps no other field of study benefits more from the theory of supergeometry than that of the paranormal. Presently, paranormal researchers have no common set of scientifically oriented principles by which to organize, interpret and communicate their individual findings, nor any means to correlate these findings with other disciplines. Supergeometry offers such a uniform set of principles and terminology that can serve as a common foundation for researchers. Supergeometric theory furnishes for the first time a coherent and consistent model of paranormal mechanics, and reveals the inner relationships between all supernatural events. What's more, it finally provides paranormal researchers with a systematic and comprehensive means by which to reach beyond the current confines of their discipline into new scientific and spiritual vistas.

Transmentation

Remember that for transmentation to operate, there must exist a non-local means by which information can be transmitted to and from a human mind over vast distances of time and space. Years of research have failed to identify any such means within the physical realm, and so the mechanism must reside outside normal space-time. In the superphysical realm of the patriverse, information is indeed stored and transmitted outside space-time in the form of supergeometry. All things in the universe—people, places, and even thoughts—each has its own supergeometric pattern containing all the information necessary to reproduce its physical counterpart.

But how does the mind access this seemingly infinite store-house of information patterns? We know that the human mind has the unique ability to transform intangible data into tangible physical reality. In this way, the creative process of the mind mimics the very process by which intangible supergeometry and diffluence combine to create our tangible, physical reality. There is every reason to conclude that the creative faculties of the mind and the creative processes that give rise to the physical universe operate along the very same principles. In this way, the human mind can act as a portal or gateway between the superphysical and the physical, and can both recognize and assimilate the patterns of information it receives from either side of that gateway. And in the great mental cauldron we call the imagination, the number and type of patterns that can be generated and/or recognized appears almost limitless.

One of the challenges of telepathy is explaining how it operates over the vast physical distances that often separate the source of information and the recipient. Yet such dimensional barriers do not exist in the patriverse. Above the speed of light, temporal and spatial dimensions have not yet unfurled, and so distance and time have very little meaning. Many great thinkers, philosophers, and religious figures past and present have repeatedly asserted that all things in the universe are interconnected, no matter how much physical space separates them. Telepathic detection of another's thoughts, clairvoyant remote viewing of distant places and events, and precognition of events in the future or past display this interconnection. Transmental phenomena reach though some inner doorway within us and upward into the patriverse where the guardians of space and time have no jurisdiction.

Translocation

When objects move through the air of their own free will, one gets the eerie suspicion that the laws of gravity are being violated. Yet it may simply be that translocational phenomena applies those laws in ways with which we are not yet familiar.

As described earlier, supergeometric gravity is the result of the flow of diffluence across the light barrier into dimensional space. A large object like a planet has a correspondingly large surrounding diffluential field. When smaller objects like a meteor enters into the planet's surrounding diffluential bubble, its own smaller bubble is caught up and carried inward toward the center of the larger bubble, taking with it the physical mass of the meteor. Consequently, the movement of the meteor toward the planet's surface is caused by the gravitational effect of the larger object's diffluential field over that of the smaller object, which then carries the meteor along the resulting bending of space-time down to the larger object's surface as if caught up in the current of a river.

This supergeometric gravity presents us with a different set of laws that not only describes every characteristic of classical gravity, but also facilitates paranormal translocations without breaking any rules. In instances of telekinesis or mind-over-matter, a person's ability to reach across the space-time barrier telepathically and move a material object only appears to defy known laws because it applies an aspect of those laws not yet recognized. The object is moved through the manipulation of its diffluential field, and so it works by controlling gravity at its very source before its classical laws are fully unfolded.

Researchers of poltergeist phenomena in a house have often attributed the associated levitations with a particular family member, especially a young girl entering puberty. In such cases, it is believed that the person who is the focal point of activity unconsciously releases some kind of nervous energy that causes objects to be "thrown" around. But how could a conventional energy field manifest with such intensity to shove a heavy book off a shelf, or with such focus as to not displace adjacent books, without any visible or otherwise detectable *physical* mechanism to generate or direct such a field? It can't—at least not without breaking other well-established physical laws. But if the space surrounding the object is bent superphysically, it could easily be translocated without the need for a physical energy field. As discussed earlier, this same set of laws is at work in the translocation of both photons and air molecules to produce visual and auditory paranormal phenomena.

In some hauntings, the source of translocations appears to be a spirit. Supergeometry allows for such spirits, since it asserts that superphysical patterns can exist independently of their physical counterparts, and changes to those patterns can indeed cause physical effects. Kirlian phantoms show that the pattern of a living thing can manifest itself even after its physical body is cut away or destroyed. The notion that humans each possess their own unique supergeometric pattern is virtually identical to the traditional concept of a person having a spirit or soul. Presumably, such a spirit would maintain an image of its consciousness (which is part of its overall supergeometric pattern) even after being separated from its body. A conscious, sentient spirit dwelling in the patriversal realm of supergeometric and diffluential elements would naturally be in an ideal position to manipulate the diffluential field of an object in the physical realm, causing it to be moved by invisible hands.

Transmutation

Recall the discussion of supergeometric evolution, where a change in the pattern of an individual results in the appearance of a new species. Such a change occurs by the same process as a paranormal transmutation, in that the altered supergeometry automatically results in a corresponding change to its physical counterpart, so that the very molecular structure of a substance undergoes a metamorphosis into a different physical form.

Just as in translocational phenomena like telekinesis, transmutations can also be purposefully produced. A good example of this is psychic photography, where images of remote objects are recorded on film. These images are obviously not made in the conventional manner, since reflected light from a remote object cannot possibly reach the lens of the camera. The only explanation is that somehow the mind of the photographer is manipulating the film itself, thereby creating the image. And since it has already been demonstrated that telepathic signals are not transmitted physically, the image can only be produced by manipulating the superphysical pattern of the film. It may be more accurate to state that the supergeometry of the object in the photograph is somehow overlaid or superimposed onto the supergeometry of the film, which then transmutes the molecular structure of the film to produce a corresponding image.

Transmental phenomena show that the human mind has the power to receive and assimilate supergeometric forms from the patriverse. Transmutational phenomena such as psychic photography indicate that our minds have the ability to also transmit or project supergeometric patterns through the patriverse and back into physical space-time.

Spontaneous healing through prayer or the laying on of hands is another example of transmutation brought about by human agency. However, faith healings are probably not a case of superimposing a new supergeometric pattern over the old, but of restoring or re-enforcing the original supergeometry of the body, thereby bringing the body back into alignment. The sudden healing of a broken limb or the spontaneous disappearance of a tumor requires no supergeometric alteration, since the blueprint for the original healthy body already exists. This may be the reason why psychic and alternative healers do not describe the process as one of shaping or manipulation, but instead often speak of restoring the natural balance and flow of forces through the body, thereby bringing it back to its original state of health. Healers also often speak of inducing a flow of energy, even though it cannot be measured with conventional instruments. What they are actually inducing is an increase in the flow of diffluence, which would indeed have physical consequences both to the subject and any surrounding energy fields.

Transmigration

Transmigrations are certainly the most radical and mysterious of all paranormal phenomena. While other phenomena are caused by subtle adjustments in the supergeometric system, transmigration actually reverses the normal creational process, yanking the subject out of space-time and plunging it back in at a different location.

A simple model can be used to illustrate the mechanics of supergeometric transmigration. Imagine a very thin sheet of rubber stretched vertically. The sheet is so thin that if you were to push against it with a finger, every detail of your fingerprint would be visibly impressed into the rubber. Now place an apple against the left side of the rubber sheet and push in, making a depression in the rubber. Again, the rubber is so thin that it conforms around the apple so that every detail is clearly visible through the opposite side. In this model, the rubber sheet is the space-time barrier; to the left of the sheet is the superphysical patriverse and to the right is the physical universe. The apple is a supergeometric pattern, and the force pushing the apple into the sheet is the flow of diffluence across the space-time barrier. The pocket of rubber sheet surrounding the apple is a diffluential field bubble. An observer in the physical universe (on the right) sees the apple materialized as a hard physical object, complete in every detail, while the processes occurring on the other side of the sheet remain invisible. [Figure 8.5, next page]

351

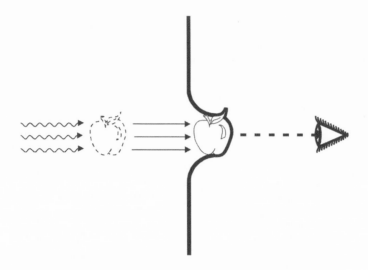

Figure 8.5 — Normal Materialization. The flow of diffluence across the light barrier creates a diffluential field bubble in which the apple materializes.

Now let's reverse the flow of force that holds the apple into the rubber by pulling it out of the sheet. The depression in the rubber disappears, or in other words, the diffluential field bubble collapses. The apple is no longer pressing into the rubber, and so its image becomes invisible to the observer in the physical universe. This is an example of a dematerialization. [Figure 8.6, next page] Remember that even though the apple has physically disappeared, its supergeometry is still intact in the patriverse.

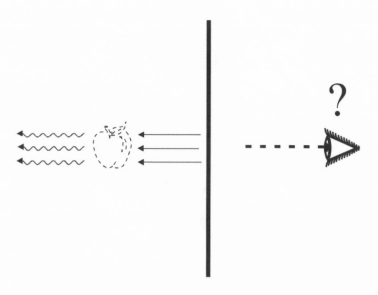

Figure 8.6 — Dematerialization. Reversing the direction or polarity of the flow of the diffluential waves causes the bubble in space-time to collapse, and the apple to dematerialize.

Now move the apple to a different point on the rubber and press it in again. The apple now rematerializes at a different location in space-time. These two examples taken in sequence —the dematerialization of an object from one location, follow-ed by its rematerialization at another location—paint a working picture of teleportation. As long as the supergeometric pattern of an object remains intact, it can be re-introduced at any location along the fabric of space-time. [Figure 8.7, next page]

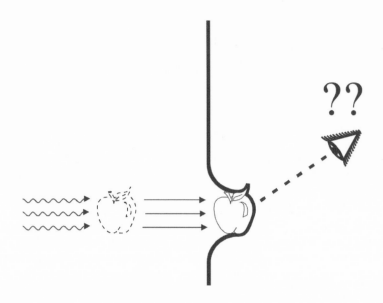

Figure 8.7 — Teleportation. The flow of diffluence is redirected toward a new location in space-time and the apple rematerializes, thus producing the effect known as teleportation.

What if two separate diffluential streams are simultaneously directed at the apple's supergeometry? As the two flows of diffluence reach their respective destinations on the rubber, diffluential field bubbles begin to form at both sites, and an image of the apple appears in each. This is bilocation. [Figure 8.8, next page]

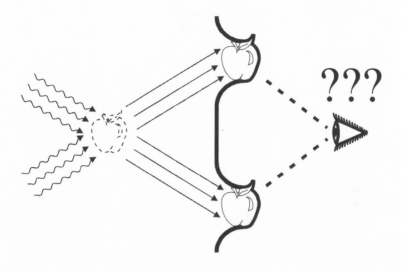

Figure 8.8 — Bilocation. A second flow of diffluence is directed through the supergeometry of the apple, causing it to bilocate in two different places in space-time.

The supergeometric mechanics of transmigration might also shed light on the phenomenon of levitation. Recall that the word *presence* was previously used to represent the degree in which an object is physically manifested in space-time. An object in its normal state (fully materialized) is considered to have full presence in our universe, while an object taken out of space-time (dematerialized) is considered to have no physical presence. An object in between these two extremes is understood to be in a state of partial presence. The degree in which an object is partially present can vary widely, from a hard concrete object to a transparent ethereal ghost. If an object were reduced to only partial presence in the physical plane, the overall surrounding bubble of gravity will likewise be reduced, and so it might begin to levitate or float, even though it would still appear visually like any normal object.

Synchronicity

Based on what has been covered so far, the source of synchronicity is fairly obvious. The all-encompassing pattern of grand supergeometry that determines the nature of time, space, matter, and events is internally synchronous by nature. The entanglement of all things through this supergeometric network goes largely unnoticed, since we cannot directly observe the underlying web of interconnections outside the physical plane. But on occasion, we catch a brief glimpse of its synchronous patterns when a series of seemingly unrelated events appear to us as "coincidental" in some meaningful way.

Investigating the Paranormal

I believe that paranormal activity affords us the opportunity to study the supergeometric effect in real time as it unfolds. By applying our new model of paranormal mechanics, researchers can gain fresh insights into how their techniques might be modified to obtain more meaningful results from their investigations. Such a systematic and rational approach also presents mainstream scientists with a compelling reason for becoming actively involved with paranormal investigation. Experimental physicists can bring to the paranormal table resources, ideas and perspectives that the majority of laypeople who regularly conduct these investigations cannot.

A standard set of equipment has evolved from decades of paranormal investigations that include video and still cameras, motion detectors, sound recorders, EMF meters, infrared and thermal detecting devices, and even "white noise" generators that appear to give disembodied spirits a voice with which to converse with the living. However, I believe this collection of technology has reached its full potential some time ago because of the faulty model of paranormal mechanics employed by researchers to analyze the gathered data. As a result, investigators today are limited to traveling from one location to another, recording the very same types of phenomena over and over, year after year, without achieving any further advances in understanding.

So now what? How much of this identical and repetitive data do we need to accumulate? Believers are already convinced, skeptics won't believe until they experience it for themselves, and deniers will refuse to believe even if they see it with their own eyes. It's not the evidence that is the challenge, but the conditions under which it's collected. A haunted house crawling with amateurs (from a scientific view) operating without a detailed understanding of basic physics while laboring under faulty preconceived notions will never satisfy the criteria of a controlled experimental environment. This doesn't mean, however, that these efforts are for naught. There is always a chance that some investigative team will record a piece of evidence that is so compelling and so revealing that its study will serve to help advance the field and convert skeptics. But for the most part, we're just plodding the same outworn paths.

Most paranormal research to date has focused primarily on what a phenomenon *does*. We need to shift more of that focus to what a phenomenon *is*. The problem has been that no framework existed that was both logical and broadly applicable in which plug all this data so that scientifically sensible hypotheses could be formulated and then tested. Without this essential element, most explanations have revolved around speculations about spiritual considerations like deceased persons, "stuck" souls and demons, and nebulous notions of spirit realms, other dimensions or parallel universes. None of these ambiguities lead to the kind of sound, sober reasoning needed to effectively explore the processes behind the physical manifestations associated with these phenomena.

Supergeometry can provide researchers with a functional framework with which to probe for reasonable answers. Here's just one example how supergeometry can present us with new insights into the mysteries of the paranormal. Observers often report a feeling of "heaviness" in the vicinity of paranormal activity. Almost everyone uses this exact same word to describe the feeling, so the sensation must be very pronounced and distinct. Since we are all familiar with the feeling of overcoming gravity in carrying both our own bodies and other objects, I accept this universal description of heaviness as an accurate assessment—things really *are* heavier. No one to my knowledge has ever provided a reasonable explanation for what causes this. But recall that, according to the supergeometric model, a paranormal event is preceded by the creation and expansion of a diffluential field bubble in the fabric of space-time. One of the characteristics of such a bubble is that it generates its own gravity field as it warps space. If that's the case, then this instinctive sense of heaviness reported by witnesses is quite literally true!

Most people have experienced the added G-forces that push you back in your seat when the car you're riding in accelerates very quickly. Imagine being in a standing position with this many Gs on you and how heavy your body would feel. Imagine the sensation of trying to walk forward in it. It would be as if you were walking through a thick fluid. This feeling is exactly what paranormal investigators describe.

To test this hypothesis, I suggest the construction of a new apparatus for field investigators called a *gravometer*. This would comprise a rigid hollow sphere with a mount so that it can be secured to a foundation in a fixed position to prevent even the slightest movement. In the center of the sphere would be fixed a highly sensitive motion sensor suspended by delicate elastic cords or springs from multiple point. When a diffluential field bubble begins to form in the vicinity, the sensor will be pulled in the direction of the center of the emerging gravity well and will record the degree and direction of deflection.

Another consequence of expanding or contracting diffluential field bubbles are the disturbances they will produce in the surrounding atmosphere. Investigators should then also bring with them a barometer to measure these disturbances. Combining the use of a barometer and the new gravometer along with the more traditional EMF meter would better help investigators isolate and identify the location, size and intensity of these spatial depressions as they form.

Other observations defying explanation in the vicinity of paranormal activity are sudden spikes in electromagnetic fields (EMF), heat signatures, cold spots, and the failure of electrical devices. As previously mentioned, these cannot result from the conventional premise of spirits drawing energy from the surrounding area to visibly manifest—the physics for it just simply isn't there. It also raises other contradictions like the rise in EMF levels frequently detected at the location of paranormal activity. If a spirit draws electromagnetic energy (the kind of energy carried in batteries) from its surroundings to manifest, wouldn't we then observe a *drop* in surrounding EMF instead of a rise? This clearly makes no sense.

However, these kinds of observations illustrate quite well the various effects an expanding diffluential field bubble might have on its surroundings. Consider the elevated EMF readings recorded at the sites of paranormal reports. An expanding bubble of space would indeed create a form of piezoelectric effect at its surface. It's not difficult to visualize this if you think of the visible shock waves seen in the films of explosions during aerial bombardments (of course, the effect of a localized, expanding spatial depression would not be so dramatic as an exploding bomb, since it occurs on a much smaller scale). Based on our model of an expanding diffluential field bubble, we would expect its leading edge to compress and excite the air molecules it encounters, thereby generating elevated amounts of EMF, heat and sometimes even light. It's easy to see how this might cause the often-reported effect of goose bumps or hair standing on end to a person making physical contact with an expanding bubble. The amount of EMF, heat and light actually generated would depend upon the size of the bubble and the rate of its expansion. The length of time in which these measurements persist at a given location would indicate the relative stability of the forming bubble. A bubble of sufficient volume and stability would be necessary to manifest a paranormal event for more than just a fleeting second.

The fact that these kinds of energies are being generated only at the surface of the bubble where it interacts with the surrounding environment would explain why thermal images recorded of specters do not fully mimic those from a physical living creature. The thermal signatures of living persons, for example, have a striking variation of intensity across its surface. Exposed flesh radiates far brighter than clothing. Even on the flesh itself, outer areas like cheeks, noses and ears display much darker than warmer areas receiving more hot blood flow. This is because the extreme hot spots recorded at the skin's surface are being produced by the biological heat-generating machine at the core of that person's physical body, which is then carried to the surface by the blood. But the thermal images of apparitions do not manifest like this. Even though these can sometimes display a surprising amount of detail, the thermal signature is much more even over the entire surface of the image. This is because the supergeometric processes taking place inside the diffluential bubble are not like the processes that generate heat inside a living body. Instead, the heat processes of the bubble occur at the surface where it interacts with its surroundings. Since we would expect this process to be fairly even over the entire surface of the bubble, the heat signature of an apparition would be similarly even over its entire perimeter with only minor variations in surface geometry. This is exactly the kind of signatures we see in these paranormal images.

The generation of EMF at the leading edge of an expanding diffluential bubble provides a solution to yet another anomaly sometimes observed at the site of paranormal activity, namely, that batteries in electrical devices appear to temporarily drain or the device is otherwise rendered non-functional. We know that certain kinds of EMF can act as a dampening field that will interfere with the normal operation of electrical systems. In fact, weapons already exist that produce this exact same kind of damage or disruption of electrical devices with EMF pulses. Satellites and even entire electrical grids can all be crippled with the right kind of EMF. It is quite possible that an expanding diffluential bubble could indeed produce the right kind EMF with sufficient intensity to occasionally cause this effect in electric devices and their batteries. This would also explain in a scientifically sound way why these devices usually return to normal operation once they are removed from the vicinity of the activity. This is yet another example of how supergeometric theory provides a better explanation for these phenomena that is more reasonable than the thermodynamic impossibility of ethereal spirits draining power to physically manifest.

Another important feature of a diffluential field bubble's surface is that it can occasionally achieve sufficient density to reflect ambient light like a normal object, so that the resulting apparition has a similar appearance and with the same relative brightness as other objects in the immediate vicinity. There are also instances where this surface can instead absorb the entire light spectrum in the same manner as an object painted black, thereby producing what's commonly known as a *shadow ghost*. Remember, if all objects in the universe are formed within these spatial depressions or bubbles, then the paranormal apparitions formed within these same bubbles will display the same kind of optical effects as the reflection and absorption of ambient light from the surfaces of normal objects.

Up to this point, we've been focusing on the effects at the leading, convex edge of the expanding surface of a diffluential bubble. We also need to consider what effects might occur at the trailing, concave edge. For example, while the leading edge of the advancing depression exerts pressure on the opposing air molecules, the receding edge would create more of a suction or vacuum behind it. Isn't the detection of a passing breeze with no apparent source among the manifestations occasionally reported in association with paranormal events? If the rate of the bubble's expansion was sufficiently quick, there would not be enough time for the air pressure building at the outer, advancing edge of a forming bubble to gradually equalize with the vacuum building within the bubble behind its inner edge. The sudden sucking of air into the growing vacuum would produce the same kinds of breezes reported by observers where there is no apparent source like an open window or door.

Does it sound like we're onto something here?

Now let's talk about the drops in temperature that are also recorded at the sites of paranormal activity. We've already surmised that the supergeometric process within a forming bubble does not generate its own heat. Lacking any such internal heat source within its own relative bubble of space-time, whatever heat energy might be present within the bubble's interior would have to be drawn from the surrounding air by means of thermal induction. But what if the bubble expands so quickly that there is insufficient time for the temperature within the bubble to equalize with the temperature outside? In instances where the expansion of the depression is so rapid that heat transference cannot occur fast enough to maintain thermal equilibrium with the adjacent areas, temperatures within the depression would be quite a bit chillier than the surroundings. Keep in mind, however, that this would not negate the production of a heat signature at the very surface of the expanding bubble where the molecules of the air are being excited. If heat generation was only taking place at the outer surface of the bubble, but its interior was markedly cooler, this would perfectly explain how a thermal imaging camera might detect a heat signature in the shape of a figure (i.e., a diffluential field bubble configured by a supergeometric pattern into the shape of a figure) while at the same time a thermometer at that location records the opposite effect of a significant *drop* in temperature in the same area.

Supergeometry's ability to provide a singular model that can be used to explain the myriad of paranormal observations in a uniform and consistent way is unprecedented, and so furnishes the conceptual breakthrough needed for advancing paranormal research to the next level. The belief that a spirit is peculiarly endowed with the power to draw energy from its surroundings by completely inexplicable means (a skill that's acquired in the process of dying?) in order to physically manifest in defiance of all know physical law, and in direct contradiction to other phys-ical evidence gathered at the time has served as a sort of mental roadblock behind which we've been stalled for years.

Orbs? They are small diffluential field bubbles. They simply lack the necessary supergeometric pattern to shape them into recognizable forms like apparitions. Their outer surfaces excite the surrounding air molecules, causing them to emit enough energy to make the "shell" of the bubble visible under certain conditions, either by emitted or reflected energy. Although they are little balls of energy in a certain sense, this energy is only at the outer surface, and so they are not quite as researchers have traditionally perceived them.

Kirlian Phantoms

Supergeometric mechanics can give us an idea as to what is actually being presented by the phantom leaf effect images in Kirlian photography. As we discussed earlier, one of the effects of a diffluential field bubble is the generation of an electro-magnetic field at its leading edge. Of course, this effect would be much more pronounced with the kinds of spontaneously expanding and fluctuating bubbles associated with paranormal phenomena than with the relatively subtle EMF effect for a stable physical object like a tomato leaf. When the experiment-er removes a section of the leaf, the portion of the steady, stable bubble associated with the removed section persists for awhile as part of the larger field bubble of the whole leaf. The smaller section is sustained by the leaf's greater overlaying supergeo-metry, which is superphysical and therefore unaffected by the removal of its physical counterpart. The combination of both a persisting bubble and supergeometric pattern in the area vaca-ted by the leaf section produces a "phantom" on the resulting photograph.

But how could this image be recorded on film, since it is superphysical and thus invisible? The film image is likely the same effect that causes apparitions to become visible and EMF meters to react to paranormal events, in that the outer edge of the leaf's diffluential field bubble is reacting with the surround-ing environment sufficiently for the film to record. The Kirlian apparatus is then not recording the actual diffluential bubble, but the interaction between the EMF at the outer surface of the bubble and the electrical field across the charged glass plate on which it is placed.

Another amazing aspect to the Kirlian phantom is that the small section severed from the main body of the leaf *also* dis-plays its Kirlian pattern when photographed separately. This has incredible implications. It means that the main leaf and the separated portion both have the same pattern presented in two different places at the same locus in time. We are seeing the actual physical manifestation—and thus the evidence—of bilo-cation. Because both the leaf segment's supergeometry and its associated diffluential bubble is now breaking forth into the physical at two different locations in space-time, the necessary superphysical elements are in place to yield full bilocation of the physical leaf segment at both locations. All we lack is the scientific understanding to technologically replicate the missing portion from its supergeometric pattern (we'll talk more about this in the next chapter).

CONCLUSION

This theory of supergeometry derived from the three-fold study of physical anomalies, paranormal evidence and Biblical principles has been put to the test and found to offer reasonable answers to the mysteries posed to it. Some of these solutions have proved to be more workable than existing theories. The correlation of paranormal phenomena, scientific anomalies, and Biblical principles within the framework of the supergeometric model provides for the first time a coherent and consistent foundation in which all three disciplines can finally stand together in co-operative harmony.

It is time to explore the possible applications of this new theory, and see where it may lead us.

Behind The Cosmic Veil

10

Fantastic Possibilities

Super-Technologies of the Future

> 'Nonsense' is that which does not fit
> into the prearranged patterns which
> we have superimposed on reality.
> There is no such thing as 'nonsense'
> apart from a judgmental intellect which
> calls it that.
>
> —Gary Zukav

Viewers of the famous *Star Trek* television series and its off-shoots were treated during its run to a dazzling world of science fact, fiction, and fantasy—ships that fly at superlight speeds, teleportation of personnel and objects across empty space, and food replicators that serve up meals out of thin air. Incredible alien talents also fired the imagination, such as the transmutational shape-shifting of the Founders, and the telepathic mind-probing of the Betazoids and Vulcans.

But is all this merely the fruit of an overactive imagination, or are these supernatural and technological miracles a real possibility? Could they actually represent a realistic if not fanciful glimpse into our future?

For the most part, traditional science does not provide for such marvels. Infinite energy would be needed to propel a ship at the speed of light, let alone the incredible superlight velocities achieved by the fictional starship *Enterprise*. In the case of teleportation, we'd have to overcome the seemingly impossible challenge of converting a physical human body into an energy beam containing its entire pattern, including the exact position and type of every subatomic particle (the uncertainty principle of quantum physics would in itself declare this unfeasible), then converting that beam back into a living body of physical matter while duplicating in exact order the original pattern of molecular structure, mass, energy level, temperature, blood flow, etc. Food replication, and the creation of hard, fleshy holographic projections also fall victim to these very same complications. And we already know what mainstream science has to say about such "nonsense" as telepathy.

Yet virtually all these scientific objections are based on the assumption that the whole of reality is defined only by what is physical, and thus bound by the immutable laws of space and time. Supergeometric theory, on the other hand, defines an additional component of reality called the patriverse, a parallel realm that is both superphysical and superdimensional. Such a super-dimensional realm would not be limited by the normal physical constraints. The supergeometric model of creation suggests there is indeed a way to bypass the classical laws of physics and achieve what was previously considered by mainstream science to be impossible.

SUPERGEOMETRIC TECHNOLOGY

The ability to re-shape matter into almost any imaginable form is a characteristic trait of *homo sapiens*. Some primates employ simple tools. Beavers build dams that alter the environment. Microbes break down substances into various chemical compounds. But all these are merely the rearranging of existing items. Humanity's ability to first conceive and then shape a previously non-existing article from the raw materials of this planet is without parallel.

Yet, in spite of the seemingly limitless number of forms and devices we produce, our creative prowess is confined to merely re-configuring the physical elements that already exist. Supergeometry offers the promise of a second, more direct way to alter matter by manipulating the supergeometric patterns from which the very physical structure of reality is derived. Through this, it would be possible to not only shape the cosmic clay, but also change its fundamental nature.

What if we were to attempt to build an apparatus to manipulate material patterns based on supergeometric principles? Unfortunately, it's unclear how a supergeometric device could be constructed using today's technology. Just as contemporary measuring devices can only detect things physical, an apparatus based on current technology would be unable to pierce the cosmic veil of space-time into the superphysical realm of supergeometry where any such pattern manipulation would have to take place.

This doesn't mean, however, that such technology could not be developed at some future date. As is often the case with most advances in our technological history, theory precedes practice. A process must first be identified and understood (at least on some rudimentary level) before technicians ply their skills at finding a practical application. The principles of electromagnetism had to first be understood before dynamos and generators were built, $E=mc^2$ before atomic reactors, and jet propulsion before moon rockets. Being a pragmatic species, we tend to look only for what we believe we'll find. Supergeometry proposes there is indeed something beyond the physical to find for those who have the vision and determination to look for it and conduct the necessary research.

Actually, an apparatus already exists that could prove an excellent model for the design of this supergeometric device. There is every indication that the human brain has the capacity to send, receive, alter, or even create supergeometric patterns. The many instances of clairvoyance and precognition demonstrate the mind's capacity to penetrate the barriers of space and time to retrieve recognizable and accurate images. Some of these images are so vivid (as in lucid dreaming) that there is little doubt real physical objects could be fashioned from them. Indeed, the very fact that we can hold such an image in our minds, then use our hands to fashion an article based on that image, is the hard evidence that these mental patterns can serve as blueprints for actual physical creation. Sculptors often say that they envision the already completed statue embedded inside the block of stone, and they with their tools and hands merely remove the superfluous material that covers it. The challenge is to discover a device more efficient than our mere flesh-and-blood hands to manipulate these mental images into their physical equivalent. By replacing the human hands with the proper apparatus, supergeometric patterns in the mind could be converted directly into physical reality.

Hungry? Picture a big, juicy red apple. My, that looks good. Now plug yourself in, and poof! Enjoy.

Unfortunately, such a creational mechanism could not only have severe limitations, but also serious liabilities. The human mind can be quite unpredictable, and so a device built to convert human thoughts directly into their physical equivalent might generate some unpleasant and chaotic side effects. After all, how many of us are truly masters of our thoughts? For this reason, a machine emulating only that portion of the mind which generates supergeometric patterns while eliminating all our behavioral "static" would be much preferable. If we truly understood the workings of the psyche, we might be able to construct a device based on its design. Supergeometric patterns could then be generated in a stable and predictable way unhindered by the tumultuous ramblings of our fickle imagination and passions.

370

Creation of Matter

For this hypothetical device to be fully functional, it must also be furnished with a supply of raw material for shaping into objects. Remember that matter consists of both form and substance—the form of supergeometric patterns and the substance of diffluential waves. We would need to discover a way to harvest the same diffluential waves that yield the hard material from which the physical world of space-time is made.

The challenge is to fabricate a mechanism out of physical materials that will generate something superphysical like supergeometric patterns and diffluential waves. Although this might seem at first too daunting a task, our current technology may be closer to solving this than we might think, at least when it comes to the diffluential part of the equation. During their research into the dual nature of light, physicists discovered that all physical things have corresponding matter waves. Although these matter waves are accepted today as a fundamental part of physical reality, physicists have yet to discover exactly what these waves might actually represent. Louis de Broglie, who first proposed the theory of matter waves in 1924, could only conclude that these waves "correspond" to matter, but could offer no explanation as to what they might be, nor even why matter has such waves. Supergeometric theory now defines these matter waves as the "echoes" left by the superphysical diffluential waves that form dimensional matter.

The supergeometric principle of primal conflict provides us with another clue. It suggests that diffluence is a uniform substance containing within it the potential for all possible matter waves. What causes diffluential waves to morph into almost any form is not any variations in the diffluence itself, but the supergeometric patterns with which the diffluence combines. In other words, generating this pre-creational substance is a separate process than the shaping of it. We should then only need to find a single method to induce a flow of diffluence for any

371

and all purposes to which we'd apply it.

To illustrate this more clearly, let's look at the physics of vision, specifically, the seeing of colors. Sunlight carries with it all wavelengths of the spectrum from ultraviolet to infrared. But when this light strikes an object, some of these wavelengths are absorbed while others are reflected back, so that a green plant primarily reflects wavelengths in the green spectrum while absorbing the majority of the others. Diffluence is likely similar in that its raw form contains all possible matter waves, which are then "filtered" according to the specific supergeometric pattern with which it interacts. Although the pattern of an oak leaf is quite different than that of a squirrel, each has the same spectrum of diffluential waves interacting with its supergeometry, which then shapes it into different forms. But the substance of the diffluence is the same in both.

Here's an interesting "proof" of how the same diffluential wave frequencies can be used to create different physical forms. Consider the ringing in one's ears resulting from being struck in the head, often caricaturized in cartoon by a halo of tweeting birds. I can personally attest to the accuracy of this metaphor (rest assured—the ideas in this book are not directly related to this dizzying experience). The sound is so much like that of a woods filled with life that the phenomenon cannot be easily dismissed as coincidence—singing birds and chirping insects fill your head in startling fidelity. This medley of waves playing through the human brain must therefore be very similar if not identical to the waves playing through the forest canopy.

What if the reality of this is exactly what it appears to be? What if the sounds in the head and the sounds in the forest are truly one and the same? The source of these frequencies would then be identical, and would play the same tune throughout the cosmos. The only difference would be in those material forms around which this cosmic melody plays. In our example, the brain and the woods each have a very different supergeometric pattern—one shapes the diffluence into synapses, neurons, and vessels, while the other mints insects, birds, and trees. But the diffluential waves and their associated frequencies are identical for each, and therefore produce the exact same "echo" in both the head and the woods.

Look at the naked branches of a typical northern tree in winter. Then look at a model of the human vascular system. Coincidence? Or do both arise from the same intrinsic order?

This relationship between diffluence and matter waves may hold the key to developing our hypothetical apparatus. While the superphysical waves of diffluence themselves might lay beyond the reach of current technology, the physical matter waves they produce are not. Physicists currently possess instruments capable of detecting or generating virtually any physical wavelength. If wave-like functions are at the heart of physical reality, then by broadcasting the correct number and kinds of waves simultaneously, we should be able to tap into the raw diffluence necessary for the creation of matter. There may indeed be some cosmic melody whose playing would open a rift between the realms of physical dimension and superphysical supergeometry, and so expose the proverbial gateway to another dimension.

An example of two waves projected together to produce an entirely new wave can be found in many pneumatic (air-driven) pipe organs. The lengths of its various ranks of pipes determine the range of octaves that can be played. The longer the pipe, the lower the octave. A very high octave is produced by a one-foot series or rank of pipes, the next lower octave by a two-foot rank, the next by a four-foot rank and so on, the length of the ranks being doubled for each successive lower octave. Because of the space required to house the huge, lowest-pitched pipes, most organs are limited to having a sixteen-foot rank as their lowest octave. Yet there are certain compositions that call for notes to be played in the even lower thirty-two-foot octave. To play these contrabass notes, many organs have a *theoretical rank* called a thirty-two-foot *resultant*. Activating this rank causes two different sixteen-foot pipes to be played simultaneously. If these two pipes are tuned just right, they resonate together to produce a resultant, an entirely different note that is an octave lower than the two original notes. This resultant is a true thirty-two-foot octave note, even though there is no physical thirty-two-foot pipe playing it.

Another example of waves being used to produce a resultant is a process known as *sonoluminescence* [*sono* = sound, *luminescence* = light]. Simply put, sonoluminescence is the process of converting of sound into light. H. Frenzel and H. Shultes of the University of Cologne first discovered the process in 1934. In the original experiment, a container of water was immersed within an intense field of sound waves. At a particular frequency and amplitude, the waves agitated the water, creating clouds of expanding and collapsing bubbles. As the bubbles collapsed, they emitted a brief but discernible flash of light. Frenzel and Shultes concluded that the flashes were produced by a buildup of static electricity that discharged when the bubbles collapsed in much the same manner as a spark discharges when touching something after shuffling your feet across a carpet. However, subsequent experimentation by others failed to confirm this or any other explanation for the phenomenon. To date, the underlying mechanism by which bubbles of air can be induced to emit light through the use of sound waves is uncertain.

The significance of these examples is that a resultant wave can be produced by the use of other waves instead of by direct means—thirty-two-foot octaves without a physical thirty-two-foot pipe, and light waves without a physical light source. In a similar way, our supergeometric device may be able to produce waves of diffluence by the simultaneous projection of known, conventional waves. This would eliminate having to invent a means to generate superphysical waves directly. Granted, there are a staggering number of possible wave frequencies from which to choose. Every particle, planet and star in the cosmos dances to its own symphony. Extensive research would be needed to determine the exact combination of wavelengths required for diffluential field generation. Since diffluential waves give rise to every physical wavelength in the universe, it may even be necessary to play *all* physical wavelengths in specific proportions to create a diffluential resultant.

Still another exciting possibility may be that we do not need to produce diffluence at all. Diffluence is the result of primal conflict, a process that has been at work since the beginning of time. It may only be necessary to harvest the existing diffluence by tapping into it at its source, then containing it in a suitable vessel, in this case a space-time depression. By simultaneously projecting the correct combination of waves, it may be possible to induce a focused flow of diffluence across the space-time barrier. The flow would then warp the fabric of space-time as it penetrates the barrier, creating a pocket or bubble into which diffluence would be drawn and suspended. Such a warp bubble filled with raw diffluence (i.e., a diffluential field bubble), would serve as an ideal crucible in which to forge material objects.

The notion of creating an opening in our physical universe leading to some higher realm is by no means new. This theoretical opening has been offered up many times under various names: gateway, portal, doorway, window or rift. But to date, no one has been able to describe precisely what form this opening might take. Supergeometry can now define this portal as a pocket or depression in the fabric of space-time induced by a localized, focused flow of diffluence. The resulting depression—a diffluential field bubble—protrudes into dimensional space, creating an opening leading directly to the superphysical realm. It is within these bubbles that material objects can be formed.

Physical Presence

In order to reproduce the various effects associated with paranormal phenomena, our supergeometric device must also be able to manipulate the degree to which a material object manifests itself in the physical plane, or in other words, the degree of its physical *presence*. For example, imagine a scale of zero to ten, ten being a completely manifested, hard physical object with full physical presence. If somehow the object were completely removed from the physical universe, our imaginary scale would read zero, having no physical presence at all. Now what about an ethereal, quasi-physical manifestation such as a ghost? Although visibly discernible in the physical realm, ghosts are not quite fully physical, which is why they often appear transparent and are also able to pass through solid walls. A ghost therefore only has partial physical presence, and so falls somewhere between zero and ten on this scale.

Supergeometry describes a progression of creation from a superphysical, superdimensional state to one that is fully physical and dimensional. A supergeometric device would need the ability to advance or reverse this process, causing an object to recede back into its superphysical state or forward again into full physical presence. This would be accomplished by altering the direction of flow or the *polarity* of the diffluential fields that surround all physical objects. As the polarity of an object's diffluential field begins reversing, the presence of that object in space-time decreases. The object grows lighter in weight as its presence diminishes, and will even become transparent as if it were fading away (which is actually happening in a physical sense). Eventually, the object's physical presence will be so reduced as to completely disappear from space-time. By restoring the normal polarity of the object's diffluential field, the surrounding bubble once again expands, and the object will then begin to gradually re-materialize in the physical plane until it again achieves full physical presence.

It is important to remember that throughout this process, the object's supergeometry remains unaffected. Even though the object may be completely removed from the physical plane, its supergeometric pattern remains preserved outside of space-time. This pattern serves as the blueprint or template from which the original object can be exactly re-created.

To sum up, our supergeometric device will comprise two basic components or sub-systems, each performing a distinct function. The first sub-system will induce a focused flow of diffluence by the simultaneous emission of the right number and combination of physical wavelengths. The emitter will also control the diffluence by increasing, decreasing, or even reversing the direction of its flow. The second sub-system consists of a patterning device designed along the same principles as the human mind's imaginative faculty (which is indeed an imaging device made from flesh-and-blood). This component will act as a combination scanner, rectifier, generator, and projector of supergeometric patterns. It will scan existing supergeometric patterns and store them to memory from where they can be recalled on demand or altered in some beneficial way. The unit will also be capable of generating new supergeometric patterns bearing their own novel and distinct features. Finally, it will be equipped with an emitter to project the patterns stored in its memory to a spatial depression formed at the desired location.

By creating a controlled flow of diffluence and then focusing it around a supergeometric pattern, the device will be able to generate an almost infinite variety of physical objects.

APPLICATIONS

Some would dismiss as too fantastic the idea that the device being described could ever be built. Yet philosophers have maintained for centuries that all things are possible, and that we can accomplish whatever we can imagine (using the brain's same imaging mechanism that gives rise to all human creations). Our supergeometric device is simply a technical expression of these widely recognized human capabilities. With this device, one could duplicate virtually all paranormal or supernatural phenomena, as well as most of the technical wizardry presently confined to the realm of science fiction.

The Paranormal

Our supergeometric device would be most adept at performing transmigrational effects. It was described earlier how this device could achieve dematerialization through reversing the flow or polarity of an object's diffluential field. Rematerialization occurs when the field's polarity is restored to its original orientation. The supergeometric pattern of an object remains unaffected during the dematerialization process, and so serves as a template from which the object can be perfectly re-created during rematerialization.

The ability to dial into an object's supergeometric pattern and project it to a desired location in space-time also gives the device the power of teleportation. Once dematerialized, an object's pattern can be guided elsewhere to a receiving station where it will be rematerialized, thereby effectively teleporting the object. Remember that in the realm where supergeometry dwells, time and space play a relatively insignificant role. The supergeometric pattern of the Eiffel Tower may be as spatially close to New York City as it is to Paris. A device in New York need only scan the patriverse for the pattern matching the Eiffel Tower, then induce a flow of diffluence through that pattern to cause the tower to materialize there.

Bilocation is a similar process except that more than one copy of the object is materialized using the same supergeometric pattern. Keep in mind, however, that a bilocated object is more than just a "copy" of the original—it *is* the original, but is materialized at multiple locations in space at the same location in time (this is one of those thought images that challenges the limits of our ability to conceptualize). To accomplish this, our supergeometric machine would first need to induce a flow of diffluence against the fabric of space-time, creating a diffluential field bubble. Then, by projecting the original object's pattern into the bubble (and consequently in the path of the diffluential flow), the diffluence coagulates around the pattern and the duplicate materializes. The number of objects that could be re-created would be limited only by the number of diffluential field bubbles the device could produce. In such a way, nourishment for the masses might be provided by replication—thousands of people could be fed with a mere handful of food. The opportunities for catastrophic misuse would likewise be enormous.

Transmutations can be performed through the device's capacity to manipulate and alter supergeometric patterns. Once an object's pattern is altered, the physical object itself will change in accordance with the new configuration. The sheer number of applications for this feature is staggering, being limited only by the imagination.

The supergeometric pattern projector in the device could also produce transmental effects. The transmitting of information via a superdimensional realm (where spatial distances are irrelevant) would allow communications from distant satellites and spacecraft to be instantaneous, since there would now be no need to cross the physical expanses of space. We might also transmit supergeometric patterns directly to the human mind, achieving a sort of telepathic link between human and machine. Similarly, a machine equipped with a supergeometric pattern scanner could in turn receive images directly from the mind, enabling complex instructions in the form of pictographs or symbols to be transmitted "telepathically" to the machine. The symbiosis between mind and machine might become so close as to make one a mere extension of the other. Be careful what you think.

Medical Applications

Supergeometric technology could have a multitude of applications related to the field of medicine. Take for instance just the single disease of cancer. Scanning the body for any foreign supergeometric patterns would make the detection of abnormal growths almost instantaneous. Once such a growth is detected, it can be teleported out of the body without the need for invasive surgery. One of the most devastating characteristics of this disease is the process called metastasis, where individual cancerous cells separate from the original tumor and migrate to other parts of the body to begin forming new growths. With supergeometric technology, the cells in the original tumor can first be scanned for their unique supergeometric pattern. Then the patient's body can be scanned for any cells that carry the same supergeometric signature. The individual cells can then be teleported out of the body, leaving the patient free from the disease, and thus truly cured.

Both the phantom limb effect experienced by amputees and the phantom leaf effect observed in Kirlian photography are powerful evidence that the superphysical pattern of a limb remains intact even after the physical limb is removed. These patterns will serve as the blueprint from which to manufacture replacement limbs by rematerialization. The need for transplanting organs like the heart, lung, or kidney from a donor would be eliminated, as an exact original can be replicated. There would be no problem of tissue rejection, as the immune system would recognize the replacement as being identical to the original—it will, in fact, literally be the original. In the case of less severely damaged organs and limbs, it may be simpler to use transmutation to adjust them back to their original healthy state by regeneration.

Time Travel

Most physicists are of the opinion today that time travel is unfeasible. This belief is based on certain limitations inherent to dimensional space and time. However, such limitations are irrelevant in the realm of the patriverse. Remember that in the superphysical, time and space are not the hard, distinct dimensions they are in the physical universe. In such a timeless realm, past, present, and future are practically indistinguishable from one another. Just as the supergeometric pattern of the Eiffel Tower is no closer to Paris than to New York, the birth of Christ may be no more distant from us than the events of a few moments ago.

Paranormal evidence indicates one can indeed touch past or future events while standing in the present. Clairvoyants called in by police to help solve crimes have demonstrated in documented cases that it is sometimes possible to see events of the past with uncanny accuracy. The recorded accounts of accurate prophecies indicate that the same is true for future events. Such prophetic visions can cross the expanse of time in much the same way as telepathic images can cross vast distances of space. Both are transmitted from the source to the recipient in the form of supergeometric patterns that bypass the normal space-time barriers.

What's important here is that accurate premonitions of the future and clairvoyantly detecting the past are both examples of supergeometric patterns traveling through time. If supergeometric patterns can be rematerialized in the present as they are with teleportation, then they can also be rematerialized in the future or the past. If so, then there is nothing in theory to stop us from achieving time travel. A dematerialized object exists only as a supergeometric pattern, and so like a telepathic image can travel more or less unaffected by the barriers of normal space and time. At some point in the future when humanity develops the necessary supergeometric technology, time travel could become a reality.

UFOs

No discussion of supernatural technology would be complete without addressing the subject of Unidentified Flying Objects. UFOs are without a doubt one of the most puzzling and bizarre enigmas of our time. Explanations range from mass

381

hysteria to electromagnetic disturbances to highly sophisticated spacecraft.

What if the third possibility is true? The thought of building such spacecraft using supergeometric theory is by no means absurd. Supergeometric technology could easily account for all the mysterious behavior observed in these strange objects. They certainly seem to display the characteristics of many other paranormal phenomena—they spontaneously appear and disappear (transmigration), move in a way that seems to defy gravity with no visible means of propulsion (translocation), alter their size and shape (transmutation), and otherwise casually violate every known law of physics. There have even been reports of persons having established a sort of transmental link or sympathy with these objects so that their behavior seemingly responds to the person's changing thoughts. Aircraft employing supergeometric technology could easily accomplish such feats.

Of particular interest is how UFOs achieve their fantastic flying skills. Their reported speed is such that they literally fly rings around the fastest jets without creating any atmospheric turbulence, and without producing any audible sound or sonic boom. Such a spacecraft must have a means to overcome the normal effects of air resistance to move so silently and effortlessly through the atmosphere. By employing supergeometric technology, a UFO can reverse the flow of its diffluential field, thereby reducing its physical presence. Like a ghostly specter drifting through a solid wall, the UFO with its reduced presence would still be visible, yet would drift smoothly through the atmosphere, leaving little or no disturbance in its wake. The UFO's reduced presence would also result in lessening the effect of gravity on the craft, making its amazing aerial acrobats all the more feasible.

A common argument against UFOs being extraterrestrial spacecraft are the vast distances they would have to travel to reach earth in a reasonable amount of time. Mass cannot be propelled at the speed of light without applying infinite energy, which is not possible—the total volume of energy in the entire universe is still not infinite. All interstellar travel would then have to be at sub-light speed so that any such trip will take very many years, even from the nearest stars. Several ideas have been suggested to overcome this obstacle, like creating an artificial wormhole, or somehow folding space so that the distance between two regions is greatly reduced. But because of the incredible volume of mass needed to bend enough space to accomplish either of these tricks according to standard physics, they remain the stuff of science fantasy.

The difficulties arise from the belief that such a journey can only be made within the confines of dimensional space-time. However, a ship employing supergeometric technology would be capable of duplicating the same kinds of effects observed in paranormal phenomena, since the mechanisms behind each are the same. A ship from a distant star could transmigrate to our solar system by withdrawing its presence out of space-time, and so simply bypass vast expanses of space by flying "over" them instead of through them. The process would utilize the same paranormal mechanics that govern dematerialization, teleportation and rematerialization.

Supergeometric theory also provides a way by which a UFO might use a form of antigravity to obtain its incredible speed and maneuverability with no visible or audible means of propulsion. Recall that supergeometric gravity begins with a flow of diffluence into the fabric of space-time, producing a depression. Objects that are caught up in the flow are carried into the depression, thereby generating the effect of gravity. A localized diffluential stream focused directly in front of the craft would create a gravitational depression into which the UFO would be drawn. As the on-board generator increases the flow, the depression becomes more pronounced, increasing the speed at which the UFO "falls" forward into the artificial depression. As the depression advances, so does the UFO, riding the crest of the accelerating pocket like a surfer riding a wave. This supersedes conventional technology, which requires a physical object to be forcefully propelled through the air and across space and time with roaring engines. Instead, by simply bending the fabric of space-time in front of itself, the UFO is continually drawn forward into the advancing depression, attaining incredible velocities in total silence. The UFO encounters no atmospheric resistance because it creates its own surrounding pocket or buffer of space-time, which moves along with the UFO as it rides the advancing edge of the depression. There is no need in this scenario for "inertial dampeners" to cushion the passengers from the impact of these sudden, violent accelerations. Being in their own relative bubble of space-time, the interior and its occupants are not moving at all relative to the surrounding space-time, so in a real sense they are perfectly stationary.

If UFOs indeed prove to be the advanced flying machines they appear to be, then the supergeometric device described in this chapter may already be a working reality.

11

Are We There Yet?

To my mind, there must be at the bottom of it all.... not an utterly simple equation, but an utterly simple idea. And to me, that idea, when we finally discover it, will be so compelling, so inevitable, so beautiful, that we will all say to each other, "Oh, how could it have been otherwise?"
                                    —John Wheeler

All truth passes through three stages: First it is ridiculed. Second, it is violently opposed. Third, it is accepted as being self-evident.
                                    — Arthur Schopenhauer

The search for Truth has taken us to many wondrous places. We have challenged the dogma of conventional reason, confronted the mysteries of time and space, and dared to think the unthinkable.

But have we discovered Absolute Truth?

Before attempting to answer, let us first take stock of what has been accomplished.

With the theory of Supergeometry, a set of principles has been presented that reconciles seemingly dissimilar and sometimes contradictory fields of study, just as was the case with the theories of evolution and relativity in their respective fields when they were first presented. Before the theory of evolution, biology was confined to the cataloging of individual species and studying their respective behavior. Evolution revealed how the various species related, not only to each other, but also to their environment, thus transforming a collection of disconnected data into a coherent system. Whereas a forest was once seen only as an aggregation of individual flora and fauna, we now know it to be a single ecosystem, having many complex inter-relationships that evolved together over time. The theory of relativity similarly demonstrated the interrelationship between various branches of science previously considered to be separate. Supergeometric theory in turn lays a foundation on which science, religion, and the paranormal can peacefully co-exist for the first time within the same cosmological system.

The supergeometric model of the cosmos has also helped de-mystify the world of the paranormal. The theory demonstrates in a consistent and logical way the hidden processes behind supernatural events, and explains the causes for the bizarre manifestations observed. Armed with this theory's uniform set of principles, definitions, and terminology, we are now able to discuss all aspects of the paranormal in a rational, systematic manner and with a uniform approach across all phenomena, free from the spiritualistic sensationalism and the ambiguous ideas and terminology that has dogged this field for so long.

Supergeometry has moreover established a means by which we might expand the frontiers of our current sciences and technology. It furnishes valuable insights into a number of cosmic conundrums, among which are the nature of gravity, the dual nature of light, quantum entanglement, evolutionary anomalies, and time dilation. It additionally provides the conceptual foundation from which we might develop amazing technologies such as time travel, teleportation, and even the spontaneous generation of matter. Like Da Vinci's prophetic drawings of helicopters, battle tanks and submarines, the supergeometric model may be a primitive, dim foreshadow of some distant future super-science.

So indeed, much has been accomplished. But have we really discovered Absolute Truth?

If we are to define Truth as a single set of principles or laws by which the true nature of *all* things can be described, then the answer must be a disappointing no. There are still observable phenomena that cannot yet be explained by this or any other system. We can only say that supergeometry appears to have indeed brought us a few steps closer to that ideal of Absolute Truth.

Any discovery, no matter how many puzzles it solves, brings with it a whole new series of questions. Supergeometry certainly has its share. How is time measured in the pre-temporal, superphysical patriverse between the eternal absolutes and the fully temporal universe? How can supergeometry be used to find a mathematical expression of gravity in the four dimensions of space-time, or does it render the search for such a formula irrelevant? How can a physical object be "destroyed" while its superphysical pattern remains unaffected? Why is it that diffluential field bubbles seem to form spontaneously at the locations of paranormal hauntings, while in other areas the fabric of space-time appears very stable? There are many more such questions for which I have yet no workable explanation. I simply do not know.

Even Einstein didn't have all the answers to the questions raised by his relativity theories. He formulated his theories, not with laboratory experiments or a particle accelerator, but with an instrument far more formidable—his mind. He believed in a creation of order, and accepted without Newtonian prejudice the experimental data and anomalous observations available in his time at their face value. He was then able to contain in his incredible genius all this vast information, gather it into the one logical assemblage where all the pieces smoothly fit together in contiguous order, envision a complete stable image of this giant cosmological model, and persistently hold that vision in his head. And he accepted that model as the only possible logical conclusion, no matter how fantastical it seemed. But he also struggled with the mathematics, and lacked the equipment necessary to experimentally confirm every aspect of his universal model of reality. His hope had to rest on future generations of mathematicians and physicists who would continue where he left off. Time has proven his hopes well-placed.

My hope is no different, although I'm in a less fortuitous position. Though educated, I am not a member of the scientific elite, nor a paranormal field investigator, nor a degreed theologian. Regardless to what powers of deduction and reasoning I may possess, I am neither a mathematician nor an experimental physicist. But no matter what might be made of my credentials, there's something of unquestionable substance to this vision of supergeometry—it answers too many questions across a broad spectrum of disciplines in a consistent and uniform way to be easily dismissed. It accommodates existing observations without prejudice, as well as satisfactorily predicting why certain anomalous phenomena behave in precisely the way we observe them. Because of this, the concept of supergeometry does in fact meet the scientific book criteria for a legitimate theory. My hope is that some sincere and open-minded physicist, mathematcian and/or paranormal researcher will recognize its merits and take on the task of continuing what I started.

A theory can only be as sound and complete as the information used in its construction. By our own admission, the sum total of our current knowledge—and thus the total body of evidence we have for examination—is limited. What if black holes are one day indisputably confirmed as a source of decreasing entropy? Or what if some fortunate physicist actually discovers a graviton, and by doing so demonstrates that gravity is in fact a conventional physical force? What if it's finally demonstrated that the *Higgs boson*, a hypothetical particle believed to impart mass to other particles, actually exists? This would give us a conceptual formula (according to the standard model) of *Higgs boson + particles = mass = gravity*, as opposed to the formula *diffluence - velocity = space-time = gravity = mass* indicated by our current theorizing. What would be the consequences to the supergeometric model? It would most likely survive, since it still answers too many questions that other systems cannot (or will not), although it would no doubt require adjustment in the same way existing physical theories do when new discoveries are made. Nevertheless, the point here is that we cannot today say with absolute certainty that the properties of black holes are exactly as our current science *believes* them to be, or that no one will ever discover a graviton. Until such speculations are finally put to rest with verified knowledge, then supergeometry, like other similarly devised physical theories that appear to solve critical scientific quandaries but lack solid physical proof, must be taken as a possible representation of reality based on the body of human knowledge available today.

It is likely that the limits to both our human perceptual and conceptual abilities will also prevent us from ever fully realizing Absolute Truth. The various supergeometric models presented in Chapter Eight are but one example of these limitations. Multiple diagrams were required to fully illustrate the mechanics of supergeometry, each demonstrating only a single aspect of this immense and almost incomprehensible superphysical machine. It is impossible to conceive of any single model that is adequate to represent in the human mind the entire system of reality known as the omniverse. How can we possibly express with three-dimensional ink and paper that which is not fully confined to those dimensions, or understand with a reasoning faculty bound by dimensional thinking that which is boundless?

Consider for example the earlier discussion of the tesseract, a theoretical geometric figure existing in four spatial dimensions. Although we can describe this figure in mathematical terms, we cannot represent it physically. Try as we might, no

matter what image we can conjure in our mind, sketch with
pencil and paper or project on a computer screen, the resulting
figure will always be definable by three dimensions. To *fully* visualize the reality of a superdimensional tesseract is beyond our
limited comprehensive ability.

This book itself is crippled by its very spatial and temporal
limitations. Entire volumes could be written on the specific
subjects of each individual chapter, let alone the many novel
ideas touched on within each of them. Addressing each concept
down to its most infinitesimal detail might well span an entire
library. But I had to reduce all this to a single book that could
be practically bound, reasonably sold, fit on the shelf of any
bookcase, and not require years to read. I doubt that any building or even digital database, no matter how huge, could ever
house a library-of-everything comprising every detail of all that
is the universe.

If we were able to separate ourselves from the cosmos that
confines us and soar above it so that we might survey what was
below, perhaps then we might catch a glimpse of the grand
scheme underlying the Creation, and grasp its meaning in some
elemental way. But unfortunately, we ourselves are an integral
part of that cosmos, and so we are truly captives inside it. It's
like the old metaphor of a single blood cell trying to comprehend the entire body in which it dwells. Computer scientist
David Wolpert has actually devised a theoretical proof to this
axiom that no device (including the human brain) can ascertain
with certainty the absolute state of any system in which that
device is a component, but instead can only derive inferences.
The best we will ever likely achieve is to arrive at a Theory Of
Almost Everything, or a TOAE. We cannot rise up from among
its trees to behold in its entirety the cosmological forest. This
does not, however, stop us from trying. Nor should it.

Let us return to that age-old philosophical dilemma on
which many generations have before pondered: "What was God
doing before He created the universe?" The question seems

reasonable enough on the face of it. But just as Augustine concluded, closer examination reveals it to be almost entirely irrational. Remember that time existed only *after* the creation process began. Before that first moment, there was no time. Therefore, any word indicating a temporal reference is non-functional and irrational. Now look again at the question and consider each word carefully. We must discard *was*, for it is a designation of time (past tense), and cannot be meaningfully used in discussing a state before time existed. *Doing* must also be disqualified, since it is in the present tense, and so too is an expression of time (just like the past tense *have done* or the future tense *will do*). *Before* and *created* likewise must be eliminated, falling victim to the same temporal stumbling block. We're likewise forced to reject *what* and *the universe* as indications of things, none of which existed before the moment of creation. We must therefore resign ourselves to the embarrassing and pitiful conclusion that our very minds and lips do not possess the integrity to even formulate or speak the question intelligibly! We mere mortals cannot adequately describe with our temporal brains and mouths that which is eternal. The only word we can speak from this primordial puzzle that truly makes any sense here is *God*, for at the "time" in question, He "was" "all" "that" "there" "was."

This brings to mind the account in the book of Exodus when Moses asked God how he should depict Him to the Israelites. God replied, "*I AM WHO I AM*.... Say this to the people of Israel; '*I AM* has sent me to you.'" Any other characterization would be both meaningless and futile.

Only the Mind of the Creator is sufficient to grasp the Absolute Truth concerning the cosmos that He Himself created. For in the end, it is that Mind which is Truth Itself.

Index

393

16767653R00233

Made in the USA
Charleston, SC
09 January 2013